Our Biosocial Brains

Our Biosocial Brains

The Cultural Neuroscience of Bias, Power, and Injustice

Michele K. Lewis

LEXINGTON BOOKS
Lanham • Boulder • New York • London

Published by Lexington Books
An imprint of The Rowman & Littlefield Publishing Group, Inc.
4501 Forbes Boulevard, Suite 200, Lanham, Maryland 20706
www.rowman.com

6 Tinworth Street, London SE11 5AL

British Library Cataloguing in Publication Information Available

Library of Congress Cataloging-in-Publication Data Available

ISBN: 978-1-4985-8353-4 (cloth)
ISBN: 978-1-4985-8355-8 (pbk)
ISBN: 978-1-4985-8354-1 (electronic)

∞™ The paper used in this publication meets the minimum requirements of American National Standard for Information Sciences Permanence of Paper for Printed Library Materials, ANSI/NISO Z39.48-1992.

Contents

Acknowledgments

Words cannot express my gratitude to my Dee. Your love and support are always encouraging, especially when my biosocial brain is frustrated and fatigued. I would also like to thank my family members and colleagues who regularly inquired about my progress, and shared kind words. I am grateful to editors and reviewers who read the early draft and provided invaluable feedback to strengthen this project. Thank you to the Center for the Study of Economic Mobility at Winston Salem State University for funding the research on the local Black women challenged by poverty. Thank you to all scientists, surgeons, and physicians who study and treat our biosocial brains. I am inspired by you all. Lastly, I acknowledge all victims of violence, greed, marginalization, exploitation, and dehumanization throughout the cultures of the world.

Preface

At the time of this writing in 2019, examples of police brutality have appeared in media for several years in the United States and other parts of the world. At the time of this writing in 2019, parts of the Amazon rainforest in Brazil have been burning for days, even though the rainforest is known as among the Earth's greatest natural treasures. Now, indigenous humans and plant life there are at risk. As well, in 2018, a longtime physician was sentenced to life in prison for years of sexual abuse of young women and girls in professional gymnastics. In 2017, the year ended with *Time Magazine* selecting women of a *#MeToo* movement against sexual assault as person(s) of the year in the United States.

Repeatedly over several years, juries have decided against indictment of police officers for the killings of unarmed Black human beings. In each case, the parents of the murdered, protesters, and other citizens have considered the actions of the police to be use of excessive force. As well, some of the killings and bodies of the deceased have been shown in graphic depiction on the news, reoccurring loops similarly to a movie trailer for an upcoming entertaining film. Parents have stated in the United States, their children are fearful of getting shot at school, and proactively think of how they will shield themselves or escape the terror. Does chronic exposure to this information and negative images have an impact on the brains and behavior of all who repeatedly view or hear about these events happening in their culture? What changes have already occurred in childrens' brains when they express fear and the associated neurotransmitter and hormonal releases at the thought of going to school to potentially face gun violence?

Frantz Fanon in his iconic 1961 work, *The Wretched of the Earth*, includes an opening chapter entitled, Concerning Violence, in which he makes several points regarding power and privilege. He makes several statements regarding colonizers and the colonized, statements about relations between wealthy and lower socioeconomic classes of people, and statements regarding relationships between white Europeans and people of color. Within the chapter, policing is presented as a tool of colonization and oppression. Fanon also wrote of violence as being inevitable in the process of change that may produce something completely new with respect to challenging the oppression. Since 1961, these same social problems have continued to exist on an international scale. This book attempts to detail the significance of these events in the study of the brain as a biosocial organ influenced by these events. All people, irrespective of where they reside on planet earth, are embedded in a culture which shapes their reactions, decision-making, and perceptions.

Fanon's words, though written decades ago, have remarkable relevance to the Black Lives Matter protests of 2014 and the Occupy Wall Street movement which began in September 2011. There are many other examples, such as the Grenfell Tower fire in England and the forcible land grab disputes among members of *quilombos* (settlements of runaway enslaved people) and developers in Brazil. The Black Lives Matter protests were initiated in response to the deaths of Black men at the hands of police. This movement was largely initiated by young people in major cities. The Occupy Wall Street movement was initiated in Liberty Square in Manhattan's Financial District. This movement was initiated in response to the corruption and power of major banks and multinational corporations. Its aim is fighting back against the richest 1 percent of people who toppled the global financial industry, thereby globally affecting millions of ordinary peoples' financial well-being into the foreseeable future.

The organizers of the Occupy Wall Street movement used the slogan, "we kick the ass of the ruling class!" The slogan was aggressive, though the protests were nonviolent. This is different from Fanon's message, which advocated for an aggressive and even violent response to oppression. However, to be clear, Fanon was not (as he has been mistakenly described by some writers) advocating for violence for the sake of violence. Yet how instinctive have violent reactions become in the face of human frustration, greed, or attempts to solve problems? How does chronic exposure to violence (gaming, movies, sports, current events) impact the biosocial brain? How have the sociocultural worlds of the different generations from Baby Boomers through Generation Z impacted the brains and behavior of humans? How have humans' brain capacity for humane vs. inhumane cognition and behavior been impacted across these changing sociocultural contexts?

The Black Lives Matter and Occupy Wall Street movements, have been comprised of youth in the 21st century, calling forth the historical Marxist use of the term, lumpenproletariat. In the 21st century, millennials and Generation Zs have been frequently dismissed as too self-centered to be collectively useful to greater societal movements. Thus, in terms of their perceived usefulness to an organized movement, they can be compared to those that Marx referred to as the lumpenproletariat in his communist manifesto. This can be said because Marx described the lumpenproletariat as the disengaged, unorganized, lowest levels of the human population who are unskilled, dispossessed, and unemployed. Yet, youth have been significant in the Black Lives Matter movement, as Fanon suggested should happen. The outcasts or dismissed, he suggested, must join the revolutionaries to bring forth liberation. Who are the people today, who are most often perceived as the outcast, dismissed, "ratchet," despised? If we are watching and listening to national and international news, then we can guess the answer to this question. On a related note, we may also gain insight to the answer by noting who are the people absent from mainstream scientific brain research as participants of interest and as researchers.

Fanon wrote of the psychological effects of colonization for both the colonized and colonizers. To be colonized, means to be geographically, mentally, emotionally, and culturally invaded and taken over by a powerful other (aka colonizer). The original values of the marginalized and their native customs, languages, minds, and behaviors then disappear. They no longer know who they are nor truly understand what has been done to them. Although this may sound extreme, it is a historical fact that continues to be relevant in the form of threat-based neural activation patterns and lived experiences of marginalized peoples and their oppressors into the present. It is not uncommon for threat-based neural activation of the sympathetic nervous system to occur when some Black teens and adults initially encounter law enforcement officials, even if they are innocent citizens. Due to the state of the sociocultural world that humans inhabit, such as situations where police officers and young Black men encounter one another, their feelings of fear may be reciprocal. Cultural neuroscience to date has not thoroughly interrogated these facts outside of a standard Eurocentric paradigm. This book will address these events and others by using the physical, psychological, and spiritual as emphasized in Black/African-centered psychology.

Although controversial to many, Fanon advocated for justified violence by the oppressed, as a means of obtaining liberation. However, this is not the focus of *Our Biosocial Brains*. This book examines the cultural neuroscience of the oppressed and of the powerful. It is argued, that using non-western or African-centered psychology is necessary because it is not rooted in racist, classist, and patriarchal methods as that of mainstream Euro-American psychology. Thus far in the biopsychological and neuroscientific literature, scholars have not ventured forth to deeply address how cultural neuroscience coupled with non-western psychology can inform about the inhumane behaviors that occur on a global scale.

Oppressed people and their oppressors have been psychologically affected, and still require healing as Fanon addressed in his writings. The underlying science to be learned from current events and the burgeoning field of cultural neuroscience, will be articulated here, inspired by Fanon's writings on the psychology of oppression. The information here is intended to highlight the connection between cultural neuroscience and African-centered psychology, to understand the abuse, violence, and disregard enacted upon disenfranchised oppressed groups of the world. White males of privileged status are also included for analysis of their acts of violence which may also stem from a lack of psycho-spiritual wellness. Such behaviors have manifest as isolation, disconnection, and abandonment from others. The men are discussed within the context of patriarchy and sub-optimal masculine ideological beliefs which may contribute to violence against others and themselves.

The aim of this book is to focus attention on the marginalized, specifically in relationship to violence, disrespect, othering, micro-aggressions, environmental injustice, health, and general disregard. Using hundreds of peer-reviewed studies or reviews, the brain-based scientific research is integrated with cultural studies of diverse populations, to foster understanding of the impact of cultural experiences of marginalization and dehumanization on brain processes. For example, via examination of areas of the world where people experience daily lack of access to clean, healthy, plentiful water, the significance of spiritual and cultural coping practices in some of the regions is included. This has biopsychological and spiritual relevance to cultural neuroscience.

Fanon's *Wretched of the Earth*, and his ideas as a different kind of psychiatrist inspired this book. In each chapter, background information and facts are presented regarding affected people and their experiences, incorporating what is known from published works. This includes cognitive and brain research regarding perceptions of some humans as subhuman by those in power or with privilege. As well, an objective here is to transgress surface level mainstream media coverage about highly publicized news stories to discuss the relevant science. Lesser known stories are also included, and some older well-known cases (DC snipers and Columbine shooters) of relevant behaviors are analyzed.

Another aim is to also inform a wider audience beyond typical university settings. Therefore, in addition to hundreds of peer-reviewed articles and books, I have included news stories from local, national, or international newspapers, reports, science magazines, and research groups. Thus, a wider variety of sources exists here than what would commonly be found in works about any aspect of neuroscience. The mainstream neuroscience journals remain lacking in the type of diversity presented here for the framing of this book; neither researchers nor research participants in neuroscience represent the diversity of people on the planet. Thus, it is intentional that I have not exclusively referenced journals of neuroscience and other closely related disciplines when connecting the brain science to cultural studies and the more humane African-centered/Black psychology. This is a deliberate act of resistance to the promotion of a sub-optimal worldview regarding contributions considered worthy of this subject matter.

I invite the public to read this book in its entirety. View this book as an eclectic African-centered psychology and cultural neuroscience project that focuses on culture, brain, behavior, and thinking that can shed light and offer possible direction for innovations and advancement of cultural neuroscience. I invite others to learn, share, and dialogue in community, classrooms, book clubs, conferences, bookstores, and religious and civic organizations about the information here. Understanding the brain for how it is impacted by our sociocultural world is knowledge that can be widely useful beyond neuroscientists, psychologists, and academics. We all carry around this fascinating organ, the human brain. All humans can benefit from learning more about how the brain is shaped by the world around us. I am excited for the advances already occurring in neuroscience, and remain hopeful that health and social problems may be further addressed. I am optimistic about the developing neuro-technologies and data-driven science that can be produced by a more diverse population of researchers and research participants.

Michele K. Lewis, Ph.D.
Winston-Salem State University

Chapter One

Still Wretched

The word "*wretched*, when used to refer to a person or people, means to be in a very unhappy or unfortunate state. It is specifically regarding this meaning, that the Black Martinique psychiatrist, Frantz Fanon, used the word "wretched" to refer to poor, disenfranchised, and oppressed people who were then (as now) experiencing ongoing violence from their oppressors. Today there remains violence, disenfranchisement, and the added dimension of various social media outlets to distract or desensitize humans from the breadth and depth of these circumstances. For example, less than 24 hours apart, there were two mass shootings in the United States in El Paso, Texas, and Dayton, Ohio, in August 2019. The young White male gunman's manifesto in the El Paso case referenced his motives as a way to stop "Hispanic invasion"; he also referenced his vision that the nation should be divided into territories according to race, with interracial marriage being one of his disdains (Abutaleb, 2019). Although the shooting in the Ohio case was not labeled a hate crime nor domestic terrorism, but referenced as preoccupation with violent ideologies, the majority of the victims killed were Black human beings.

These types of hate-based violent behaviors and sentiments are not new, but how we research and attempt to interpret them requires innovative and more expansive studies. For example, functional magnetic resonance imaging (fMRI) has been used to study willingness to fight and die for sacred values in Spain, examining a sample of radicalized Islamists (Hamid, Pretus, Atran, Crockett et al., 2019). The findings implicate a role of the dorsolateral prefrontal cortex (DPFC), inferior frontal cortex, and parietal cortex. Other scholars of the nonpartisan research and policy Center for the Study of Hate and Extremism (CSHE) at California State University, San Bernardino have reported on the relative lack of research, public attention, and acknowledgement of White supremacist domestic terrorism in the United States which shows the same radicalization as what garners more attention when identified radicals are non-White and from other nations (CSHE, 2019).

Many licensed therapists of varying fields of study (psychiatry, psychology, social work) and researchers are not members of the perceived to be "wretched" classification. Researchers may be trained in how to design racially sensitive studies with diverse ethnic minority and LGBT populations, yet some would argue that this too, is a White supremacist implicitly biased perspective. It presumes the knowledge of how to research White hetero-attractional cisgender people is the standard. It implies all researchers will be White and unfamiliar with the strange and "wretched others." It affirms that from this worldview, there is a standard normal approach for researching White hetero-attractional, middle-class, cis-gender people as norm, and upon whom the literature can be based.

Likewise, brain science appears to presume studies can be generalized to everyone, although they are primarily based upon the narrow population of White western-acculturated persons studied. Brain research and publications in neuroscience have often reflected the Manichean world of division into the oppressors and the oppressed. Such structure is also well-ingrained into the socio-cultural historical and contemporary world that has permeated the human mind (Harrell, 1999), impacting human neural reactions, perception, and treatment of the marginalized. Research in cultural neuroscience can address this history and how it relates to the reality of the brain as a complex biosocial organ. It is time to explore this more critically, as outlined in this current text.

WHO WAS FANON?

In *Wretched of the Earth*, Frantz Fanon stated that any case of neurosis and abnormal behavior or excessive emotional sensitivity or reaction in the body to a stimulus is the product of one's cultural situation (Fanon, 2005). The part of the body at the center of explanations of the initiation of perceived threat is the brain. The human brains of oppressed people, and their oppressors, are negatively affected by the culture of White supremacy (Fanon, 2005; Fanon, 2008). However, before turning attention to understanding the behavior of oppressors and the oppressed in relation to cultural neuroscience, it is imperative to have a basic understanding of Fanon's framework which inspired the current work.

In the opening chapter of *Wretched of the Earth*, entitled Concerning Violence, Fanon repeatedly used the concepts of settler and native to refer to the power and privilege of white Europeans (settlers) relative to the masses of colonized Black people (natives). For purposes here, this frames the discussion of the oppressive conditions of large populations of disenfranchised and marginalized groups around the world. For example, one analysis of a U.S. Police-Shooting Database using county-level predictors revealed racial bias in police shootings emerged in police departments in larger metropolitan counties having low median incomes and numerous Black residents (Ross, 2015). In these contemporary times, Black urban residents are comparable to those Fanon referred to as "native." When members of various police departments enter neighborhoods of Black residents, it is they (the police) who are the outsiders with the privilege to harm, and to evoke feelings of anxiety, fear, and mistrust in the communities; this has been regarded as a public health concern in Black communities (Oh, DeVylder, & Hunt, 2017).

Throughout his opening chapter, Fanon (2005) addressed the tensions that rise under such oppressive conditions. He also further explicated how this reality of oppression often produced tension within the community and cathartic reactions in the form of Black on Black crimes, and eventually sometimes retaliatory violence against the "settler" (i.e., police) as an act of defiance in pursuit of liberation.

Fanon was born on the island of Martinique into a middle-class Black family. Like many people of African descent throughout the Black world (Diaspora), Fanon experienced psychological and emotional distress resulting from White supremacy. Though he was born and raised on an island nation of primarily Black people, a European (French) worldview controlled and dominated how Black people in Martinique thought and behaved. Therefore, Fanon knew very well the psychology of oppression. He referenced health, law enforcement, and education as being similar and connected within the realm of inequality and bias (Bulhan, 1985). The legacy of his work lives on through the writings he gave the world, which unfortunately are still reflective of modern-day social ills of power, negative bias, and inhumane treatment. While books on oppression are not new, the deeper analysis of maltreatment from a cultural neuroscience, African-centered Black psychology framework, as used here, is a novel approach.

When Fanon completed writing *The Wretched of the Earth*, he was in his final days of life due to terminal cancer. It is often perceived as Fanon's finest work, a masterpiece. Although *The Wretched of the Earth* was published in 1961, predicaments in the world are presently very similar to what they were in his lifetime, and during the turbulence of the 1960s. Though *The Wretched of the Earth* focused on the specific colonial imperialistic case of French colonization of Algeria, the psychology of Black inferiority/White superiority based beliefs presented in *Black Skin, White Masks* (Fanon, 2008) is still relevant in today's world (Alexander, 2012; Blanchett, 2006; Pettit & Western, 2004; Oliver & Shapiro, 2006). Other marginalized groups beyond Black people, such as Native Americans, transgender people, LGB people, and people in poverty face bias, powerlessness, and inhumanity. Black people as well, have intersecting identities with all these other identities of marginalization. Fanon's contribution to the world through his writing was a call to pursue a psychology of liberation (emotional and mental emancipation) to transform the social circumstances of oppressed, despised, marginalized and "othered" people (Bulhan, 1985).

Cultural Neuroscience

The social problems of imperialism, racism, and other isms are addressed across a multitude of fields of study. Such social problems seem intuitive to fields such as sociology and social psychology; however, even in these fields, many of the frameworks and methods of analysis have centered Eurocentric worldviews and conclusions. The fields of neuroscience and quantum physics have been relatively less visibly integrated with cultural studies in western scientific literature. However, psychologists who have African-centered behavioral, clinical, and neuroscientific backgrounds, do exist. Such scholars have provided invaluable contributions for the development of further understanding and empirical explorations of topics such as the functions of neuromelanin in the central and peripheral nervous systems (Moore, 2010; Bynum, 2013). The work of these scholars inadvertently destigmatizes use of the words Blackness and darkness, given that these words are associated with negativity in the English language (Burgest, 1973). The works of African-centered scholars are relevant to this book because they have delineated the role of neuromelanin in the brain regarding its benefits to all humans. They educate about the ancient wisdom of Egyptian scientists who understood the brain, the soul, and higher cognition and consciousness. In western culture, Egyptian scientific knowledge was later incompletely and inappropriately attributed to Eurocentric theorists for scientific consumption throughout the western world. As well, the existence of institutionalized global social problems such as anti-Blackness, can impede openness to scholarship about the benefits and significance of the brain's dark/black matter. Relatively speaking, such discussion has been largely marginalized within mainstream psychology and neuroscience.

Cultural neuroscience is regarded as still emerging as a discipline in western cultural scientific contexts. It is understood in western science, that humans vary in cultural experiences and at the level of neural activation, genomic processes, and psychological processes (Chiao, 2009). Emphasis placed on the brain as a biosocial organ, references the bidirectional nature of humans' biology and socio-cultural experiences as emphasized in cultural neuroscience. As a result of this bidirectionality, the behaviors expressed, thoughts, and emotions may be culturally specific across humans, even as humans are also similar. Scholars of cross-cultural psychology and cultural neuroscience search for etic (universal) and emic (specific) characteristics among humans across the globe.

Cultural neuroscience (CN) holds great promise for understanding more about power, bias, and inhumane treatment because of its integrative theoretical and methodological approaches. The emerging field may benefit by expanding its reliance upon diverse disciplines such as cultural psychology, neuroscience, anthropology, sociology, women and gender studies, LGBTQ studies, behavioral and neural economics, epigenetics, and African-centered/ Black psychology to understand how the brain is shaped by sociocultural impact. Chiao et al., 2010 state that the research in cultural neuroscience focuses on two questions of human nature: how do values, beliefs, and practices stemming from cultural background (nurture) shape humans' neurobiology (nature) and behavior, and how do neurobiological mechanisms prompt the emergence and transmission of cultural traits? A critique of CN is its lack of examination of a diversity of cultural experiences when attempting to address the two questions.

By using Fanon's framework of psychology of liberation from oppression and situating his framework under the umbrella of African-centered/Black psychology (ACBP), this is not an advocacy for an essentialist stereotyped view of Blackness. It is important to state this because some scholars of CN warn of the mistake of studying cultural stereotypes rather than culture itself (Chiao et al., 2010). Here, I do not argue that Black people and other marginalized groups are monolithic, in support of stereotypes nor essentialism. Instead, a premise is that many Black people of the diaspora know the long history of cultural experiences of inhumanity, bias, and vilification of Blackness as it exists around the globe (Hart, 2018). This is evidenced by inhumanity, bias, and power differentials for Black men, women, and children of many geographic regions. However, what is not thoroughly examined within traditional neuroscientific research is the neural impact of chronic oppressive experiences of marginalized people who suffer or are resilient in the face of chronic negative experiences.

Chiao et al. (2010) listed several key challenges to conducting cultural neuroscience research. They stated it is an error to conceptualize nation or race as a proxy for culture; they detailed, that to do such, is a gross and inappropriate characterization of culture. Chiao et al.'s position is not a view derived from an African-centered psychological framework. African centered/Black psychology recognizes the interconnectedness of all things in the universe, the salience of collectivism, and the mental health benefits of communal self-knowledge which is characteristic of the cultural histories of Black people (Nobles, 2015; 2006; Association of Black Psychologists, n.d.). The absence of the cultural knowledge of culturally appropriate methods and questions to be incorporated in the cognitive sciences can be considered unethical or erroneous. One example of this is to study the racial classification of faces based on the faces' perceived proximity to whiteness, such has been published in highly regarded peer-reviewed western literature without appropriate critique (Halberstadt, Sherman, & Sherman, 2010).

If people can be deemed to be of a racial identity other than White, based upon just their phenotypic deviation from phenotypic whiteness, then racial identity is not being treated as a social construct but as a hierarchically based physical identity. Halberstadt, Sherman, & Sherman (2010) never quite adequately address race as a social construct at all. However, the researchers did define the historical meaning of hypodescent or the one drop rule created under White supremacy. Hypodescent in the United States mandated labeling any person with a Black identified parent or ancestor as a member of the Black race, and incapable of claiming White identity. Halberstadt, Sherman, & Sherman's (2010) research findings reflected how White participants evaluated stereotypically non-White phenotypic features via grouping all such perceived persons to be separate from White. The brain is what allows for perceptual capability, yet cultural experiences shape how people and other stimuli are processed in the brain. Thus, though Chaio et al. (2010) warn against using race as proxy for culture, in society, humans of "non-white" phenotypic appearance may in fact share similar cultural experiences of social bias and inhumane treatment based on their perceived race, they then may share patterns of sociocultural experiences that impact their neural activation to stimuli.

From a collective or communal perspective, ACBP scholars and associated organizations address the shared cultural experiences of inhumanity and oppression for the people deemed non-White. In the field of CN, this has not been adequately studied. So, although marginalized groups around the globe may differentially experience oppression (e.g. anti-Blackness, transphobia, classism), nevertheless they consciously or unconsciously do experience it. CN can be a part of understanding more about neural and epigenetic impact of oppression. There remain several research challenges for CN, which Chaio et al. (2010) have detailed. From an ACBP perspective, the researchers' list of challenges may be critiqued as follows:

> Culturally appropriate experimental tasks may not be the sole method for gaining information to build a more inclusive CN literature. When experiments are done, by necessity they must be cultural appropriate; incorporation of additional innovative methods is worthwhile.

> Available brain templates from neuroimaging statistical analysis packages and standard brain atlases have been normed on white individuals, even though brain research exists that provides evidence of variability amongst White Westerners compared to East Asian groups (Chee et al., 2010). Such evidence suggests CN funders and researchers must consider development and use of culturally appropriate brain templates to conduct cross-culturally valid re-

search studies. Consideration of diversity beyond comparing Eastern to Western culture is still lacking. Many groups that will be discussed in this text as oppressed groups (e.g., lower income status, LGBTQ) have not been mainstreamed into CN studies or brain research in general; the field is primarily developing based on hypotheses which compare eastern cultural to western cultural responses to stimuli, in which the western participants remain overwhelmingly White-identified.

Researchers have addressed the source of error stemming from comparing brain responses of participants who have been tested at different sites that use different brain imaging scanners. However, less recognized is an accompanying and equally valid critique that diversity of persons being scanned has not yet occurred in the studies. Many diverse groups of most marginalized people are not being tested at all by any type of imaging scan.

Chaio et al. (2010) state two CN research challenges that are particularly relevant to this book 1) the need for identification of functional polymorphisms that have evolved alongside cultural customs and experiences of either trauma, health compromise, or resilience and 2) over 90 percent of peer-reviewed neuroimaging studies come from homogenous cultural regions. The CN studies to date also disregard diverse emphasis on the brain as a biosocial organ. Thus, how can we learn more about the neural and epigenetic impact of chronic exposure to powerlessness, social bias, and inhumane treatment with such narrowly focused science?

The circumstances of the modern day oppressed were set in motion many centuries ago with socio-cultural creation of Eurocentrism, imperialism, and the accompanying patriarchy, capitalism, heterosexism, and White supremacy. Research on implicit bias has revealed that such racial and ethnic bias persist, even among healthcare providers (Hall et al., 2015). This is particularly alarming as an example of the complex interplay of sociocultural and biological processes that impact humans (Sasaki & Kim, 2016). As another example, there are young persons who can read words on a page but may avoid doing so relative to the reading behavior of people in the 1960s (Twenge, Martin, & Spitzberg, 2018). Specifically, regarding enslaved ancestors of African American people, they were not legally allowed to read. However, today, many of the marginalized may have less (relative to White students) intrinsic motivation to read, and stronger avoidance (relative to White students) of reading; such has been found that African American students were more averse to and ambivalent to reading than their white counterparts (Twenge, Martin, & Spitzberg, 2018). Under a Eurocentric psychological paradigm, there is an absence of non-westernized explanation of these findings to adequately address the sociohistorical factors of systemic oppression, such as erasure of one's own history from many books due to institutional racism, and internalized racism that may relate to such demotivation.

In the more "color-blind' society of the Americas today, youth may be less aware of the Manichean nature of the world's historical organization since the onset of European domination. Such is relevant when some oppressed persons seek to deeply integrate and immerse themselves in values and contexts of their oppressor; this poses a risk such as having an encounter experience with the potential to shake their world, i.e., racial trauma, associated neurotransmitter and neuroendocrine responses (Cross, 1971; Sasaki & Kim, 2016)

Solely Eurocentric discussions are problematic as they can promote victim blaming and negative attributions for research findings. Fanon explained how blaming the victim works to rationalize an unjust world, ordered according to White supremacist heterosexist capitalist patriarchy. He also argued that blaming the victim assuages the guilty conscience of oppressors. For the oppressed who are attempting to cope with inhumanity, bias, and powerlessness, they sometimes develop internalized racism, which in Fanon's terminology he referenced as auto-colonization (Bulhan,1985).

Psychological liberation and healing require empowerment that comes from a shift of a sub-optimal belief system such as auto-colonization to an optimal Afrocentric worldview (Myers et al., 2018). Optimal psychology references a conceptual system that has the potential, via application, to combat many of the ongoing social injustices seen in systems such as education, health, land rights, and state-sanctioned violence against marginalized groups (Myers, 1993).

Scholar Linda James Myers has written about and utilized optimal conceptual theory for decades (Myers, 1993; 2003; 2006; 2009). Myers et al. (2018) extol the harmful impact of suboptimal Eurocentric worldviews on the thinking, emotional expression, and behaviors of both the oppressed and the oppressors. Myers' body of work aligns with the framework of Fanon as he wrote of the psychology of oppression as it impacts the colonized and the colonizer.

For those who are resilient and thrive despite chronic exposure to maltreatment and disregard, Myers detailed explanations for this resiliency and healthy way of being. Her work predates the advent of positive psychology in Eurocentric westernized psychology. For persons who change from suboptimal to optimal worldview, what are the accompanying changes in their neural activation patterns and at the molecular level of the brain cells? How could this be mapped and even better understood and applied for the health benefit of the wider communities of people who are currently suffering (e.g., the oppressed, or the oppressors suffering from their own false beliefs in their own superiority)?

In this book, the African-centered/Black psychology perspective is used in conjunction with Fanon's ideas. Less prevalent in the science literature, is an application of African-centered psychological perspectives to developing fields such as cultural neuroscience. Thus, this book aims to make this connection through examination, critique, ACBP, and cultural re-interpretation to expand upon conclusions derived from mainstream research. Theories such as optimal conceptual theory (OCT) were developed for the healing of non-immigrant African Americans; however, Myers et al. (2018) have also written that OCT has the capacity to heal humanity at large.

Discussions are reoccurring about mass shootings, as these have pervaded media and political discussions in the United States; frequently the discussions have included mental health. Yet, the discussions have been from a western Eurocentric worldview, not that of the worldview of Myers et al. (2018) as they have detailed the more optimal way of thinking and relating to one another as human beings. As described, the optimal conceptual theory outlines the shift in worldview that could potentially heal the cognitions and emotions relevant to inhumane behaviors.

Fanon's words about negative perceptions and the vile treatment of Black people, have since continued to apply to people of African descent throughout the African Diaspora and other marginalized groups into contemporary times. For example, in the 21st century in the United States, Black people are still experiencing grave health disparities, lower socioeconomic status, lower educational attainment, and high rates of criminalization (Oliver & Shapiro, 2006; Pettit & Western, 2004; Blanchett, 2006; Alexander, 2012). One can tune into any social media feed, podcast, cable, or internet stream and learn about daily occurrences of violence, disregard, and injustice by those with power, against oppressed people of the world.

In addition to institutionalized racism, this book explores the bio-psycho-culturally-based, scientific explanations for disregard for some humans' existence. The objective here is to critically examine and explain how and why incidents occur, going beyond the headlines and talking points. Racism and other social problems have seeped into many human minds because it is in the fiber of world cultures. Questions raised here will explore from whence derives anti-Blackness, hatred and fear of transgender people, disdain for people living in poverty, disregard for indigenous peoples and other intersecting examples of marginalization and oppression. Although in part, topics here have been addressed in the body of work of a mainstream neuroscientist (Sapolsky, 2017), it is the Eurocentric worldview of his presentation that makes it different from the current perspective. Yet, the approach taken here does align with Sapolsky's discussion of the brain as not only biological, but also cultural and tribal. The current approach brings together African-centered liberation psychology and cultural neuroscience. It is important for people in the science world and beyond to gain an understanding of how power, privilege, bias, racism, heterosexism, sexism, and transphobia occur in the behaviors of everyday ordinary people around the globe from the perspective of what humans' brains absorb, resulting in the dehumanization of people.

Conclusion

In present times, interdisciplinary scholars might pursue, what is the best way to engage the masses of disenfranchised people regarding defining and understanding themselves for themselves? What is the best way to understand the brain and radicalization, as it relates to masculinity, White supremacy, and domestic terrorism? Discussions about the pursuit of science, technology, engineering and math (STEM) careers among more diverse groups of men and women is ongoing. However, the privileged, have significantly influenced many fields, including neuroscience. The STEM fields remain very male and very White western comprised. Such lack of progress in this area, within the field, keeps the work and the frameworks very narrow. I argue that future directions should aim for a radical ethno-cultural neuroscience that includes people of the world who have largely been omitted from brain studies, or have been evaluated based on templates that are culturally inappropriate for their lived experiences. Fanon argued, the colonized are resented whenever they assert personhood, humanity, and right to freedom. If there is to be any hope for the people to be liberated, deeper awareness and understanding are needed, followed by unification of the people most endangered. A more diverse cultural neuroscience requires a shift in worldview that could bring solutions to world cultures' most vexing social problems.

Chapter Two

Subhuman to Superhuman

Cultural Neuroscience of Illusory Blackness

An officer in Ferguson, Missouri, compared a young Black male teenager, Michael Brown, to Hulk Hogan. He described his experience of holding onto Brown's arm, as feeling like he (the officer) was just a five-year-old holding onto a bulky professional wrestler. Darren Wilson is the Missouri police officer who fatally shot Brown in Ferguson on August 9, 2014. Wilson's statements were publicized in November 2014 following the grand jury decision that he was not to be charged for killing Brown (Sanburn, 2014). The reason being, Wilson convinced the jury he feared for his life. He described Brown as having deliberate intent to intimidate him. The following are words of Wilson about Brown, as reported in Sanburn, 2014:

> And then after he did that, he looked up at me and had the most intense aggressive face. The only way I can describe it, it looks like a demon, that's how angry he looked.

> It looked like he was almost bulking up to run through the shots, like it was making him mad that I'm shooting at him. And the face he had was looking straight through me, like I wasn't even there, I wasn't even anything in his way.

Wilson's words represent an ideology of "othering" or "otherness" when he perceived Michael Brown. A close examination of his words reveals Michael Brown was not perceived as human, but more akin to the fictitious Incredible Hulk figure from the comic series and the real-life world heavyweight professional U.S. wrestler, Hulk Hogan. With such a perceptual suspension of reality and superhuman categorization by Wilson, the fact that Michael Brown was fatally shot is not surprising.

Michael Brown was an 18-year-old unarmed teenaged Black male; he was shot six times, including four shots from the front into his arms and two shots from the front, to the top of his head (Robles & Bosman, 2014). Wilson's claim is that Brown was charging at him and trying to take his weapon; thus, Wilson said, he was afraid and fired in self-defense. A medical examiner concluded the shots did not appear to be fired at close range (Robles & Bosman, 2014).

OTHERING

Literary writings, social science writing, and the words of Black consciousness thinkers have described how "othering" of Black people has been used across time as a cognitive vehicle of objectification; "othering" in part stems from a socio-culturally constructed phenomenon labeled "white gaze" that has had a powerful impact on the behaviors and cognitions of both people of African descent and their oppressors (Fanon, 2008). "Othering" begs the fundamental question in African-centered psychology: What does it mean to be human (Nobles, 2015)?

Nobel prize-winning author Toni Morrison posed questions relevant to "othering" in her work, *The Origin of Others* (Haas, 2017). Delivered during her 2016 Norton lecture series on race and skin color, Morrison asked, What is race and why does it matter? What motivates the human tendency to construct others? Why does the presence of others, make us so afraid (Haas, 2017)? Morrison's questions addressed motivation and emotions; she asked about the tendency to construct others in the mind. She also referenced fear, when speaking of the emotional reaction to others. This relates to the two perennial questions posed in motivational science: What motivates a behavior to start or stop? Why do motivated behaviors vary in their intensity (Reeve, 2018)? To attempt to answer such questions posed by Morrison and within motivational science, novelists, sociologists, psychologists, and Black consciousness thinkers prompt humans to acknowledge the social and cognitive construction of race and racial identity. Morrison has also asked how one moves from the non-racial womb to the womb of racism? She referenced race as, "genetic imagination" (Nguyen, 2016). Darren Wilson's genetic imagination of Michael Brown proved fatal for Brown.

Likewise, South African anti-apartheid activist Steve Biko, in defining and extolling the social and cultural benefits of developing Black consciousness in Black people, explained the need for Black people to achieve psychological liberation from their self-perceptions as merely appendages to and inferior to White persons (Kaindl, 2013). Biko indirectly addressed the concepts of "othering" and "otherness" by calling for Black people's discovery of their own genuine culture. Biko called for Black people's actual identities to manifest, as opposed to the negatively manufactured fictional Black identity in existence through othering, created by White supremacist ideologies and illusions. Fanon expressed these sentiments in his writings as well.

White Gaze

In his classic 1952 clinical analysis, *Black Skin White Masks*, Fanon interrogated the unconscious minds of "the Black man" and "the White man." At the outset of the text, he makes specific statements about White men slaving to reach a level of being human, relative to Black men striving to be White. Though he acknowledged there would be Black and White persons who would not recognize themselves in his text, he made it clear that this could not negate the reality of this phenomenon (Fanon, 2008).

This chapter focuses on the perceptions of Blacks primarily by Whites (though Black people may also perceive other Black people with a gaze of internalized anti-Blackness) across time and space. Though Fanon stated his words were specific to his time and to his observations of Blacks of his native Antilles, his words within *Black Skin White Masks* remain timely in the 21st century for the African Diaspora at large. Through a series of topics, Fanon (2008) laid out the tools used by Black people to attempt to gain acceptance and bestowal of human status from Whites. For example, Fanon mentioned the motivational strivings of some Black people to love and engage behaviors perceived as White, based on their knowledge of white gaze. It is documented that Black people have been historically perceived by race scientists as being an evolutionary step towards humanness, closer to monkey than human, i.e., sub-human (Fanon, 2008; Winston, 2004; Guthrie, 2004). The following quote is a representation of the psychological implications of such social cognitive perception:

> The negro enslaved by his inferiority, the white man enslaved by his superiority alike behave in accordance with a neurotic orientation. (Fanon, 2008, 60)

In the history of psychiatry/psychology during Fanon's time, neurosis was once a common diagnosis. As of 1986, the term was removed from the *Diagnostic and Statistical Manual of Disorders* (Torgensen, 1986). Though today, no one is diagnosed with neurosis, the thoughts, feelings, and resulting interracially based anxious behaviors mentioned by Fanon still exist.

Numerous scholars have elsewhere detailed the history of othering and dehumanization of Black people (Baldwin, 2017; Ani, 1994; Kilomba, 2010; Yancy, 2012). White gaze and perceptions of Black people as feared and subjugated objects have been sustained. Yancy (2012) advocates "flipping the script" to a practice of "Black gaze," with the aim to make whiteness visible rather than insidiously invisible to many people who identify as White. In calling for this flipping of the script, Yancy references the world of white gaze as follows:

> It is the social world of white normativity and white meaning making which creates the conditions under which black people are always already marked as different/deviant/dangerous. (Yancy 2012, 4)

Such is evident in the ideology of Darren Wilson presented at the beginning of this chapter.

Calmore (2005) takes an alternative approach to flipping the script. As an act of status protest of white gaze from the margins, Calmore has argued against Black assimilationist ideology when in the presence of Whites. Instead, he has advocated for both being oneself and consciously performing Blackness in a manner that resists white gaze and respectability politics. Though scholars have addressed white gaze and white othering, the scientific literature is lacking in treatment of such as being a deeply historically rooted cultural phenomenon that has impacted the biosocial brain. White gaze, othering, and black subjugation as cultural realities are pertinent to discussions of biology of mind as impacted by socio-cultural input. Cultural neuroscience can be used to interrogate Darren Wilson's brain processes, as impacted by cultural immersion in white gaze and othering.

Yancy (2012) articulated the ideological fantastical notion of illusory whiteness as a social problem, creating dangerous life-threatening dehumanizing experiences for Black people; this has relevance for the cases of Michael Brown and many others. Fanon (2008) and Baldwin & Peck (2017) have detailed the crisis that is Black people being perceived as sub-human other. The "n-word" archetype created by White society as a means of power and superiority is a partly sustaining component of the notion of illusory whiteness and its related potentially fatal consequences. Scientific theory of human perception sheds light on the cultural neuroscience of race as an important means of understanding racism as a biosocial problem.

Yancy (2008) discussed cognitions of White women as they have perceived Yancy when he enters an elevator where a lone White woman awaits arrival to her floor. The barrage of media images and messages across time of Black men as criminal, hypersexual, violent, wicked, dangerous, scary dark things not only sustain illusory whiteness but can result in these paranoid delusions in the elevator or in the world. Such illusory human-made perceptions may result in innocent Black people killed or harassed with the threat of death.

On May 8th, 2019, Clarence Evans was shown in an online video, in which police showed up to his Texas home as he was playing in his front yard with his children. In a five-minute video, Evans can be seen and heard saying multiple times to an officer who is mistakenly attempting to arrest him, that his name is not "Quentin" (Hutchinson, 2019). Quentin is the name of a Louisianan Black male suspect who the officer was seeking. Evans is an innocent citizen and father who was playing outside with his children. Evans asked the officer if his Blackness and hairstyle (dreadlocks) were reasons for suspicion. Also, in the video, viewers see and hear Evans commenting to the officer,

> You're shaking like you're scared or something. . . . I'm not finna let you put me in handcuffs. (Hutchinson, 2019)

Evans' words are critical as evidence of the physiological response the officer was having during his engagement with Evans. The officer's fear is irrational, initiated by the officer's own self-generated human illusory perception that all Black men are dangerous and relates to the previous concepts of genetic imagination and othering.

When the officer eventually produced a photo of actual suspect, Quentin, on a cell phone, the officer said to Evans,

> Here's the deal, doesn't that look a lot like you? (Hutchinson, 2019)

Evans explained that the suspect wore dreadlocks and had a similar complexion to him, but otherwise did not look like himself, who is a much younger man than the Black man in the photo. Evans also shared he was terrified for his life, because the officer was convinced he was the Black male suspect in the photo.

There is existing research evidence which relates to what happened to Evans. Researchers have investigated a phenomenon known as the-other-race effect, which emerges by six months old and is well-established by nine months of age (Kelly et al., 2007). The other-race-effect is described as a perceptual narrowing developed due to having primarily same-race interactions within the first year of life. Researchers tested three-, six-, and nine-month-old White infants' ability to discriminate faces within their own racial group and within three other-racial groups (African, Middle Eastern, and Chinese). Between the ages of three months old and nine months old, the evidence showed that White babies became less flexible in visual recognition of faces that were not White. This perceptual narrowing towards same race bias is gradual, reflecting that by six months old, White babies have narrowed recognition to White and Chinese faces. However, the White babies were exclusionary of recognition of African faces by six months. This early onset narrowing persists to adulthood, resulting in the "they all look alike" phenomenon (Kelly et al., 2007); thus, according to research findings, Black male Clarence Evans did look like Black male Quentin to the White officer who attempted to mistakenly arrest Evans.

Eurocentric mainstream descriptions of the other-race-effect are presented as apolitical; the racism has been downplayed as explanatory for phenomenon such as the other-race-effect, even as there are findings that the other-race-effect is stronger in White perceivers than in Black perceivers. Black people, because of institutional racism, will have greater involuntary exposure to perceiving White faces within the White-dominated cultural milieu. As a racialized minority, a Black baby would have less opportunity within western White supremacist cultural spaces to avoid early processing of faces of White persons. Western-trained authors and scholars of a Eurocentric worldview have warned against referencing the-other-race effect as racism; they explain it as being a science-based cognitive developmental phenomenon (Swarns, 2015).

Tyrique Hudson, a 22-year-old Black male native of North Carolina, moved to Maryland after graduating from North Carolina A&T State University with a computer science degree. Hudson was fatally shot two months after he was denied a protective order against a White male neighbor who had threatened to kill him. In the petition filed by Hudson he stated the shooter had said to him that Hudson "knew this day was coming," and that Hudson knows what he did (Mann & Prudente, 2019). Hudson reported he did not know what the man was speaking about. Hudson had also told his mother the shooter seemed to have a strange look and Hudson was perplexed by the White male neighbor's fixation. The shooter had indicated a death gesture to Hudson by using his thumbs across his throat as symbolic of ending Hudson's life.

A judge in Maryland denied Hudson's request for a sustained protective order, stating Hudson could not meet the burden of proof; Hudson was only able to secure a three-day temporary court order. Two months later Hudson was dead while the shooter is still alive following a 10-hour standoff with police. The shooter was charged with first- and second-degree murder, first- and second-degree assault, and using a firearm in a felony crime and reckless endangerment (Mann & Prudente, 2019). Though the shooter was referenced as suffering from paranoid schizophrenia in his bail hearing, a close examination of the incident and background on the shooter revealed he also had a history of protective orders against him, including one granted to an ex-wife (Mann & Prudente, 2019). However, when Hudson reported feeling unsafe due to threats of violence, his request was trivialized and dismissed by the judge, resulting in his murder by the neighbor two months later. The White female judge's reasoning and decision in this case sparks the following questions that may be relevant to her decision-making. Can a 22-year-old Black man unquestioningly be perceived as afraid of a 53-year-old White man? Can a 22-year old Black man truly be in danger due to a threatening older White man? Isn't it supposed to be the reverse; the young Black man is the threat? Hudson's request for protection was denied; he and the shooter were told by the judge, that as neighbors they simply needed to try to get along better. Hudson is dead, shot in the stairwell of his apartment, after coming in from taking out his trash; the older White male shooter was seen standing over his body (Mann & Prudente, 2019).

Yancy (2008) made the point, it matters not how a Black body is dressed nor the comportment. Thus, it matters not that Tyrique Hudson was a young promising engineer. What is significant is Yancy's (2008) description of sweaty palms and racing hearts of White women who become afraid in the elevator in Yancy's presence; he commented as well on his own sensory neuronal firing of action potentials when he is in their presence in an enclosed space. This is the substance of cultural neuroscience that has not been given enough depth of attention for the biosocial ramifications of systemic cultural and institutional racism that it represents. These reactions in the bodies of Yancy and the collective White female bodies he describes are examples of cultural and historical racist experiences seeping into humans' neural activation patterns. It is argued here that white gaze and prescriptive White supremacist ideology are emblematic of a grand western cultural narrative having implications for cognition, cultural neuroscience, and behaviors.

The Neuroscience of Race

Researchers have written about the neuroscience of race which relates beyond the words of the officer who murdered Michael Brown, but more generally to the existence of white gaze and subsequent effects of "othering." As human beings by necessity move about the world, inevitably they encounter out-group members as a part of their human experience. Noted scholar of African-centered/Black psychology (ACBP), Dr. Wade Nobles, references human experiences as a necessary component of divine spirits' existence within a physical container, i.e., the body (Nobles, 2015). The physical container which humans inhabit, varies in the responses it evokes, based upon the culturally determined ways implicit racial attitudes impact neural activation (Kubota, Banaji, & Phelps, 2012). This has been measured by brain imaging techniques and other physiological measures. Upon reviewing studies dating back to the 1990s, Kubota, Banaji, & Phelps (2012) reviewed research revealing a cluster of brain regions that are most relevant to the brain's processing and perception of Black-White race. The studies reviewed relied upon blood oxygenation level–dependent (BOLD) signaling throughout the brain in reaction to Black-White facial stimuli. The commonly studied brain areas are amygdala, anterior cingulate cortex (ACC), dorsolateral prefrontal cortex (DPFC), and fusiform gyrus. Areas of the cortex such as ACC and DPFC are needed for higher order thinking and decision-making.

Amygdala

The amygdala is an area of the limbic system in the anterior temporal lobe, that has been most frequently discussed in studies of race that test for differential reactions to Black versus White faces (Kubota, Banaji, & Phelps, 2012). Given cultural shifts across time in the United States regarding polite conversations about race, the methods in which many of the Black-White racial stimuli of faces need to be tested has also shifted. Therefore, as expected, studies of neuroscience and racial attitudes measure implicit racial associations' impact on decision-making and behavior. Somewhat consistently, implicitly classically conditioned associations have been revealed that represent negative fear-based attitudes regarding Black versus White faces. The findings overall have been complex regarding variation of bias shown among Black participants towards Black faces, as well as for White participants towards Black faces.

Findings in this realm of research, can be interpreted as a toxic culturally produced seeping of anti-blackness into the brains of citizens, irrespective of participants' race. Black and White citizens may be classically conditioned to fear Black people, favor Black people, discriminate negatively against Black people, or to be neutral in reactions to Black versus White faces. Researchers have concluded too that there are overlapping systems and responses of both an implicit and explicit nature regarding neural activation shown via BOLD to Black versus White faces. The small group of nuclei that make up the amygdala evolved in brain development to be vital for animals' and humans' encoding, storage, and learning through classical conditioning to fear threatening stimuli. However, nowadays we must study these areas of the brain, not merely for their evolutionary significance, but also for how they have been molded and shaped in response to chronic institutional racism. There is empirical research to be analyzed and critiqued with an aim of possible use towards solutions and intervention to remove even implicit forms of racial bias (Lai et al., 2016).

In the case of high-profile murders of unarmed Black males at the hands of police officers, the emotion of fear of the officers has been evident. Officers can either be heard speaking in a terrified trembling tone on audio (e.g., the murder of Philander Castile) or officers have been referenced as being shaky and nervous by unarmed Black men who were forced to engage with the police (e.g., Clarence Evans). In the murder of Michael Brown, the officer admitted he was afraid of Michael Brown. Though the ontogenetic existence of a brain structure vital to the divine spirit's experience of fear during human experiences reflects the wisdom of any human body regarding survival, for Black people's lives, the evolutionary psychobiology has repeatedly worked against their survival. A once rational fear-based reaction of the amygdala became irrationally conditioned over time to manifest due to a sociocultural creation of illusory othering and fear of Black people often deemed less than human.

Anterior Cingulate Cortex and Dorsolateral Prefrontal Cortex

It is possible to feel an emotion that does not align with a thought that one has; it is also possible to have competing response options regarding reacting to a single stimulus. Therefore, cognitive monitoring and cognitive control are necessary for many life situations which require rapid decision-making or action. Without an optimally directed anterior cingulate cortex, humans would be unable to successfully engage the executive control needed to act counter to subcortical feelings in favor of thoughtful, more intentional rational behaviors. A vivid example of a situation in which amygdala activation may have overridden the cortical is the case of the 2016 shooting of Charles Kinsey by North Miami police officer Jonathan Aledda. It is plausible that implicit anti-Black attitudes may seep into the minds of officers due to exposure to toxic anti-Blackness within the wider culture.

Charles Kinsey worked as a caretaker of a severely autistic Latino man, Mr. Rios. Mr. Rios had run into the street and sat in the middle of the street holding a toy truck. Officers were called to the scene by a witness who reported that Rios may have been armed. Kinsey, the caretaker, is a Black male. Kinsey may have made the decision to lie on the street with his hands up to attempt to avoid being shot by officers arriving onto the scene. Kinsey also tried continuously to get his client, Mr. Rios, to sit still and be calm (Ovalle, 2019). Despite Kinsey's proactive efforts to avoid harm to himself and harm to Mr. Rios, Kinsey was shot in the leg by Officer Aledda, who shot from a distance behind a parked car across the street.

Aledda stated in his trial that his heart was pounding out of his chest as he contemplated that he would have to shoot Mr. Rios in order to protect Mr. Kinsey, who he thought Mr. Rios was going to "shoot" (Ovalle, 2019). Mr. Rios was unarmed; other officers testifying in the case reported, that as they arrived on the scene Mr. Rios appeared to pose no threat. When Mr. Kinsey asked officer Aledda why he was shot, the officer's response was, "I don't know." Aledda's reference to his heart pounding out of his chest indicates fear-based sympathetic nervous system arousal, and activation of his amygdala. It is possible that Aledda may have consciously wanted to be fair, rational, and intentional in his actions. Yet, faced with two ethnic minority males who are "othered" as "wretched" under a White supremacist patriarchal culture (with a cognitive seed planted that one man might be armed), Aledda was unable to successfully activate executive neural control in the situation. He therefore shot an unarmed man who was lying in the street with his hands up in submission.

However, Aledda still thought he saw a weapon instead of a toy truck in possession by Mr. Rios; Aledda thought Mr. Rios was about to turn a gun on Mr. Kinsey; Aledda though, does not shoot Rios, but instead shoots Kinsey. In this situation, rapid visual and auditory processing were occurring while Aledda's adrenal glands were also pumping cortisol through his body, due to the activated sympathetic nervous system in the situation. Ideally, the ACC would establish and maintain executive control to optimally manage the fear and human illusion (perceiving a toy truck as a gun) which promoted a shooting of an innocent Black man, Charles Kinsey. It is the ACC in a situation such as this, that has the capability to evaluate an irrational thought, dispose of it, think something different, and then choose among an acceptable vs unacceptable course of action. In Aledda's case, perhaps the stress of the cultural neuroscience of perceptions of Black and Brown men contributed to his misperception and faulty life-threatening implicit decision to shoot in the direction of the two harmless men, injuring one. He misperceived the toy held by a non-White man, because of conditioning in a socio-cultural world, and then he reacted from this irrational fear.

The outcome in this situation also relates to the significant role of the dorsolateral prefrontal cortex (DLPFC) in conjunction with the ACC. Imaging and other physiological research reveals from closely examining the neuroscience of race bias and conflicting thoughts and actions to racial stimuli, the need for further studies of the DLPFC (Kubota et al., 2012).

The DLPFC governs self-control. Aledda's behavior represented a failure to accurately perceive his error, resulting in an inappropriate action of shooting a defenseless harmless Black man. The conclusions from neuroscience of race studies suggest that Aledda's DLPFC was not optimally active to control the unwanted implicit racial associations made for Kinsey and Rios. Aledda's verbal response to Kinsey, stating he did not know why he shot him, may be taken as evidence that the shooting stemmed from implicit negative racial attitude and dysregulation of self-control, typically governed by the DLPFC.

Fusiform Gyrus

The fusiform gyrus area (FFA) has also been studied by scientists interested in the neuroscience of race, specifically to assess how research participants readily identify faces of people outside their racial group (Kubota, Banaji, & Phelps, 2012). Generally, the FFA has been discussed as a face recognition area of the brain. Persons who have difficulty recognizing faces have no trouble distinguishing a face from a stimulus that is not a face. However, damage to the FFA affects the ability to distinguish the detailed components of faces, thereby making recognition of the faces of even familiar people difficult to do. The FFA contributes to quick processing of racial information; it shows a stronger response activation when research participants see faces of persons from within their racial group. This is not surprising, given the existence of the other-race effect in which research participants have reported perceiving all people of the same race to look alike. There is room for increased innovation in these studies of the fusiform gyrus, as the literature is limited in analyzing this area, beyond noting its role in recognizing faces. However, given the lingering presence of nuanced manifestations of White supremacist racial preferences, how might future studies of the fusiform gyrus be incorporated into experimental implicit bias studies of colorism (Reed, 2017)?

Race as a social construct is the central message of critical race theory; the consequences of this social construct are grave for how it impacts what our brains perceive and react upon. The perception of "racial other" as object, rather than as human is critical to the way marginalized people are treated. Ani (1994) makes this case by stating that the greater the perceived distance of a marginalized racial group member from the European culture, the greater the perception of the marginalized person as an object as opposed to a human. Ani explains that once rendered sub-human or object, the marginalized person can be easily ill-treated or even murdered with no empathy (Ani, 1994).

Human-Made Illusions

What is the rendering of a human into an object, if not an illusion of human brain perception? Wilson (1993) wrote of the seemingly apolitical nature of standard theoretical and empirical writings in psychology. As example, he described the way standard introduction to psychology authors present classical conditioning to the reader. In their typical descriptions of dogs conditioned to salivate to a bell, or the case of Little Albert being conditioned to fear a small white animal, the presentation of classical conditioning is wholly depoliticized.

Considering Wilson's position, upon examining standard psychological sciences texts, one will recognize that classical conditioning as it relates to social problems is not presented in the standard Eurocentric curricula. Instances of racial othering of Black people's bodies via classical conditioning is not incorporated into the lessons of standard Eurocentric curriculum. It would be easy to include the classical conditioning of race-based threat as example of Blackness being associated with danger, violence, and predatory behavior The resulting death from such conditioning is perhaps deemed too political or controversial.

Juxtaposed to discussions of salivating dogs and conditioned anxiety in an infant, such vexing examples of classical conditioning of the violence enacted against oppressed people are avoided or perhaps deemed irrelevant. Wilson's argument is that Eurocentric presentations of learning theory depoliticize the theories. The same can be said for standard Eurocentric publications in psychology about human perception (Carbon, 2014). Embedded in the seemingly apolitical language of theories of human perception, is clear science which explains the psychology of how a human brain would become enculturated and conditioned to accept illusory White supremacy and could perceive a racially marginalized human to be a dangerous object. Although conspicuously devoid of discussion of race-based homicidal examples of cognitive processing, Eurocentric scientists who study perception have stated that objective perception is impossible; they have stated that inherently, perception is an illusion (Carbon, 2014).

One poignant example is the homicide of Philando Castile in July 2016. Castile was a Black male cafeteria worker in a local school in Minnesota. On the day he was fatally shot by a Minnesota police officer, he was riding on the passenger side of an Oldsmobile with his girlfriend and the girlfriend's 4-year-old daughter in the backseat. The officer initiated what was thought to be a routine traffic stop; it was later reported that the officer believed Castile to be a suspect wanted in an unrelated search, so he stopped the vehicle (Berman, 2017). The Castile shooting went viral when his girlfriend posted the immediate aftermath of Castile's murder via Facebook livestream. The officer who shot Castile was questioned and gave his perception of events. His perception can be analyzed for how the words represent another example of racism as a biosocial problem, particularly as the human brain is capable of human-made illusions (Carbon, 2014).

Repeatedly, the officer stated how Castile's hand kept moving. The officer repeatedly stated that the movement and positioning of Castile's hand appeared to be wrapped around a gun that he perceived Castile to be pulling from his pocket (Berman, 2017). Repeatedly the officer says Castile was not following his instructions and only doing what Castile wanted to do. The officer also says he smelled marijuana in the vehicle; this further socially constructed a perception of criminal, drug user, drug dealer. He questioned Castile's character because he was in possession (legally) of a gun, because he perceived the smell of marijuana, because he said, he feared for his life. The officer feared Castile was reaching for a weapon to shoot the officer. Castile had revealed to the officer that he was licensed to carry a gun and stated he had the licensed gun in his possession.

When the officer asked Castile for his ID upon stopping the vehicle, this is when Castile informed the officer he had the licensed weapon; Castile was following orders of reaching for his requested ID. However, the officer still feared for his life, he stated, because of the fear of the moving hand in search of ID, he perceived to be Castile pulling out a gun. On the audio of the incident, the officer's voice is nervously hysterical. The officer also said, he just was not sure what Castile was going to do with his moving hand. The St. James Minnesota police department made an agreement with the acquitted officer, by which the officer could voluntarily separate from the police department with monetary compensation. It was reported that the St. James police department felt this was the best way to wrap things up as quickly as possible, given the emotionality of Castile's murder, and need for community healing (Forliti, 2017).

Human perception involves our brains filling in any missing data with what is believed to be the most plausible information based on our experiences. Particularly with visual processing, it is often perceived as reality-based, although it too is affected by stress and otherwise compromised mental bandwidth. When the officer who stopped Castile provided his perspective of the events, he stated that he just did not know what Castile was going to do when he perceived Castile to be wrapping his hand around a gun in his pocket. If a brain has been culturally immersed in anti-Black racism, it is plausible that an officer could erroneously fill in missing data (what object he thought Castile was wrapping his hand around inside his pocket). Also, for cases in which unarmed Black men have been fatally shot while holding a cell phone or wallet perceived to be a firearm, these cases too are examples of human-made illusions that stem from a culturally constructed world of anti-Black racism. When officers fill-in missing data about Black persons who they stop and detain, in such situations they may develop hypotheses about what is happening in the situation at the moment, and how they believe the situation will evolve (Carbon, 2008). However, if such hypotheses are misleading or incorrect (e.g., culturally influenced racist expectations about what Black people are likely do), then the underlying decision-making in the situation will be problematic. Subsequent actions that stem from the erroneous initial hypothesis (e.g., Black people are inherently dangerous and will behave as dangerous criminals), in many cases can lead to fatal decisions such as the murder of Castile, and others such as Tamir Rice.

While 12-year old Black male, Tamir Rice, was playing outside with a toy gun, he was fatally shot by a police officer. This can be analyzed in accordance with race-based top-down processing by the officer. Such a shooting may begin from a false premise of Blackness as either sub-human or superhuman. Socially constructed images of Black people have negatively affected realistic perceptual processing of Black people in the brain (Eberhardt, 2019).

Perception is socially constructed, and the way it is socially constructed is based in evolutionary psychology's explanations of survival or promotion of a species. The human brain rapidly constructs reality of what we are perceiving to make quick judgments of a whole situation, person, or object to take quick action. Depoliticized explanations of top-down processing, however, are devoid of applications to social problems such as the murder of Tamir Rice. However, an examination of the nature of top-down processing provides clues to racist-based fatal shootings of unarmed Black people. Carbon (2008) explains that top-down processing of our world and the objects and people in it, are guided through information we have gained over the years. As well, there are several cases in which the top-down processing was guided by cognitions of a prejudicial and interpretive nature. The whole image or scenario is rather quickly constructed to make snap judgements of categorization, decisions, and action. Depoliticized evolutionary psychology would reference this as vital to human survival (Neuberg, Kenrick, & Schaller, 2011); yet in the case of Tamir Rice and others it worked against his survival.

Steve Loomis, former president of the Cleveland police patrolman association, deemed it insignificant information to be dispatched, that Tamir Rice had a toy, not a real gun in his possession. However, research regarding the neuroscience of race suggests this would have been important given the magnitude of processing and decision-making needed during the encounter in which Tamir was fatally shot. The social construction of reality means we change the meaning of a scene towards what we expect (Carbon, 2008). An important question is, what has the social world taught one to expect from a person deemed sub-human or superhuman?

In November 2014, Cleveland Ohio police officers responded to a 911 call, dispatching them to Cudell Recreation Center. The police were told that a man in the park had a gun and was waiving it around, pointing at people. The emergency dispatcher was subsequently suspended for eight days for omitting information. The dispatcher failed to notify officers that the suspect could have been a child with a fake gun (Ali, 2017). Video footage showed that within 2 seconds of arriving to the scene, an officer fatally shot the 12-year-old Black child who was holding a pellet gun.

The officer who shot the boy reported he had to make a fast decision to shoot because he and his partner were in immediate danger as easy targets. He perceived, due to their positioning in the car, that they were sitting ducks (Ali, 2017). Thus, informed by research, Tamir could have been perceived as larger and more threatening to the officers in this instance, because the shooting officer believed his own positionality put him at a disadvantage. The officer perceived his own capabilities as more inferior to Tamir's. The officer perceived himself as incapacitated in the presence of a Black suspect perceived to be a large man (Fessler, Holbrook, & Gervais, 2014).

Tamir Rice was described as a grown man between the ages of 18 and 20 by several different witnesses, although he was just 12 years old (News 5 Staff, 2017). Psychologists have revealed through experimental research that Black males are perceived as stronger, bigger, and more formidable (Wilson, Hugenberg, & Rule, 2017) than similarly sized White males. In the research, possible racial biases in judgment were examined. Wilson, Hugenberg, & Rule (2017) had the following hypotheses, of 1) research participants would misperceive young Black men as physically larger and more formidable than young White men of comparable size, 2) race-based bias in perception of physical formidability could lead to race-based biases in decisions about the use of force.

The researchers conducted seven studies to test these hypotheses. Findings were that young Black men were perceived as taller, heavier, more muscular, and more physically formidable and more capable of physical harm than similarly-sized young White men. According to Wilson et al., this bias in perception of Black men's physical size can influence the amount of force used against them. An example of this is obvious in the statements from Steve Loomis, saying the following regarding Tamir Rice (Schultz, 2015),

> Tamir Rice is in the wrong. He's menacing. He's 5-feet-7, 191 pounds. He wasn't that little kid you're seeing in pictures. He's a 12-year-old in an adult body. Tamir looks to his left and sees a police car. He puts his gun in his waistband. Those people—99 percent of the time those people run away from us. We don't want him running into the rec center. That could be a whole other set of really bad events. They're trying to flush him into the field. Frank [the driver] is expecting the kid to run. The circumstances are so fluid and unique.

Note Loomis' use of the "othered" reference to "those people." His language may represent implicit or explicit bias. Loomis' reference to "those people" is indicative of a slur-type reference to a group of bodies not perceived as law-abiding humans. Loomis vacillates in his statements, from referring to Tamir as menacing and not a little kid, to giving a final statement of "expecting the kid to run." It is as if in his logical mind, he knows Tamir was a kid; however, in his racist perception of a Black child's physicality, Tamir could not be a kid. Reports from the day's events showed that Tamir Rice laid bleeding on the ground for four minutes before anyone came to his aid. He later died in the hospital. Likewise, Michael Brown's body was left lying in the middle of Canfield Drive in Ferguson, Missouri, for at least four hours after he was fatally shot by a police officer (Bosman & Goldstein, 2014).

Steve Loomis' description of Tamir Rice is consistent with the findings of Wilson et al. (2017) in one of their studies which found that perceivers overestimate young Black men as taller and heavier than young White men; they couple Black men's faces with larger, more muscular, and more formidable physiques when attempting to match a Black male face to a body that they perceive fits the face. The validity of the studies done by Wilson et al. is reflected in the researchers' large sample size and their method of presentation of the stimuli.

Over 900 participants rated color photos of White and Black men who were of equal height and weight. The participants, when asked to estimate height and weight of the men in the photographs, consistently showed bias in perceiving Black men to be larger and stronger than White men. As well, Black men with more stereotypically Black facial features produced a stronger effect of bias regarding their perceived physical strength and likelihood of being perceived as a threat. The consequence of such perception is that unarmed Black men and boys may often experience excessive force at the hands of law enforcement. Tamir Rice's body size was mentioned repeatedly in a police report of the incident. The fact that his and Michael Brown's bodies lie unattended after they were shot are further testament to their being dehumanized.

Researchers interested in moving beyond merely discussing the history of dehumanization of Black people, empirically tested for dehumanization via use of experimental manipulation of the "Negro-ape metaphor" (Goff et al., 2008). The Negro-ape metaphor has deep historical roots beginning with European philosophers' descriptions of a continuum of human development that renders the White man as the most evolved human and Black people as the least evolved human. Goff et al. (2008) designed studies using priming, to test whether in modern times college students would still implicitly associate Black people with images and thoughts of an ape.

The findings were the students did in fact have Negro-ape cognition. The Negro-ape metaphor was also influential in participants' greater support for violence against a Black suspect relative to a White suspect. The power of media's use of the Negro-ape metaphor, even subtly, influences attitudes towards Black defendants and jury decisions to execute Black defendants (Goff et al. 2008). One of the Goff et al. studies also acutely revealed the power of white supremacy, as researchers found that cognition of a White person as an ape was an inhibited association in the minds of the participants.

From Sub-Human to Super-Humanization Bias

Using standard depoliticized theory and concepts from the study of human perception, cases of homicide of Black men can be clearly related to race-based perceptions of sub-human objectification or at the other extreme, superhumanization. Superhumanization is the attribution of supernatural, extrasensory, and magical mental and physical qualities to humans (Waytz et al., 2014). Superhumanization has been investigated for its association with how Black identified persons are perceived. It increases endorsement of police brutality against Black people and reduces altruism towards Black people. Superhumanization is another example of othering. Until the Waytz et al. (2014) studies, superhumanization was largely an empirically unexamined phenomenon.

Ironically, people may view superhumanization characteristics as positive and complimentary, even as these characteristics can cause harm to ordinary humans who are erroneously considered to be so tough and so strong they do not feel pain. Waytz et al. explain the concepts of moral agent and moral patient. If a Black person is shown as a moral agent, the person will be viewed as capable of either helping or harming another person. Depending on the label of helpful or harmful, the outcome is the Black person will be perceived as an extremely benevolent mystical being, or an extremely strong, aggressive, and monstrous being. Researchers report that once a Black person is typed as a moral agent, it is not possible for them to subsequently be viewed as a moral patient, which would be a human being capable of receiving help or a person capable of being harmed.

Across a series of 5 studies, researchers investigated the existence of superhumanization bias perceptions of Black people. White participants implicitly and explicitly superhumanized Black persons versus White persons, using Black target stimuli of both genders. The superhuman qualities identified from the series of studies were mental control, running at the speed of light, expectation of heightened abilities due to strength or magic, and generally expectations of mysticism or supernatural capabilities. Overall, the studies revealed a robust effect of superhumanization bias as social cognition about Blacks, among the White college students tested. The implications of this research: once they are viewed as a superhuman, Black people may receive less empathy when they need assistance, such as when they have been injured. Their experience of pain may also be dismissed.

Cultural Neuroscience, Dehumanization, and the Freddie Gray Case

Freddie Gray, 25, was arrested "without force or incident" on April 12, 2015, for alleged possession of a switchblade knife, though the knife was legal. It is uncertain why Gray was stopped by police. Gray ran upon seeing police but had not committed any crime. Given maltreatment and murders committed against unarmed Black men, Gray's reaction was likely a conditioned fear-based flee from seeing the police, once his amygdala and sympathetic nervous system were aroused. A week after the arrest, Gray died due to injuries sustained while in police custody. The autopsy revealed Gray's death to be the result of a "high-energy injury" to his spine. Neurologists define a high energy injury as an acute, traumatic cervical spinal cord injury that occurs from motor vehicle trauma (McCarthy et al., 2011). Therefore, his death was ruled a homicide attributable to acts of omission of the police (Bertrand & Sterbenz, 2015).

The medical examiner deemed Gray's injury comparable to injury one might sustain if diving into shallow water. The injuries sustained were to the lower left side of his head, believed to have occurred when the police were driving Gray around in the van while shackled by wrists and ankles (Bertrand

& Sterbenz, 2015). The police made several stops, often stopping short likely causing Gray to fall unsupported; he was shackled and placed into the van on his belly and he was not secured with a seatbelt. During his transport by police van, Gray suffered a medical emergency that severed his spine 80 percent at his neck. The medical examiner wrote that Gray's spinal cord injury possibly occurred when Gray was partially reclining or if he was trying to change his position on the floor of the van after falling from the rough ride (e.g., defined as abrupt acceleration and deceleration without seat-belt while shackled).

It was reported that several times Gray stated to officers he needed medical assistance and stated he could not breathe. Despite asking for help, requesting his inhaler, and screaming in pain, Gray was not given consideration. This treatment of Freddie Gray aligns with research findings regarding the dismissal of Black persons' pain (Hoffman et al., 2016) and aligns with research that has incorporated the stereotype content model (SCM). The SCM explains that some prejudice is worse for certain groups; for example, extreme out-group members stereotypically perceived as hostile and incompetent (e.g., homeless people and drug addicted persons), are more likely to be dehumanized. Experienced by Africans throughout the diaspora, afro-pessimism and anti-Blackness are pervasive to the degree that some people of African descent may be perceived as members of an extreme out-group.

Using functional magnetic resonance imaging of the medial prefrontal cortex (mPFC), it has been found that research participants showed no mPFC activation to extreme outgroup members, though it is typical that social cognition regarding humans would activate the mPFC. It was concluded from the research that extreme out-group members may not actually be perceived as human, similarly to the perception of objects rather than humans (Harris & Fiske, 2006). Instead of activation of the mPFC, the perception of extreme out-group members produced reaction in the amygdala and insula areas of the brain; these areas typically activate as a result of disgust (Harris & Fiske, 2006). Therefore, when media coverage of shootings of unarmed Black people have occurred, whose bodies laid deceased in public for several minutes or even hours, this has not been discussed in connection to brain science. This does the public a disservice. It is imperative for the public to understand the science underlying the objectification and dehumanization of Black bodies. When this occurs, it can manifest at the level of the brain, specifically the insula and amygdala because the persons are not viewed as human.

The Harris and Fiske (2006) study provides evidence that people could feel disgust evoked by someone such as Freddie Gray, resulting in his dehumanization. Gray grew up in an impoverished neighborhood by the name of Sandtown-Winchester on Baltimore's west side. Gray and his family inhabited a home with high levels of lead-paint (Cox, Bui, & Brown, 2015). Seven years prior to his death, a lawsuit had been filed on his family's behalf because of the lead-paint in his residence. The suit was filed against the owners of the home where he and his family lived. He was the recipient of settlement payments referred to in his community as "lead checks." These payments were Gray's source of income, paid to him by the government, due to the excessive lead poison he was exposed to during his lifetime. Cognitively he was also four grade levels behind in reading; he and his siblings were rendered dysfunctional as a result of the lead poisoning. This is consistent with findings from a longitudinal study of the harmful impact of exposure to lead as an environmental toxin (Stewart & Schwartz, 2007).

In addition to lead exposure throughout Gray's childhood living in poverty, his mother was reported in court papers to be disabled, illiterate, and addicted to heroin (Cox, Bui, & Brown, 2015). These are intersectional classifications that could render some humans to be perceived as less than human in the minds of people Fanon referred to as the proletariat class. In media stories of such high-profile cases of social injustice such as with Freddie Gray, the relevant culture, history, and science of human perception are not linked to the events. Yet, the relevance to the science of perception is evident in the details of the backgrounds of such dehumanized people, and the behaviors directed towards them.

Tancredo Neves/Beiru Neighborhood (Salvador da Bahia, Brazil)

In the nation of Brazil in impoverished Black neighborhoods, the subject of this chapter is also relevant. In Beiru (officially renamed Tancredo Neves, to honor a White Brazilian politician), a neighborhood in the city of Salvador, Bahia, Black people have endured random open fire upon them by the police. Police have been described as enacting violence in neighborhoods of Brazil where the poorest and Black persons reside (French, 2013). Officers have entered certain neighborhoods such as Tancredo Neves and opened fire into the streets, sending residents scurrying, or leaving dead bodies of anyone unfortunate to escape via running into side spaces. Therefore, residents commonly walk hurriedly and closely along the fronts of buildings when walking to their domiciles, particularly at night. The residents do this preemptively in event the police should appear, and they must run from the sidewalk to a slightly more secure area. This constitutes random unsolicited and unwarranted open fire on Black Brazilians that scholars elsewhere have addressed (Smith, 2018a). The police typically cannot be held accountable because officers may report the incidents as retaliatory gunshots in self-defense. In the aftermath, residents' bodies can be removed from the scene and planted with weapons or drugs as the police deem it necessary for cover-ups. Black human beings are thus being treated as though they are objects on a screen in a recreationally violent video game.

Conclusion

The history and trajectory of othering in the form of dehumanization and superhumanization is a long path. While many scholars across various disciplines have written extensively about this history, the integration of it with the understanding of cultural neuroscience, social cognition, and the stereotype content model research has not been pervasively at the forefront of scientific writing. Yet, when cases are researched regarding the details of the killings of unarmed Black men in the United States, coupled with actual quotes from their murderers or those otherwise complicit, there is ample evidence that some humans are not perceived as ordinary humans or even human at all.

In impoverished Black neighborhoods of various locales, dehumanization and superhumanization ideologies put Black lives at risk. Superhumanization research has already revealed how harm can come to Black people who are not viewed as moral patients, but instead as mystical, magical, superhumans. In the 21st century, U.S. based media has heightened the visibility of Black superheroes in the form of the Black Panther, Black Lightning, and Black Superman. As millions of people around the world have absorbed the images of these characters (including the developing minds of children), it may be informative to understand more about the impact of these images over time. The image of Black people becoming increasingly visible in mainstream media as superheroes has the potential to impact perceptions of Black people and Black lives. Yet how this may impact white gaze and othering is unknown. More longitudinal brain studies of these phenomena and other social influences via multiple methods of inquiry are needed. More extensively funded research of exposure or interventions that can disrupt negatively biased responses in brain areas such as the anterior cingulate cortex, dorsolateral prefrontal cortex, medial prefrontal cortex, and amygdala is critical for future research directions.

Chapter Three

Cultural Neuroscience and Poverty

Emotional Emancipation Circle for Black Women

Cultural neuroscience (CN) and behavioral economics (BE) are areas of study that have highlighted the influence of environment, culture, poverty, and context on persons' thinking and behavior. CN and BE are both interdisciplinary areas of study. For example, CN combines the study of culture, psychology, and neuroscience (Han et al., 2013). Therefore, CN researchers explain that people who have developed in different cultures, often process and perceive stimuli and contextual backgrounds differently (Han et al., 2013).

BE combines psychology and economics. Behavioral economics deviates from the standard or traditional economics, which historically has been anti-behavioral. Research in behavioral economics has consisted of two areas: 1) identifying the ways in which persons' behavior may differ from the predictions of the standard economic model and 2) making clearer why the behaviors of humans are, in fact, significant to studying economics (Mullainathan & Thaler, 2001). Thus, the decision-making and resulting behaviors of persons in poverty might also be better understood by studying behavioral economics.

Standard economists have not given attention to the consideration of concepts such as bounded rationality, bounded willpower, and bounded selfishness (Simon, 1955). Rationality, so-called willpower, and selfishness have boundaries. Traditional economists remain disinterested in human behavior and decision-making, despite the reality that many human beings must utilize immense brainpower throughout each day. Brainpower, however, is not infinite, such that attempts to solve difficult and persistent problems may mentally, emotionally, or physically tax people. Bounded rationality, bounded willpower, and bounded selfishness are more of a reality under these challenging circumstances. Thus, Simon (1955) used the term bounded rationality to label the limited information processing capabilities of humans. One result of being cognitively overwhelmed may be the use of quicker "go-to" strategies that humans use to "save on" use of cognitive faculties (Mullainathan & Thaler, 2001). A consideration of such strategies is particularly relevant to the behavior of economically disenfranchised people. Why? Because all humans, but particularly humans living under a persistently stressful life of poverty, have been known to experience cognitive impediment (Mani, Mullainathan, Shafir & Zhao, 2013).

The work of BE researchers can be used to help explain why people challenged by poverty, may not always behave in their own best interests, and why they may make predictable and recurring cognitive, emotional, and social errors regarding economic stability (Mullainathan & Thaler, 2001). Researchers have found that a decision that is perceived as irrational by the affluent, could seem completely rational to persons challenged by poverty (Mani, Mullainathan, Shafir, & Zhao, 2013). Based on lessons learned from CN literature, poverty literature, and the behavioral economics literature, one can argue that the cultural context of cognitions and resulting behaviors are related to the sub-optimal environment of impoverished living. In consideration of culture and poverty, the following have been identified as cognitive analytical devices relevant to persons living in poverty (Small, Harding, & Lamont, 2010):

Cultural capital—people of different cultural environments privilege different tastes, habits, and styles

Narratives—accounts of how persons living in poverty view themselves relative to others; narratives are central to how people construct their social identities. Narratives impact actions. People will choose actions that they think are consistent with their personal identities and personal narratives. Example: "*I'm broke, so I have to go to the pay day loan office.*"

Repertoires—people living in poverty do not possess different values from the rest of society but rather have access to a different set of "modes of action" and meanings

Values—these vary based on different conceptions of culture, institutions, boundary work, i.e., limits on types of work that may be thought of as possible or relevant for career pursuits

Frames—how people living in poverty behave, depends on how they perceive themselves, the world, or their surroundings; frames also include expectations about the consequences of their behavior and the relationships between various aspects of their social worlds. By understanding the frames that people living in poverty bring to their social interactions and decision-making, we can begin to understand variation in their interpretations and understandings.

CULTURAL NEUROSCIENCE

Cultural neuroscience as a specifically designated field is only a decade old. Over the course of the 10 years, researchers in the field of CN have presented detailed information as to how the brain is a biosocial organ (Han et al., 2013). Research findings have reflected how different cultures react differently to situations including trauma, and how the situations vary in effect on neurotransmitters and hormones, such as cortisol, the stress hormone (Sasaki & Kim, 2016). Culture impacts the information processing of the brain because the brain is shaped by experiences. An example is the behavior of research participants from collectivist cultures who show similar brain responses when thinking about "themselves" as when they think about another person such as a relative (Han et al., 2013). This exemplifies brain evidence for the phrase, "I am because we are"; "I am a person because of other persons." Hans et al. found that the brains of people from individualistic cultures do not show this same brain pattern of collectivism.

Interestingly too, the executive functions of the frontal lobe may also shape cultural style (Azar, 2010). For example, once the brain's functioning has been shaped by experiences and environment (such as living in an impoverished community), the poverty-influenced executive functioning of the brain may lead to predictable and persistent adaptive repertoires used within the stressful environment, i.e., economically disenfranchised communities (Azar, 2010). This may explain why often, persons living in poverty are viewed as having similar frames, repertoires, and values (Small, Hardwood, & Lamont, 2010).

Cultural Neuroscience: Power, Motivation, and the Brain

Specifically, reduced power has been found to be associated with increased threat, punishment, and social constraint, and thereby activates inhibition-related motivation (Galinsky, Magee, Inesi, & Gruenfeld, 2006; Boksem, Smolders, & De Cremer, 2012). The lives of many people living in poverty, are characterized by powerlessness and voicelessness, which bounds their choices; poverty also defines and impacts the quality of how they engage with current and potential employers, markets, the state, and even non-governmental organizations (NGOs), (Narayan, 2000).

Socially powerless people display neuroscientific output that is an opposite pattern of activation than that amongst powerful people and may have compromised executive functions due to lack of power (Smith, Jostmann, Galinsky, & van Dijk, 2008). Powerful people have shown increased right frontal lobe activation representative of approach motivation (Carver & White, 1994; Guinote, 2007; Boksem, Smolders, & De Cremer, 2012). These findings suggest that persons living in poverty and experiencing powerlessness may be neuro-cognitively more inhibited from optimal decision-making to engage in more optimal behaviors that increase opportunities to advance the economic ladder. This has been elsewhere discussed as cognition and behavior that represents the influence of the science of scarcity (Mullainathan & Shafir, 2014). This could possibly be addressed by intervention with adults via culturally sensitive community-based healing and empowerment experiences that could boost group-oriented self-determination and action (Association of Black Psychologists & Community Healing Network, Inc., 2016).

A review of the literature in CN reflects an absence of applied community-based research that focuses on culture, poverty, and decision-making, as possibly related to engagement in optimal/healthy motivation among people of African descent. However, there is data-driven evidence to support the explanation that feelings of powerlessness, which relates to living in poverty, are related to behavioral inhibition (Galinsky, Magee, Inesi, & Gruenfeld, 2006; Smith, Jostmann, Galinsky, & van Dijk, 2008). This relationship between powerlessness and behavioral inhibition is not characteristic of a people across all time and place. For example, persons who endured horrific inhumane treatment and lacked social power during periods of enslavement throughout the African diaspora, showed multiple examples of motivation to liberate themselves. Thus, the shifts in socio-cultural environment across time may influence the relevance of social power to behavioral motivation or inhibition.

Empowerment

Psychological empowerment is empowerment at the individual level of analysis (Zimmerman 1995). Zimmerman also writes that there is a difference between empowering processes and empowering outcomes; the empowering processes refer to the steps leading to people's self-determination. There are two approaches that may successfully lead to these empowerment processes. One approach is the participative ownership process, where individuals become involved and actively engaged in the programs that will impact their lives, and another approach is participatory action research (PAR), in which disenfranchised community participants become coequals in developing potentially beneficial programs and evaluation.

Empowering outcomes have been identified as research methods, including interventions that are designed to empower individuals. Empowering outcomes also refers to using research findings to generate a body of empirical literature to further develop empowerment theory. When researching empowerment, it is expected that empowerment takes different forms for different people, takes different forms in different contexts, and may fluctuate over time (Zimmerman, 1995). In other words, there is no one size fits all approach to empowering people within communities. Cognitive empowerment varies by race, such that African Americans understand more than European Americans how power functions through working in relationship with others, and through the community coming together in common interest regarding what to prioritize (Peterson, Hamme, & Speer, 2002).

Psychological empowerment also involves an intrapersonal component, an interactional component, and a behavioral component (Zimmerman, 1995). Thus, developing community programs in a participatory action format among people living in poverty, and in a manner that incorporates intrapersonal, interactional, and behavioral components is ideal. Therefore, the use of the emotional emancipation circles (EEC) in the current project aligns with this approach. Constructs to be measured by an empowerment scale are cognitive, emotional, and behavioral components (Speer & Peterson, 2000). Assessing the cognitive construct provides data about the participants' thoughts and decision-making. The cognition regards a) perception of relations to those in power, b) ideology about community, and c) degree to which residents believe power can be established through relationships with each other in the community.

For purposes of the current research, the behavioral component is a priority for long-term research. A measurement of behavioral empowerment was expected to best reflect the participants' behavioral involvement in activities relevant to self-sufficiency and gradual and persistent movement up the economic ladder. Civic engagement and educational attainment are examples of behavioral empowerment outcomes that may occur from participating in emotional emancipation circles. The behavioral empowerment measure used consisted of assessing seven items via self-report of likely community action behaviors over a three-month period. The behavioral empowerment construct assessed the following specific measures:

- Attendance at an event promoting information about community services or attending an open house for college or other educational enrollment
- Writing an email or making a phone call to influence a policy or issue
- Attending a public policy meeting to press for a policy change
- Attending a meeting to gather information about a neighborhood issue or business opportunity
- Having an in-depth face-to-face conversation about an issue affecting the community
- Signing a petition
- Arranging an agenda for a public or private meeting

- The behavioral empowerment outcomes have been stated to have implications for the following (Speer & Peterson, 2000):
- mental and physical health
- civic engagement
- public safety
- economic productivity
- educational attainment
- resilient neighborhoods
- quality of life

Psychological Well-Being

Studying persons existing within a culture of poverty and oppression, such as seen at elevated percentages in Forsyth County, NC, was expected to shed light on feelings of powerlessness and inhibition that stem from poverty and structural racism. Poverty and related powerlessness have the potential to interfere with the approach motivation needed to make optimal decisions (Boksem, Tops, Wester, Meijman, & Lorist, 2006)). Poverty experienced across several generations of families and neighborhoods may lead to a cultural neuroscience-informed inhibition that keeps the masses of the community in a cycle of poverty; specifically, this has been explained via reference to narratives, frames, cultural capital, and repertoires used by persons challenged by poverty (Small, Harding, & Lamont, 2010). It is to be expected that poverty and powerlessness could tax several cognitive, social, emotional, and behavioral capacities to focus on optimal opportunities for upliftment and advancement. The dimensions of powerlessness and ill-being that are potentially affected include (Narayan, 2000):

- Lack of education, information, and skills
- Lack of protection and peace of mind
- Discrimination and isolation
- Troubled and unequal gender relations
- Hunger, exhaustion, sickness, and poor appearance
- Weak and disconnected organizations for those in poverty
- Existence in risky, isolated, stigmatized, un-serviced places
- Assets and livelihoods that are seasonal, precarious, inadequate
- Institutions that are disempowering and exclusionary
- Behaviors of disregard and abuse by the more powerful against the powerless

Assessment of psychological well-being of persons living in poverty is recommended to inform social justice efforts on their behalf. Ryff & Keyes (1995) assessed psychological well-being by measuring self-acceptance, establishment of quality ties to others, pursuit of meaningful goals, ability to manage complex environments aligned with one's personal needs and values, continued growth and development as a person, and sense of autonomy in one's thought. As with much of the research in behavioral and social sciences and neuroscience, these aspects of psychological well-being have not been thoroughly investigated among people of African descent who are challenged by poverty.

Emotional Emancipation Circles

Emotional emancipation circles (EECs), have been created and utilized by the Community Healing Network, Inc. (CHN), in association with the Association of Black Psychologists (ABPsi) in the U.S., Cuba, Haiti, Great Britain, and South Africa. To defy the lie of the myth of Black inferiority, the Association of Black Psychologists (ABPsi) and the Community Healing Network (CHN) are partnered to establish a global network of EECs (Grills, 2013). EECs are community-based self-help groups focused on emotional emancipation, healing, and wellness specifically for Black people. The ABPsi partnership with CHN initiated in Tuskegee, Alabama. Tuskegee's mayor and key stakeholders recognized the need for a formal partnership to address racial trauma throughout Black communities.

Via this partnership, a model and framework were established for the delivery of EECs throughout the African Diaspora. The goal of EEC participation is a mental and emotional detoxification from internalized racism and racial stress, which often lies consciously or unconsciously at the root of behavioral inhibition among disenfranchised populations. EECs are not therapy; they are safe spaces for shared conversation, collective activities, and learning. The word emancipation is critical in the spaces. Participants are informed that a "freeing" is possible from miseducation and internalized racism. It is theorized that a healing, and psychological wellness is possible that will result in greater behavioral empowerment. EECs allow for discernment, dialogue, and recalibration (Grills, 2013). Long-term goals of EECs are the rebuilding of communal/relational ties, mutual support, and a way to address a host of social problems and disparities, including economic immobility. The EEC curriculum requires coverage of seven keys to emotional emancipation. The keys are not regarded by psychologists as merely affirmations, but also once internalized and understood, they have the potential to unlock action (Association of Black Psychologists & Community Healing Network, Inc., 2016).

Researching Poverty in Winston-Salem, North Carolina

Via studying persistent poverty rates in Forsyth County, North Carolina, using CN and BE informed literature, researchers aimed to gain insight regarding the economic immobility of residents. In the areas of CN and BE, researchers' explanations do not imply inherent or innate deficits in the people but critique the environments or contexts in which the people live from day to day. This includes the socio-cultural world of institutional and structural racism. The focus of the current research was the impact of the environment, racism, and poverty's detrimental influence on motivation, cognitive capacity, and optimal decision-making. It was expected that findings from CN and BE informed research might be combined with EECs to motivate people, to not only make wiser economic decisions, but also to lead more optimally empowered, collaborative, authentic, and culturally informed lives.

This research project was conceived and conducted as community participatory action-based research (Baum, MacDougall & Smith, 2006). The circle was introduced in East Winston-Salem, North Carolina, to provide a culturally sensitive, and potentially empowering and psychologically health-enhancing intervention. Other community participatory research and analysis have informed this work to understand the depth of contextual factors and other root causes that perpetuate intergenerational poverty in Forsyth County (Karim, Greene, & Picard, 2016).

The EEC experience presented here, focused on Black women of the impoverished East Winston-Salem community. The choice to focus on women was made, due to an increased likelihood of disrupting persistent intergenerational repertoires and narratives that impact psychological well-being and economic mobility. The pillar of psychological well-being is a bridge to economic mobility and was of direct interest in the current research. (Babcock, 2014).

The choice to engage mothers in this study was evidence-based; if women and their offspring can benefit from EECs being introduced to their families and communities, wide impact across generations is a possibility. For example, research focused on mitochondrial DNA reactions revealed that inflammatory responses are triggered in the body by stress; this informed the current focus on mothers in poverty as an important evidence-based research decision (Picard & McEwen, 2018).

Mitochondrial DNA is inherited exclusively from mothers. Thus, in the case of the current study, Black mothers who are stressed from intergenerational racial trauma and intergenerational poverty, can have DNA-code that remains consistently reflective of this stress across the generations of their families (Picard & McEwen, 2018). Therefore, any community interventions that enhance psychological well-being and reduce stress and trauma could potentially have positive widespread long-term consequences for families.

There is also scientific evidence to support that the engagement of single mothers in an intervention that empowers them emotionally, might also aid in their ability to show interpersonal neural synchronization (INS) with their family members and community members; the women may also emerge as leaders in their communities (Jiang et al., 2015). However, poverty negatively impacts executive functions and therefore potentially negatively impacts the behavioral empowerment and decision-making needed for economic mobility (Babcock, 2014; Babcock, 2016).

Research Question

The question of interest for this research was: How might Black adult women who are bio-cognitively impacted by poverty, process and respond to a culturally sensitive, community-based intervention aimed at increasing emotional emancipation and behavioral empowerment?

Methodology

As the principal investigator of this research in East Winston-Salem completed a training required by ABPsi, which authorized me to facilitate EECs within Black communities.

Research Participants

Eleven self-identified Black women over aged 18 (10 with children) were the participants from the East Winston-Salem NC community. Female-identified participants as heads of household are significant in number for the county (Towncharts, 2018). Positions such as certified nursing assistant, cafeteria worker, group home worker, and housekeeping/cleaning were current positions held by the women.

The EEC experience required learning about, discussing, and emoting across seven key themes; it was important that participants persisted in participating in the experience across the eight weeks. The women were compensated with a $500 gift card for their participation at the end of the night of the seventh key theme, if they attended all the meetings. All women who received the gift card attended all sessions. All the women qualified as low income and resided in Forsyth County. All but one of the women were mothers with either school-aged or adult children. Most of the women resided in a local public housing project community. A community organizer (Black woman) who was well-known to the women, and affiliated with a local non-profit organization, transported the women via van each week to the meeting place where the circle was held.

Materials

For the circle sessions, the following materials were used:

- End of circle activity evaluation
- Quotes from elders or ancestors (pre-printed or auto-timed PowerPoint presentation slides)
- Handouts or on-screen display of closing recitation
- Pre-selected music related to the theme of the day
- Audio-visual clips related to the theme of the day
- Energy stick for demonstration of Umoja/Ubuntu (community/unity/family connection)
- Dry erase markers, small notepads, or white boards (facilitator or participants may need to write thoughts)
- Pens or pencils
- Tissue as needed
- Internet access for facilitator use
- Printout of 7 Keys and corresponding action item (optional)
- Catered food to serve approximately 30 (recommended)

Procedure

Upon arriving each week, participants were given time to partake of the food provided. During one of the eight meetings, participants completed a cognitive, behavioral, and emotional empowerment scale which has been used for informing programming and public policy in support of community organizing and community change (Speer & Peterson, 2000).

The 11 participants in the EEC experience participated in seven sessions (plus 1 general opening session as a teach-in) for approximately 2 hours. Each session after the opening session, addressed one of the requisite 7 keys (e.g., collectivism, management of emotions, thoughts, behaviors, spiritual origins, history, spiritual connections) as instructed in the emotional emancipation circle leader's guide. For the initial "teach-in" session, no key was covered; the participants were oriented as to the objective of EECs during the teach-in. Participants were given background information about why EECs were created, and a timeline of historical information to inform them about the state of psychological and emotional well-being of people of African descent.

Each week, the key for the week was given to the women. A standard order of events was loosely followed for each week, according to the guideline book for facilitating EECs. Each week, the beginning recitations and meditations were the same. The central key changed each week during EECs. Corresponding videos, quotes, and music were used in accordance with the guideline book, to give emphasis to the keys. These prompts allow the facilitator to stimulate cognitive-emotional reactions from participants. The objective for each week was to engage the women in deep dialogue to promote healing or greater psychological well-being, which is one of the five pillars of economic mobility.

Data Analysis

This research included a combination of qualitative methods to assess EEC cognitive, emotional and behavioral impact, and self-report responses regarding psychological well-being, cognitive empowerment, and behavioral empowerment measures. Based on similarly published research, it was expected that given the small sample size, participant responses to surveys would be aggregated and treated at the trend level, rather than evaluated via statistical software used in inferential statistics (Anderson et al., 2018). Multiple types of searches of the complete data corpus of qualitative information and review of responses to surveys were conducted. The aim of the analysis was to describe participants' experiences and behavioral and cognitive trends.

A trend towards positive relationship was expected between the two content measures, behavioral empowerment and psychological well-being (PWB). Responses to PWB and behavioral empowerment scale were expected to trend towards an increase for the participants, following their seven sessions of circle participation. Five women were selected for longer-term follow-up engagement for at least six months following the last circle, so that their overall personal growth in the direction of greater economic mobility could be assessed.

The Significance of Psychological Well-Being

Over the course of eight weeks of detailed field notes, naturalistic observations, and discourse analysis of psychological well-being factors (Ryff & Keyes, 1995), we determined that five of the women were most ready for movement to a Phase II level of engagement in mobility mentoring (Babcock, 2014). While previous research has listed that the strengthening of all five pillars of economic self-sufficiency is necessary for sustaining economic mobility, the current results suggest a need to prioritize well-being for a group of Black female mothers, challenged by poverty and living as heads of household in East Winston-Salem.

Content analysis was generally conducted to identify themes that resulted from the coding of commentary from research participants regarding 1) Why choosing emotional emancipation and 2) weekly quotes in response to videos, ancestral quotes, or questions posed by the facilitator and taken directly from the women during circle meetings.

Use of Undergraduate Student Researchers

Two undergraduate psychology majors and one graduate of the psychological sciences department of the university of the principal investigator were involved in this research. The students were integral to the research process as scribes during the circle meetings, administration of scales, circle logistics, in-depth discourse analysis during the once-a-week day-long research team meetings, and selection of the five women slated for continuous work beyond the eight weeks. The students were also required to do systematic observations before, during, and after the circle group meetings.

Results

Key 1—African Spiritual Origins

During this opening key, the women were asked to name their strengths. Themes emerged of persistence, God, and caregiving. The following are different examples representative of the women's overall responses:

> The Persistent: My strength is not giving up; I maintain by not giving up; it gives me a chance to do it next time.

> The Determined: I am a fighter; I don't give up, no matter what I go through, I keep pushing.

> The Compassionate: I am reliable, cook, take care of people. What keeps me going is God.

> The Giver: I take care of others, even though one person has hurt me, I still take care of people. I lean on God to keep going.

> The Warrior: My children; my Blackness; my skin makes me powerful.

When asked about why they are choosing emotional emancipation, early during Key 1, it was evident that many of the women were not sure of what answer to give, and lacked experience answering self-reflective questions specific to their motives. One woman was direct in mentioning the financial incentive, while also adding other specific motives:

> The Recipient: I wanted to come because of financial benefits; I like the atmosphere and the safe zone, and it is a weight lifted.

Other women also made general reference to the need to unburden or free themselves of keeping things bottled inside:

The Seeker: Maybe it will help me to stop walking around being an angry Black woman, maybe to move into other emotions. I think that anger is the easiest emotion to handle.

The Exhausted: I choose emotional freedom because of being bundled up, and I'm tired of crying and tired of being confused. I am just tired, and I want to be free.

The Liberationist: I am with her; I am tired of keeping it in.

Another woman in response to hearing about the Black woman and anger, said the following,

The Warrior: Sometimes anger is good, because it gives us passion, and they say that men don't approach us because we are angry . . . and we are just assertive, and we are taking care of business.

Regarding "we are taking care of business," the same woman remarked in response to one of the evening's quotes,

The Warrior: You not always gone get where you wanna go; the try is more important than the fail, at least you tried.

Key 2 — Historical Moments and Movements

During this key, the women were again asked why they chose an emotional emancipation experience. During this key, the women were given an overview of history of Black people, prior to enslavement. Themes emerged of pride, surprise, and pessimism related to the historical information given. The following are quotes from women reflective of the theme:
Why are you choosing emotional emancipation today?

The Liberationist: Freedom.

The Seeker: Because I want to be at peace.

The Exhausted: To release.

The Determined: Self-transition.

The Reserved: To talk and free myself.

The women's comments during this night's key, relative to the other keys, were generally distracted and possessed limited reflective commentary:

The Recipient: I am surprised that white people studied Black people and kingdoms and determined who was good at doing what, so they would know what type of work to make them do.

The Warrior: I feel robbed of history.

The Observer: I am happy to know all the things my people did.

The Seeker: We feel a disconnection from Africa and this history of achieving, because maybe then we have to admit our shortcoming . . . creates uncomfortableness and we have to admit where we went wrong. We now crave acceptance from other groups of people. We don't care about uplifting one another anymore, only acceptance.

While many of the women were consistent regarding attestation to talking and freeing themselves as important, one woman was adamant in repeating that many of the women in the circle were not yet at the level of being able to do this:

The Persistent: A lot of these women need to open up more and share more in the group, but they may not because they still live in communities where they cannot grow.

This key was an overview of a long span of history beginning before the enslavement of people of African descent. The women received information about African people's historically long list of inventions, kingdoms, and business ventures. Using this information as a precursor, the women were also asked on this evening to think about their talents and abilities in relationship to potential job/career pursuits. They were invited to give this some thought and answer as though lack of resources and other obstacles are not an issue. The following were their responses written on notecards submitted to us:

Teaching (youth entrepreneurship, civic engagement, Arts teacher, cooking classes, financial literacy)
Cleaning Services
Substance Abuse Counselor
Health Counselor (Diabetes, Mental Health)
Children's Haircare Business
Small Restaurant
Children's Book Author
All Female Dance Group (for children)
Homeopathic Education About Food
Travel Business (International)

Community Kitchen
Bookstore
Men's Home, Women's Home
Art Expression Center
Non-Profit Organization (focus on young girls)

Key 3 — African Cultural Wisdom

A theme of the women's responses reflected self-awareness of the need to be present at the meetings, to grow for themselves and to help others (their children) to grow. The question posed was why you are choosing emotional emancipation again, as they began the third key. Below are quotes:

The Determined: I am seeking acceptance from my sisters. I feel comfortable with people who accept me for who I am today and don't judge me.

The Seeker: Because I have been talking to my children about what we have been talking about; so I want to talk to them and teach them things that we have learned here.

The Observer: Because I need it.

The Cautious: Because today I had to let my boss know that as a Black woman, I had to work twice as hard, and I still feel like I am coming up short. I feel frustrated.

When asked about this key's theme, what does it mean to you . . . the human spirit, or your divine human spirit, the following are quotes reflective of the general responses:

The Persistent: To be connected to your purpose.

The Compassionate: To be capable of having spiritual experiences and accept that we are all connected.

The Giver: To me it means freedom to be your true self."

The Observer: To me a spiritual human being means working on a closer relationship with God and doing the right thing with the right intentions."

This key's theme evoked comments related to need for happiness and peace, irrespective of past hurts and need for control over one's circumstances:

The Determined: My mama was physically, verbally, emotionally abusive, and I didn't hear her say I love you.

The Seeker: I am not happy now. I don't know what happiness is. When I was younger, my measuring stick was a lot shorter, and now my measuring stick keeps changing because goals keep changing, and I feel like they will never be met.

The Persistent: My happiness now is peace. As long as I have peace, I'm happy. When my peace feels like it is getting tampered with then that is when my happiness is disrupted.

The Observer: My happiness now is being content with whatever is happening. I had to learn to be content with whatever situation and know that all is well, no matter what.

The Cautious: My happiness now is being in a place where I know that I can control.

The women also spoke of secretiveness, history of being or feeling alone, and acknowledgement of challenges of isolation due to mistrust. They spoke of a desire to keep things private because things can be used against you; this was described as based on experiences with abuse or betrayal.

Key 4—Human Development & Learning

Quotes given here represent the sentiments of the women when asked on this night, Why did you choose emotional emancipation today?

The Persistent: I am here because it is a part of my purpose to defy the lie of what I can and can't do.

The Warrior: I choose to be free because it is important to me.

The Determined: I am here because it helps with my recovery.

The Observer: I am here because it helps me.

The Seeker: I am here to release my mind/it takes a lot of energy to be angry and I want to release.

The Giver: I am here because I want to continue with the group I committed to/to get myself together in certain areas.

Key 4 material addresses accountability, using compassion to accept one's humanity, shortcomings, and choices made to-date, while also focusing on how to improve oneself and one's community.
What is a short coming you know you have?

The Observer: Sarcasm.

The Cautious: Arrogance, because growing up, people thought I was weird.

The Seeker: I am not quick to forgive people; people are messy, and the more chances you give people the more chances they have to be messy. It just creates more problems. I hold a grudge forever; it may not be healthy, but I do it. I am 34 years old and there are people I haven't spoken to since my teenage years. I am not teaching my children to forgive others for repeatedly hurting them and to turn the other cheek; there are certain things you only have to do one time and I don't need to mess with you again. I don't think the thought of forgiving people is eating me up inside; it is what it is. It is not what old people do that makes me angry, it is about what new people are going to do that angers me.

The Determined: I don't know. How long does it take to forgive? How do you move on without forgiving?

The Giver: I like to give and don't get a lot back. I feel aggression when I feel like I don't get what I need from friends. When it starts getting frustrating, it turns into aggression, and aggression turns into something dangerous. I am a giver; when I give all the time and don't receive anything back, I get aggressive.

Key 5—Managing Emotions, Thoughts, and Actions

This key's content theme required the women to focus on taking responsibility for managing their emotions, thoughts, and actions. The following are emotions and thoughts revealed during discussion of this key's material: mistrust, lack of experience with and understanding of emotional and mental self-care, class-envy, masking sadness, emptiness inside, putting on an act to hide self-doubt, shame, and other unhealthy emotions and thoughts. The following are quotes from the women that are representative of the women's responses this evening:

The Recipient: I am always wondering if I can trust somebody.

The Giver: I don't trust anyone that tells me I can trust them, because actions speak louder than words. That's going to make me ask them, why did you say that?

The Warrior: I think, that saying of "walking dead" means when you giving up on life while still being alive, giving up on yourself.

The Seeker: When you feel hollow inside, it changes who you are.

The Observer: After wearing all these different masks with everyone, who is the real you?

The Determined: How can you practice self-care without being selfish?

When the women were asked how this key's content relates to feelings of doubt and inferiority, below are salient statements:

The Seeker: We hurt each other because we're scared to love each other.

The Warrior: We think it's alright to hurt each other because we don't know we're hurting each other.

By this stage of the EEC experience, the women had become accustomed to the EEC prompts such as ancestral quotes, questions posed, video clips, and dialogue; the emotions, thoughts, and actions they mentioned, related to the following life experiences:

Intimate Partner Violence
Depression
Adverse Childhood Experiences
Substance Abuse
Fighting/Aggression
Betrayals
Intergenerational Trauma

Key 6 — Our African Cultural Imperative (The Collective/The Community)

The focus of this key is on restoration through emphasis on the African cultural value of the priority of collectivity and community. The discussion addressed the value of connection and sense of community with others. The following are salient quotes from the women during Key 6 coverage. The comments reflected themes of community as well as themes of change and growth:

The Determined: If you and your mama ain't free, then ain't none of us free, because we're all connected.

The Recipient: I want to understand how our ancestors had businesses that were thriving. We didn't carry on the legacy, so my age group does not have those things to invest in.

The Warrior: We still got that soul our ancestors brought to us.

The Observer: It sounds like you have to relearn things. There comes a time when you have to change who you are and relearn things."

The Giver: Change is never easy. Sometimes it's not even easy to see that you can change; you have to be willing."

The Seeker: You gotta let people teach you—you have to have an open mind and be willing; you gotta see it. Sometimes when it's a different way of life, you can't see it. It's something you gotta see that you can change. If it's something you've never done, you have to trust that someone else can guide you in it and teach you. Sometimes people have to encourage you that you can change.

The Persistent: Coming from a person that constantly stayed in the streets, it took a lot of work and guidance. There comes a time when you realize you have to do something different.

Key 7—Spirit, Spirituality, & Spiritness

The focus of this key was on strength that comes from spirituality and the spiritual connection to one another. There were frequent references to God and the challenges with connecting to others within their neighborhoods or apartment complex. The following are quotes during this key's content:

The Persistent: There is a fear of the unknown. Some people don't really know who God is.

The Determined: If God is in each of us, then that means that you have more power than you give yourself credit for.

The Recipient: You can't have a conversation and connection with every-body."

When the women were asked to respond to a quote on the screen about *"lifting as we are climbing,"* below are salient responses:

The Leader: I think that this quote is about reaching back and bringing somebody with you. You're not on the journey alone.

The Warrior: As a mother, then your kids should be your strength, and if they're not then you're weak. I don't have nobody helping me lift, but I'm still fighting. If you don't fight, then you're giving up.

The Seeker: How can you know a person hasn't tried all they can? How do you know they not tired of trying? When you have less than nothing, just enough seems like a whole lot. Sometimes people think because they've done something, it's easy for the next person to do, but everyone's struggle is different. People get to a point of what more can you do? Maybe you gotta be that person to uplift others.

The Reserved: Everybody ain't strong.

The Observer: I feel like it's a each one teach one thing.

Conclusion

The present Emotional Emancipation Circle (EEC) study with Black women who are challenged by poverty, is the only study to-date of this demographic of women which uses the EEC curriculum. Additional work is needed, to be conducted over a longer duration, such as via an in-depth longitudinal study. Optimally, having age-appropriate circles beginning with elementary school-aged Black children who can experience an EEC curriculum over their developmental trajectory would be ideal. As well, studies with a greater emphasis on quantitative measures will also enrich the literature of evidence-based research on the circles. However, it must be noted, that for the more quantitative studies to be conducted, culturally sensitive and appropriately normed scales and surveys will need to be developed for use. In the next chapter, interpretations of the women's behaviors, thoughts, and emotions will be presented, with implications for policy.

Chapter Four

The Black Women in Poverty Study

A Cultural Neuroscience of Social Injustice

The relevance of the CN framework was evident throughout the eight weeks of work with the women who were the subjects of the previous chapter. Specifically, as the literature presents, executive functioning of the prefrontal cortex is worthy of discussion for poverty-challenged individuals (Babcock, 2014; Babcock, 2016). With the participants, "trying" and "managing thoughts, emotions, and behaviors" involved the same familiar repertoires. For example, their employment choices (decision-making) have not promoted economic mobility, but rather have maintained barely staying afloat, surviving but not thriving. These patterns of response known as repertoires, narratives, and pursuit of familiar boundary work (e.g., certified nursing assistant) maintain relatively low wage earning for the women and their families.

When asked to deeply reflect on potential jobs or career interests, some women's immediate responses were "I don't know"; but even with time to reflect, the women referenced jobs that are not high wage-earning aspirations. Notably, they were passionate about jobs that allow them to help others. While this is honorable, the economic mobility challenge this presents is evident. Their aspirations were for jobs that assist others personally, via human services, non-profits, or free community-based programs, but at the expense of economic mobility. We were unable to determine if such decision-making connected to understanding the economic consequences nor if this may matter. The women may have gained psychological fulfillment from these pursuits despite the money to be earned from such pursuits. Their identities as mothers and helpers were revealed as very central to their sense of self, which aligns with the African-centered/Black psychology (ACBP) framework of collectivism. Repeatedly during dialogue, the women referred to their children or grandchildren as their sources of strength, determination, pride, and encouragement.

One untapped career possibility for these women and similar women based on their desire to help others and inspire children, might be pursuit of teaching at the elementary or middle school level, following any requisite healing/psychological well-being, to complete the required education and licensure. Yet realistically, due to their relative lack of exposure to other women who have accomplished this in their communities or within their personal friendship networks, their likelihood of independently aspiring towards such a career is low to non-existent. This reality has been addressed by other researchers writing about the culture of poverty (Small, Harding, & Lamont, 2010) and the motivations of the powerless relative to the empowered.

Though more than one participant was pursuing certified nursing assistance (CNA), group homeworker, and hospice care aid, no woman mentioned interest in the fields of nursing, neither associate degree, RN, nor BSN. As well, no one mentioned interest in pursuit of a BSW (Bachelor of Social Work) degree at the outset, but one participant later envisioned this pursuit by the end of the sessions. This decision-making and behavior are informed by the cultural neuroscience literature regarding decision-making and the cultural neuroscience of person perception (Freeman, Rule, & Amady, 2009). The women are not likely to perceive other women in these professions to be similar enough to themselves. For the women in the group who were pursuing CNA certification, they were happy to complete the goal of passing certification exams to become a CNA and had connections to other women who had completed this same certification.

Research participants reported their salaries ranging from $0–$24,999. The average CNA salary in Winston Salem, North Carolina, is $30,644, reported as of September 1, 2018, ranging between $27,771 to $34,094 (Salary.com). While this would be a stable improvement in earnings based on their current income, Salary.com reports that the range of earnings for CNAs varies depending on a host of factors such as education, certifications, additional skills, and the number of years spent in the profession.

POVERTY, STRESS, AND HEALTH

Post-traumatic stress may develop at any time during a developmental trajectory. The impact of trauma on a person's brain processing depends on when it occurred. Certain brain regions have been implicated as particularly susceptible to the impact of trauma; these areas are the hippocampus, the amygdala, and the prefrontal cortex (Bremner, 2006). Key neurochemicals impacted are cortisol and norepinephrine. Reduced hippocampal size can occur as a result of chronic stress, as the release of stress hormones consistently over time can impact the development of this brain region and subsequent cognitive efficiency. The good news, however, is that the impact of trauma and stress on the developing brain is modifiable, and programs designed as interventions, particularly at earlier ages, is optimal.

During the eight weeks of meetings with the women, the impact of poverty on cognition was evident when reviewing field notes and highlights in the notes. Frequently, there were loose streams of consciousness commentary from the women. We also noted the women's frequent physical movement in and out of the circle space for cigarette breaks, phone calls, and other distractions, which aligns with characteristic decision-making and behavior mentioned in the literature (Mani, Mullainathan, Shafir, & Zhao, 2013). One woman was quick to remark during our first meeting: "don't worry, we used to doing more than one thing at a time; don't think we can't be doing a whole lotta things and still be able to know what's going on." Over time, we were able to deduce that this was in fact a norm for how the women processed information and how they move in the world. The women's comments and questions were frequently loosely connected to quotes or questions posed from the EEC materials.

The effects on cognitive processing possibly related to relative underexposure and reduced formal education were also apparent. For example, some vocabulary used in dialogues and quotes were at times a challenge for different women, i.e., definitions of the words "emancipation" and "obnoxious" had to be provided to some women who asked for the definitions. Across the eight weeks, the women's comments, questions, and behaviors appeared consistent with Babcock (2014), who has addressed the impact of poverty and stress on executive functioning. It is also consistent with the literature from CN, which explains how the brain adapts to the culture in which it develops as a biosocial organ (Han, Northoff, Vogeley, Wexler, Kitayama, & Varnum, 2013).

During Key 2, the night's session ended abruptly for some, due to a random shooting that took place in the public housing community where many of the women resided. This is an example of the neighborhood stress of the social environment in which their brains process external stimulation. Because most of the group carpooled via van each week, some of the women had to leave due to the anxiety of others who wanted to return to their homes to check on their children. Thus, the van driver transported them all home before the conclusion of the session. The session did continue and concluded with the women who were not a part of the van pool. Prior to the incident that evening at the public housing community, the women were able to provide us with their reflections on jobs/employment interests (see the results under Key 2 in Chapter 3). The shooting incident is mentioned here as a vivid example of a type of family instability relevant stress experienced by the Black women of this study. Such normative experiences have consequences for the quality of executive functioning needed for optimal and enduring behavioral empowerment and mobility along the bridge to economic self-sufficiency (Babcock, 2014; Sasaki & Kim, 2016).

Chronically stressful experiences such as the shooting incident or other chaos in the women's environment can also be discussed in relationship to health. The indicators of post-traumatic stress (PTS) include re-living trauma, flashbacks, as well as physiological symptoms including sleep disturbances (NIMH, 2001). The repeated re-living of trauma may add a layer of harm. A potential ripple effect means the violent act upon families may impact a wide social network in the local community of the incidents, requiring community level interventions (Jenkins, 2002). As Black mothers struggle with the loss and choose to speak out or not on behalf of the injustices witnessed, they may require targeted mental and emotional intervention to foster well-being (Lawson, 2018).

The traumatic psychological and physiological impact of violence may be exacerbated by the repeated viewing and dissecting of the experience, particularly if chronic exposure has occurred across the lifetime since childhood (Janusek, Tell, Gaylor-Harden, & Mathews, 2017). Adler, Cutler, Jonathan, Galea, Glymour et al. (2016) have addressed the issue of health disparities, particularly as it is influenced by socioeconomic factors. They highlighted the significance of socioeconomics regarding health outcomes and disparities. More importantly, Adler et al. (2016) reference socioeconomics as not only major but also modifiable, and therefore arguably this should be a priority social justice issue in the efforts to enhance lower income individuals' mental and physical well-being.

The results of our study of Black women challenged by poverty, reflects the women's stress and emotional experiences from housing issues, limited feelings of trust, and challenges to healthy emotional management. Each of these is an example of facets of their existence that can compromise decision-making, including health decisions and behaviors. Adler and Rehkopf (2008), in a review of U.S. disparities, describe the negative outcomes that arise from intersecting areas of marginalization such as race, sex, gender, education, occupation, sexual orientation, and housing conditions and environment. For the women living in poverty who were presented in the previous chapter, each of the variables was directly referenced in several women's life narratives. These variables appeared to have reciprocal and challenging developmental impact for the women and their families. Most of the women were mothers of young children; elsewhere, health research has revealed that patterns of outcomes are better for younger persons relative to older adults regarding reduction of inequality and raising of life expectancy (Currie & Schwandt, 2016). Therefore, because the sample consisted of women with children, there is significant potentially intergenerational impact to the findings of the study, specifically regarding the need to disrupt the cycle of poverty.

Psychological well-being must be deeply and broadly addressed with a focus on healing from racial and other trauma before pursuing programs aimed at housing, education, financial management, and career/employment long-term goals. This position is counter to the work of other researchers who have refrained from prioritizing the pillars of the bridge to economic efficiency (Babcock, 2014; Babcock, 2016). Other researchers have emphasized that strength of all five pillars is equally significant to economic mobility, whereas with our group of women, we noted as pervasive experiences, the history of adverse childhood and adult experiences among the group (see Key 5 list), leading to the women's socialization towards coping responses rooted in oppression, mistrust, and trauma (Anderson, McKenny, Koku, & Stevenson, 2018).

Key 5 (see results previous chapter) was overwhelmingly the key that resonated significantly with the women. During this portion of the EEC curriculum, the women were highly engaged, attentive, and sought to gain insight to themselves when prompted by quotes and imagery used for this Key 5 activity. This is when it was most evident to the research team that psychological well-being must be a priority for any poverty reduction and poverty elimination efforts aimed at increasing economic mobility for a similar group of Black female mothers living in impoverished communities of Winston-Salem. Educators, researchers, businesses, and policy makers may use the current research to emphasize the reality of trauma as both antecedent of and effect of poverty.

Quieting the Taxed Brain

Researchers have detailed the cognitive and health benefits of the relaxed-state brain (Vago & Zeidan, 2016). Combined, ten cortical and subcortical areas of the brain have been identified as related to resting neural states; the literature suggests that while stimulus independent thought (SIT) may be distracting in demanding situations that require focused attention, SIT may also be beneficial for those trained to go inward to quiet their minds. Mind-wandering versus mindfulness have been discussed and compared for their impact on cognition, memory, and focused attention. Mental tranquility is a healthy, beneficial default state that the brain evolved to be able to return to when possible, depending on the degree of excessive ongoing stimulation in the environment. However, because the modern social world is saturated with noise, technology, and near constant engagement with external stimuli, humans may find it difficult to naturally quiet the mind without having training.

Economically vulnerable people living in poverty have not been prioritized for brain research studies which test for related health benefits of low-frequency (<0.1 Hz) blood oxygen level–dependent (BOLD) fluctuations (LFBF) which occur in the restful brain state. Lack of empirical studies of mental tranquility among people in poverty constitutes a type of social injustice because being able to relax the human brain in respite from stress is very much needed by low income Black women such as the women who participated in the EEC. There is a psychophysical impact of acute and chronic stress. Yet, relaxing alternative and complementary medicine-type interventions such as guided imagery, acupuncture, yoga, energy healing, and massage therapies are less utilized by Black persons, relative to other racial/ethnic groups (Upchurch & Wexler-Rainisch, 2012). Middle-class people with discretionary income, rather than impoverished Black female heads of household are likely to have both money and leisure time to seek such services. Vago and Zeidan (2016) have proposed a plausible neurocognitive framework of the restful mind, via their review of the neural and cognitive benefits of mind-wandering, mindfulness, and mental tranquility; future studies should include women such as in the EEC study, to examine low-frequency (<0.1 Hz) blood oxygen level–dependent (BOLD) fluctuations (LFBF) in pre and post interventions aimed to help poverty-challenged women to quiet their brains through diverse alternative and complementary medicine approaches.

At the outset of this research project, the research team planned to work beyond eight weeks with five women to further track their behavioral empowerment and economic mobility in the areas of family stability, well-being, education, financial management, and job/career management (Babcock, 2014). Three of the women emerged early in the research as being very prepared to move to a second phase of engagement to strengthen their psychological well-being and growth towards economic self-sufficiency. One woman was slow to emerge as displaying healthy psychological well-being, due to her admitted commitment to anger and mistrust as primary coping; however, by Key 5 she had opened to deeper self-exploration and interest in personal growth beyond this emotion as a default expression. The final woman selected was very slow to warm to the sessions; she was reserved, uncomfortable with prompts and questioning in early EEC meetings. However, she was talkative, warm, and interested in growth-oriented mentoring by Key 5. As mentioned previously, due the women's history of experiences with adverse childhood experiences and other life traumas, having some women who were slow-to-warm-up and mistrustful of the process is not surprising. During our weekly research team meetings, we referenced the structures of psychological well-being and our weekly notes on each woman to further inform which five women would be optimal for further work towards greater economic mobility (Ryff & Keyes, 1995; Babcock, 2016).

We decided upon five women as the targeted number, due to what was feasible based on number of assistants and researcher availability for mentoring.

Mobility Mentoring

The brain-based intervention of mobility mentoring has been shown to be effective for boosting economic mobility among low-income persons (Babcock, 2016). The five women who we assessed for follow-up engagement via the EECs, showed resiliency and personal growth motives. Specifically, we expected those selected might be further motivated to initiate pursuit of higher-earning potential options and more stable employment that could still align with their interests in helping-centered careers.

Based on the information gathered over the 2 months of engagement with the women, we accumulated evidence to suggest that similar women's motivations in education, financial management, and career/employment are likely to be compromised if their PWB is not assessed and integrated into programming or policies. For Black mothers living in poverty in Winston-Salem, we learned from this community-based study that any economic mobility program targeting similar women is likely to be unsuccessful, if the women are not pre-screened for psychological well-being, or if psychological well-being is not a salient feature of the ongoing recruitment for programs.

However, it must be noted that psychotherapy with low-income Black female clients can be misguided if therapists are not properly trained in sensitivity as to how to meet the needs of lower income clients (Kim & Cardemil, 2012). It is also likely that participation in formalized therapy may be relatively unfamiliar to some low-income clients like the women with whom we worked; therapy may not necessarily be a culturally common repertoire or narrative easily embraced immediately if not common to the women's identity (Small, Harding, & Lamont, 2010). However, some of the women in the current study did have previous experience in groups to address racial equity issues and/or to address substance abuse recovery. Some of the women had experience in more general support group type work. In these other group experiences, the women expressed that the other experiences were not the same experience as the guided EEC curriculum, due to the learning they received, alongside the emotionally laden prompts given through videos and quotes.

During the current study, our research team noted implicit class bias in several of the recommended videos, quotes, and vocabulary of the EEC Keys' materials. Specifically, recommended video clips of lectures from prolific scholars such as Cheik Anta Diop that contain deeply meaningful knowledge, may not be an appropriate recommendation for all members of

Black communities who are being newly exposed to the depth of such more academic materials. Thus, implicit social class bias exists in the recommended EEC curriculum of activities, prompts, videos and quotes. While these materials can be substituted based on the group, it should nevertheless be noted that though the curriculum was designed to center Blackness and racial trauma, Blackness as it intersects with poverty was not consistently, consciously existent for some default materials recommended in the facilitators' guide. Psychologists have addressed the need for elimination of social class bias in research and therapy, as many psychologists receive limited diversity training specifically related to working with low socioeconomic status persons (Clay, 2015).

Retrofit Model

Retrofit housing is defined as a compact development of private homes, supplemented by shared land (Sanguinetti, 2015). The five women (and their families) from the current study who displayed the most psychological well-being and readiness for mobility mentoring and further personal growth, would be ideal for consideration for a retrofit housing opportunity. Four out of the five women spoke directly about a desire for change in current living conditions among other goals, during the EEC experience:

> The Determined: This community we live in, when certain type of people moved in, I'm always picking up trash and clothes hanging on the balcony. It don't look good. We could go down to the property manager and ask them why they started permitting that when the old property manager didn't; I had section 8; I tried to move and I couldn't move until my lease was up. The standards for the property now don't apply now.

> The Reserved: I stayed in _____ before the housing authorities came to _____. I was at the town hall meetings and ____ said don't associate my name with _____ because that's not my community. The banks came in and said y'all can keep y'all money; we gone close it down.

> The Seeker: I live in the projects. Where else am I going to go that's going to have 3 bedrooms for under $630 a month?

The retrofit model of co-housing has been primarily utilized in the state of California as a means of diversifying co-housing, but seems optimal for the group of southern Black female residents and their families of our study. For those who desire homeownership and community but have less money to invest in the purchase of a traditional co-op, the retrofit model is worth consideration. Traditional co-ops have been more class and race-specifically used by educated, White middle-class buyers of new-build or industrial and commercial development reuse real estate (Sanguinetti, 2015). The retrofit model, instead, makes use of housing stock that already exists. Retrofit housing is generally smaller and urban, making it ideal for a city such as Winston-Salem and others of its size. Based on the current study, five families could be recommended for piloting a retrofit model in a medium-sized city.

Education would be necessary to inform the women of the various legal structures to ownership, as well as incorporation of a mobility mentor into the process to help with review of forms and explanation of terms. This is because the women's mental bandwidth could be taxed by attempting to process paperwork and instructions related to retrofit housing; however, an accompanying workshop to assist with education is a recommendation.

Lastly, the retrofit model has been successful with a wider variety of types of people varying in age, marital status, race, and employment status. It has also been utilized more among those existing as renters (Sanguinetti, 2015). The women we selected for further growth and economic mobility work are recommended for piloting the retrofit model of housing. Although the women have had adverse childhood experiences and struggle with poverty-based stressors, their proactive decision-making and motivation for change was obvious by the end of the sessions. An investment in existing housing stock in Winston-Salem, to house five families with the possibility of co-ownership would be a very worthwhile investment in human capital of the city.

There is neuroscientific evidence which supports the incorporation of a retrofit model to assist Black women in poverty in cities such as Winston-Salem; neural synchrony occurs among humans engaged in collaborative interpersonal tasks and group cognitive tasks (Lu & Ning, 2019; Dikker et al., 2017). Results from these studies known as neural synchrony or interpersonal brain synchronization (IBS) research, provide scientific evidence of the fact that humans evolved to function in groups as interpersonal beings. Such research has revealed that authentic dyadic bonding during a collaborative interpersonal task resulted in interpersonal brain synchronization of the bilateral dorsolateral prefrontal cortex among the two socially engaged people (Lu & Ning, 2019). This effect occurred even though the participants in the studies were unknown to one another. Researchers were able to test their interpersonal brain synchronization (IBS) via functional near-infrared spectroscopy (fNIRS)-based hyperscanning. Social neuroscience is advanced by techniques such as hyperscanning, which allows for the simultaneous brain recordings of dyads or groups while they are interpersonally engaged with one another. Through this imaging technology, scientists have been able to understand the neurobiology underlying bonding that occurs when people are in relationship or pursuing goals together (Reindl, Konrad, Gerloff, Kruppa, Bell, & Scharke, 2019). Functional near-infrared spectroscopy (fNIRS) is used to measure local hemoglobin fluctuations by taking a high rate of samples of oxygenated and non-oxygenated cells within the cortex during active interpersonal situations. The relevance of fNIRS to the retrofit model is that fNIRS can be applied in natural settings such as a co-housing sample of families living in their natural retrofit environment. As well, when being scanned using fNIRS, persons are not restricted in movement to obtain the measurement. fNIRS has even been used to measure parent-child dyads in collaboration. Researchers discovered this brain-to-brain synchrony may be representative of a neural basis of emotional connection between a parent and child and may be connected to the child's development of adaptive emotion regulation (Reindl, Gerloff, Scharke, & Konrad, 2018).

The interpersonal brain synchronization was seen only in humans working cooperatively in an authentic manner; confederates in the experiment did not show the same neural synchrony when collaborating while only pretending to be an actual participant. IBS and cooperation increased over time in real-participant pairings, whereas they remained low and steady in dyads in which the confederate was the collaborator. These findings have implications for the Black women who were also mothers; a retrofit model of housing for them could be a novel approach for such women who are high in psychological well-being, low in trust, and bonded with only a few other women with similar economic goals. Under a retrofit model, the women would experience cooperative homeownership, responsibility, and accountability for the shared spaces with other families. Based on the brain science, as they care for their new environments and collaboratively form by-laws and other regulations within their co-op, they are likely to experience neural synchrony and cooperation with one another that will steadily increase over time. There is a history of Black southern people forming networks of cooperatives and worker-owned, democratically self-managed enterprises, that even into the present is an option for Black southerners to develop economic self-sufficiency and stability (Akuno & Nangwaya, 2017). Thus, the retrofit model of housing could benefit families' cooperation and pursuit of tasks that align with practices of cooperative economics and brain science.

Programming and Policy Implications

Emotional Emancipation Circles (EECs) must be viewed as essential public health goals. The use of EECs as intervention has the potential to lead to the establishment of circles throughout the most impoverished areas of Forsyth County, North Carolina. There is also the potential to increase the number of people who become trained to offer circles in the most impoverished areas. A long-term goal for this research intervention is to be able to offer targeted, more class-sensitive EEC content, created for teens, older adults, parents, formerly incarcerated people, and people in substance abuse recovery. Interventions should be more than stop-gap measures; there must be long-term ongoing infusion of self-determined empowerment strategies for targeted communities and groups. Referencing secondary data analysis and traditional survey data research, it has been possible to learn about poverty in Forsyth County (DataUsa.io). Increasingly needed is the micro-level up close and personal community research with people challenged by poverty in their daily living.

A related alternative suggestion informed by the current study, is that city or county governments invest in large scale training of residents who own or work for local non-profits (including churches, based on the religiosity noted among several women in the current study). Residents can be trained in the delivery of ongoing EECs through their non-profits. I had to travel over an hour to be trained; however, with the county's investment in the circles, the out-of-state trainers who conducted the training in state, could travel to Winston-Salem to offer extensive training to local non-profit owners at minimal cost to the city.

Non-profits in Forsyth County who have missions of serving low-income women are ideal for this training. Locals would then be able to offer the circles in Winston-Salem across a wider population of lower income people in Winston-Salem, for a longer time period than the current study was done. Ideally, to see potential long-term impact and wider influence among residents, more people across a diversity of settings will need to be trained to assist with this effort. As well, partnership between city/county government, Community Healing Network (CHN), Association of Black Psychologists, and a local university is also recommended. Local residents, college students and university faculty of Justice Studies, Education, African American Studies, Social Work, Nursing, and Social Sciences might partner with CHN and local governments to establish a revised EEC curriculum especially designed with mindfulness for use with lower income residents.

Community healing from poverty and the related racial trauma which affects psychological and emotional well-being must be addressed, with a keen understanding of how cognitive decision-making and motivation may be impacted. To continue to ignore the assessment of the psychological well-being of persons challenged by poverty across multiple generations is not in the best interest of public health or economic mobility. Researchers and policy makers readily address financial capital. In this chapter and the preceding, we highlighted the prioritization of deep study of human capital by addressing emotional emancipation as healing. Community healing has been defined as community members' shared responsibility for confronting and working to overcome centuries-old lies about Black inferiority, which stems from a historical legacy of racial trauma and resulting emotional pain and devaluing of Black lives (Association of Black Psychologists & Community Healing Network, Inc., 2016)

Ongoing research should longitudinally assess the impact of the circles, and the impact of policies that lead to public or private funding to train more people from the community to offer circles in schools, churches, and recreation centers. EECs are ultimately about collective action and reweaving the fragmented fabric of community networks. The objective of the EECs is to lead to local community activity focused on community development, community healing, empowerment, and community improvement as individuals of the community psychologically and emotionally heal from acute and chronic stress of racial trauma. EECs are the type of local community interventions that are needed to have a deeper, broader, and longer-lasting community healing and transformation, relative to stop-gap measures that have been more commonly employed in lower income communities of color.

Conclusion

Based on the general demographics of women with whom we worked: Black, low-income mothers living in public housing or other lower income residences in Winston-Salem, we suggest that similar women be recruited for extensive economic mobility efforts that focus on well-being and family stability. We also suggest that women who show improvement in psychological well-being addressed for at least six months, or women who enter an economic mobility program with moderate to high PWB, are ideal to begin a mobility mentoring program. The women's collectivism (though extended to just a limited, trusted group of people), desire to help others, and commitment to their children is a strength as well as adding to financial stress.

The women made several comments that were indicative of the Afrocentric worldview, such as gaining strength from their relationships with children, and wanting to pursue career interests to give back to their communities. Ethical and knowledgeable cultural neuroscience researchers who have been trained in African-centered/Black psychology will be ideally capable of sensitively and ethically studying the science of scarcity and the psychobiology of Black people in poverty. Yet, race scientists of distant and contemporary times have influenced how comfortable some may feel regarding funding and prioritizing such programs of research. Unfortunately, we are missing a huge opportunity to make significant in-roads in this area, beginning at a micro-level of the biosocial brain, but with the potential for long-term inter-generational impact on families and communities.

Chapter Five

That Female is *Ratchet*

Mixed-Slurs

Although the study of language and communication is not a new topic of investigation among scientists, the in-depth and expansive study of the use of slurs is relatively contemporary, and includes focused research and historical commentary on the controversial word *nigger* (Croom, 2014; 2015; 2013; 2011; Kennedy, 2003; Wiley, 2013). Though the usage of slurs has ancient evolutionary origins that evidence the dehumanization of others (Croom, 2013), the scientific examination of types of slurs, their in-group and out-group meanings, and the significance of the context of their usage have been relatively under-examined across diverse regional contexts. An exploration of more diverse age, regional, racial, and ethnic contexts may reveal more nuanced ways in which slurs infiltrate language, impacting our biosocial brains to subsequently prompt feelings of disgust regarding the humans to whom they are directed.

Croom (2011) has defined a slur as a disparaging remark or a slight that is usually used to deprecate certain targeted members; slurs can be used to derogate others based on their race/ethnicity, sexuality, social class, religion, or gender, or a combination thereof. As well, with each new generation, linguistic socialization results in the emergence of words that may be categorized as slurs. Via linguistic socialization, children and young adults learn how to use language to creatively communicate within their cultural environment. Researchers have suggested that all speakers are socialized into a particular linguistic community as they develop; this enables them to learn the norms of communication regarding what can be done with words within a community (Ochs & Schieffelin, 1984; Garrett & Baquedano-Lopez, 2002; Matthiessen, 2009). Thus, varying ways of enacting the use of slurs should be expected as different cultures of different regions engage in communications among themselves. This is consistent with the ways in which language has been employed as a marker of culture. Roberts, Bell, & Murphy (2008) state that young people of color can create social and rhetorical spaces to express and critically analyze the particularities of their lived experiences. Emergent words that are developed to be used in accordance with the norms of one's community become a part of the lexicon; they can potentially be linked to other older words representing derision, disrespect, or derogation within certain cultural contexts. There may be psychological implications for the emotional well-being of marginalized people who are the targets of slurs and other emotional abuse because the brain responds to positive commentary differently than to negative commentary (Otten, Mann, van Berkum, & Jonas (2017). Researchers have used the EEG to measure event-related potentials in response to participants hearing insults or compliments. The researchers' hypotheses regarded whether the brain may respond differently to the two types of comments, and whether the brain processes the comments differently when laughing witnesses are present or not. The presence of laughing onlookers was indicated to participants via a visual onscreen cue. Neurocognitively, participants' brains reacted more strongly to insults than compliments. Additionally, such reactions were even greater in the presence of laughing others who could be heard laughing immediately after the insulting comment was delivered.

TABOO WORDS AND MIXED-TYPE SLURS: A FRAMEWORK

If one has familiarity with the linguistic socialization practices of a subculture, the familiarity may inform about whether a speaker's culture-based word choice is meant to be merely descriptive, purely expressive, or a mixed-type usage of a slur. Taboo words are those that are sanctioned or restricted at the individual as well as institutional level, based upon the assumption that some harm will occur if the word is spoken (Jay, 2009). Within one's native and folk culture, individuals learn rules of etiquette regarding the avoidance of words deemed taboo. Individuals also learn the specific instances in which taboo words may be employed. Significantly, Jay (2009) also notes that in recent times (i.e., the 20th and 21st centuries), the U.S. government imposes sanctions for the use of words regarded as taboo, in accordance with citizens' right to protection from verbal sexual harassment and discrimination. As example, words such as the slurs *cunt* and *motherfucker*, can be construed as taboo words based on indecency, profanity, and obscenity (FCC, 2013). As well, the Federal Communications Commission (FCC) encourages consumers to complain about the public communication of offensive broadcasting material, even if it does not fall directly in the category of indecency.

The changing times regarding what is politically correct to utter, as well as what can be punishable on legal grounds, or within the realm of social acceptance, makes it important to consider the variations in which slurs and taboo words are used today. It is reasonable to expect that with changing times towards more progressive or accepting attitudes regarding lesbian, gay, bisexual, and transgender (LGBT) identity and multi-racial identities in more contexts, more subtle as opposed to overt instances of offensive language may occur (Nadal, 2013). Taboo words may increasingly decline in public use in favor of microaggressions appearing in language that is descriptive as well as expressive. Specifically, descriptive and expressive type slurs used in combination in one utterance, have been termed the mixed-type slur (Croom, 2011). Pierce (1970) used the term "microaggressions" to identify the subtly offensive behaviors that degrade and humiliate those to whom they are targeted. Pierce also noted that microaggressions derive from a sense of superiority that one group has over another. In such an instance of feeling superior to another person or group, a mixed-type slur may be uttered as a way of manipulating descriptive words to creatively convey an insult.

Potts (2007) focused attention on the semantic type of slur known as the expressive type. The expressive type slur is explained as the slur that is used to express intensity of emotion. An example of such is when in anger a person refers to another person as a *motherfucker*. This point is reflected in the example below:

> You *motherfucker*! I got to this parking space ahead of you. Move your car!

In the case of this example, the slur is not intended to be descriptive of labeling someone who engages in sexual relations with his own or someone else's mother as one would conclude as a literal meaning. But instead, the slur of *motherfucker* is hurled as an insult to express contempt, because the word accompanies anger in the example.

Potts (2007) also highlighted a semantic type of linguistic phenomenon known as the descriptive type statement, which is not associated with heightened emotional state. Thus, some words are used as merely descriptive. An example is given in the case of someone discussing a neighborhood:

> Many Latinos live in this neighborhood; I would not want to live in this neighborhood.

The word Latinos as used in the statement is descriptive, even though the underlying meaning of the sentence suggests ethnic prejudice. Therefore, the speaker could be accused of uttering a prejudicial remark but cannot be accused of uttering a slur. Pott's (2007) characterization of semantic types, suggests that words are either descriptive or expressive. However, Croom (2011) has argued that slurs can be characterized as a mixture of descriptive and expressive type, meaning that slurs can be used in such a manner as to be descriptive of an individual, while also being expressive with the objective and/or result being pejorative or insulting.

Mixed-Type Slurs as Microaggressions

Although the focus of Pierce's (1970) work was on interpersonal relationships between Black and White Americans in the United States, he acknowledged that the offensive mechanisms which he called microaggressions could arise in many other interpersonal interactions. Therefore, arguably they can also be used during communications of men regarding women; among persons who identify as heterosexual regarding LGBQ persons; and during communications of cisgender persons regarding transgender persons.

Yet it is also possible that a person who utters a mixed type microaggressive slur may not be consciously aware that what was said was offensive, particularly if common taboo words were not included in the utterance. As well, if a speaker uses words that he or she views as merely descriptive, then this may also result in the speaker's lack of awareness of using microaggressive language, particularly within contexts in which there is a relative lack of education and engagement regarding issues of race, class, sexuality, and gender (Fischman, 2000; Weber, 2001).

A Female Not the Same as a Woman

In the previously used example referencing Latinos, the descriptive language used was not equivalent to a slur. However, in the following sentence, a male speaker's underlying negative regard for women is hinted at in the form of a microaggressive, mixed type slur:

> When I saw my frat today, he was in a bad mood. He must have had another
> bad experience with that female who he messes with.

A close examination of the sentence reflects that there are no taboo words in the sentence. Therefore, some persons might wonder, how is this a microaggressive mixed type slur as opposed to merely descriptive? If someone uttered these sentences, it could be inferred that the person is referring to a possibly problematic woman, who in terms of descriptive language qualifies as also being female. However, one might also reflect upon the meaning of the sentence and reconstruct it as follows:

> When I saw my frat today, he was in a bad mood. He must have had another fight with his girl; alternatively, when I saw my frat today, he was in a bad mood, and must have had another fight with the woman he's seeing.

Others could argue that the previous example does not pay respect to language socialization within the culture of younger men who may be speaking in a style that is perhaps even ethnically and geographically contextualized. Researchers have found that gender primed language occurs and is particularly so in same-sex dyads (Hussey, Katz, & Leith, 2014). Therefore, if a man is talking to another man, the language that one man uses will likely prime the language that the other man uses. The original sentence used in the last example is perhaps a result of language socialization as well as gender socialization within same-sex male dyads. Croom (2011) and Kennedy (2003) have acknowledged that context is important as to whether the usage of a word is likely to be deemed offensive. Therefore, the men who are speaking to one another may not think that their language is offensive, instead they may view it as just how men speak to each other about women as out-group members.

In the previous example, it is significant to focus on the use of the words "that female." Though the word "female" is not pejorative, nor a taboo word, there are other words that could be used that denote less objectification than "that female"; similarly the words, "who he messes with" if replaced with "who he sees," "who he dates," or "who he is involved with" convey less sexist or misogynistic meaning. Another example of controversial use of the term "female" is evident in the lyrics of some rappers such as Shawtjay, whose 2014 song, "Females Ain't Shit," included the rapper repeating in the song, "I wonder why the females ain't shit" (Shawtjay, 2014).

Family resemblance of terms exists in the case of the earlier examples; specifically, according to family resemblance theory (Rosch & Mervis, 1975) "females" could connote "bitches," and phrases such as "who he messes with" could connote "who he's f---ing," as some popular cultural lyrics may have socialized some speakers to normalize the f-word.

Psychologist Susan Fiske's social neuroscience research has shown men's brains respond to women in a bikini, similarly to when pending the use of an object such as a tool to accomplish a goal (Landau, 2009). Such unconscious sexism has also been scientifically revealed through the brain's processing of images of women as fragmented forms, whereas the brain processes images of men holistically (Pappas, 2012). Thus, it is logical that sexist or misogynistic slurs might represent how the biosocial brain has been conditioned to respond to women.

Merriam-Webster online dictionary lists the following full definition of "female" as the foremost of definitions:

(1): of, relating to, or being the sex that bears young or produces eggs (2): pistillate

Thus, whether talking about a human or a plant, the word "female" is descriptive of reproductive capacity and perhaps should not foremost be used as a noun, as in "that female." While "that female" does qualify as descriptive, it also qualifies as expressive of language that could be deemed offensive due to its connotation that women's primary association should be with childbearing or pregnancy, and therefore is sexist language (Lei, 2006). Usage of the terms "females," "that female," or "the females" (i.e., as used by Shawtjay) qualify as mixed-type slurs. These examples of usage of such language correspond to the taxonomy of sexist language as mentioned in Nadal (2013), in which he specifically indicated the following three categories (of eight categories total) of gender microaggressions specific to women:

> Assumptions of traditional gender roles—women presumed to maintain stereotypical gender roles

> Use of sexist language—language that overtly or subtly demeans women

> Environmental gender microaggressions—messages that are subtly communicated through media, institutions, government, and other systems

Usage of terminology such as "that female" as opposed to other terms that are not loaded in meaning, can be viewed as micro-aggressive language.

"Ratchet": A Gender, Class, and Racialized Slur

The onset of the 21st century ushered in an explosion of new terms and phrases created and used by youth and has continued through the transition from millennial speakers to Generation Z speakers (Premack, 2018). This is consistent with the results of linguistic socialization (Garrett & Baquedano-Lopez, 2002). In some cases, the words that are strung together or created are actual terms; in other cases, one may hear a variation in pronunciation of an actual word. This may result in nuanced terminology with only a vague resemblance to an actual word. One such word variation once very popular among those who are young, contemporary, and urban-identified, is the term "*ratchet*." "*Ratchet*," in terms of family resemblance (Rosch & Mervis, 1975) and phonetics, connotes the actual word "wretched."

The *Urban Dictionary* is a crowdsourced collection of slang words and phrases on the internet. The *Urban Dictionary* is now about 20 years old and was created by a then college freshman. Though it is regarded by many as having little quality control, it has also been referenced in court cases in which street slang was a part of the criminal case being tried (Kaufman,

2013). Courts have used it because common slang terms can be found in it, and users submit and vote on definitions with expectations of relative agreement on words that are very popular in usage. Courts have been able to discern both meaning and intent of street slang by relying on the *Urban Dictionary*, as opposed to relying on standard dictionaries which cannot keep pace with the rapid changes in street slang. The dictionary has over 7 million definitions posted, and thousands of proposed new definitions are sent in each month (Kaufman, 2013). Many of the words proposed, whether rejected or accepted for inclusion, are crude and insensitive terms that may qualify as slurs. *Urban Dictionary* has received 110 million monthly page views and was identified as the 77th biggest website in the United States, according to Quantcast, a Web analytics company (Kaufman, 2013).

 Urban Dictionary (n.d.) includes the following information for "*ratchet,*" while also noting it as a mispronunciation or corruption of the word "wretched." It is a slur and slang term that is often gendered towards a woman as an example of misogynoir, which is the anti-Black racist misogyny that Black women experience (Bailey & Trudy, 2018). Although blackness is never mentioned in the definition, terms commonly connected to negative stereotypes of lower income Black women are used in the definition. The following terms are used in the definition: hip-hop person, welfare client with children from multiple parents, wears ill-fitting leggings, torn fishnet hose, loose, matted hair weave in a bright color.

 When a speaker uses the term "*ratchet*" to refer to a woman or girl, the message often conveys a specific gender and social class-based slur and is commonly racialized in use against Black women and girls. The following is an example of usage of the term "ratchet" in its gender and racialized context, as uttered from a young Black woman who appeared in a weekly reality show, *The Real Housewives of Atlanta*:

> I can't believe that I let that ratchet hoe take me there! I'm so embarrassed!

The young woman who uttered this statement did so in a mixture of anger, disappointment, embarrassment, and frustration following her verbal and physical assault of another Black woman about whom she was speaking. The speaker felt very strong and negative emotions about the other Black woman slurred. Therefore, the specific word choice of "*ratchet*" in the speaker's statement was meant to be offensive and expressive of intense emotions. As well, Black women cast members of two popular culture reality television shows, *Real Housewives of Atlanta* and *Married to Medicine* were criticized by men of the U.S. Black gay community and from activists on social media. The women were accused of mocking and slurring Black gay men (Daniels, 2014).

There is an international body of literature that has detailed lesbians' and gay men's language use; thus, it is known that among subcultures of gay men, the men have their own vocabulary, phrasing, and gender inversions during communications with one another (Johnsen, 2008; Kulick, 2000). This is done to highlight the men's important elements in their construction of gender and sexuality within their language. Johnsen (2008) defined gender inversion as using feminine words to refer to a cisgender male. Similarly, to the international and mainstream popularity of hip-hop culture, perhaps aspects of some gay men's linguistic socialization have become mainstream. It is also worth noting, that a subset of women deemed *"ratchet"* may be slurred, yet their personal sense of style and confidence of expression have the power to generate mainstream attention and influence language.

As images of Black gay men have become more visible in mainstream media, the men's language/slang has been appropriated by out-group members, i.e., being used by their heterosexual Black female counterparts. These women may or may not have actual quality interpersonal relationships with the type of Black gay men who they are imitating. The question becomes, is it appropriate for Black heterosexual women (and other out-group members) to engage in gender inversion speech when referencing a gay man, as some gay men do with each other, or is this considered offensive bias? A controversial comment, which offended some gay Black men, stemmed from one heterosexual Black woman on a reality show, who repeatedly referred to a gay Black man (with whom she had no relationship) as a queen. She did this in a manner deemed derogatory, specifically as an expressive type slur. Thus, while some gay men may reference one another as "big old girl" (Johnsen, 2008), "queen," or "bitch," it is debatable whether it is appropriate for out-group members to refer to them as such. The same has been said for words such as ghetto and use of *nigger* by out-group members to refer to in-group members who may self-identify using these terms. Out-group usage of these terms can be considered offensive (Croom, 2013; Croom, 2011). The word *ghetto*, in the *Urban Dictionary,* is defined primarily as a word used to refer to an impoverished neighborhood of a city; additionally, the word ghetto is frequently used as an adjective during informal U.S. vernacular to denote negative behavior, emotionality, and personal style among individuals whose primary human development has occurred within an impoverished community with few resources.

Ratchet and Ghetto

The word "wretched" and the word "ghetto" are actual words in the English language; however, over time these words' frequencies of use and manner of usage have changed. For example, the following foremost definitions of these words in *Meriam-Webster* dictionary are:

Wretched: deeply afflicted, dejected, or distressed in body or mind

Ghetto: a quarter of a city in which members of a minority group live, especially because of social, legal, or economic pressure

The following statement is an example of usage of the words "wretched" and "ghetto" which does not qualify as a slur, and is consistent with their traditional meanings:

> A few blocks from here is the city's ghetto; I know girls who live over there who behave wretchedly.

In the case of the previous sentence, the words "ghetto" and "wretchedly" are descriptive. Alternatively, "ghetto" and "wretched" are transformed in usage at times, to be used as slurs. The following is an example:

> There goes that ghetto chick who lives a few blocks from here; she is so damned ratchet!

The word "ghetto," depending on context of usage and who is using it, may be embraced by a speaker when self-referencing, similarly to how some members of a White in-group may use the word "redneck" to self-describe with pride in the manner of comedian Jeff Foxworthy (Thomas, 2016). "Ghetto fabulous" was used in the 1990s in the United States to self-describe with positive connotation. However, thus far in its evolution, masses of Black women and girls have not normalized a positive self-description of *ratchet*, plausibly due to the term's overwhelmingly pejorative and offensive intent as an expressive slur. Men and boys may not be as readily described as *ratchet*, though men and boys are described as ghetto. Ghetto has family resemblance to *ratchet*. Why the term *ratchet* has been both racialized and often gender-typed specifically to slur Black women and girls has not been studied, but can be related to the common explanation of institutionally sexist language being commonly directed at women when used by both men and women (Lei, 2006). Also, researchers have shown that slurs are generally judged as being more insulting when directed towards women and girls than towards men and boys (Bendixen & Gabriel, 2013), so this may also be partly explanatory. Male specific terms though, have existed for the purpose of slurring men. For example, a male slur of the past was the term *scrub*, which was used to describe a loser type male who has nothing to offer in a relationship, such as no job, no place to live, no money, and no ambition. During the height of this term's popular usage in the United States in the 1990s, women were not referred to as *scrubs*.

Conclusion

The way speakers have commonly used slurs such as *scrub* and *ratchet* are examples of how various slurs are consciously or unconsciously gender typed. There is no expressed rule that women may not be called a scrub; yet it has not been as obviously normalized to use the term to describe women or girls. While Croom (2011) has made the case for slurs existing as mixed descriptive and expressive, the literature on slurs has not often incorporated much of the literature on microaggressions, nor incorporated enough about the impact of hearing or using slurs on the biosocial brains of humans. Comparatively, the literature in the field of counseling psychology has rather extensively examined slurs (Nadal, 2013; Nadal, 2011; Nadal, 2010; Nadal, 2008; Sue, Nadal, Capodilupo, Lin, Torino, & Rivera, 2008).

This chapter has specifically examined slurs and is applicable to humans with intersecting marginalized identities. There is substantial existing literature written by intellectuals, activists, and journalists in which they debate the appropriateness of usage of the extensively interrogated slur, *nigger*, within certain contexts and among certain speakers (Asim, 2007; Nygen, 2013; Kennedy, 2002; Fairman, 2010; Williams, 2007). Others have devoted attention to questions such as who is more likely to be slurred most often; who uses slurs more often; and are all stereotypes and slurs equal in impact (Bendixen & Gabriel, 2013; Croom, 2014)? There is still a need for greater diversity of empirical studies to interrogate how diverse groups of "othered" persons have neurocognitively and emotionally responded to being slurred. Such are areas of promising future research.

Chapter Six

Negative Emotionality and Disgust Activation towards LGBT Persons

A proposed theoretical taxonomy of sexual orientation and gender identity related microaggressions includes eight distinct categories of microaggressions that may target lesbian gay bisexual and transgender (LGBT) people (Nadal, Rivera, & Corpus, 2010). Two of the eight can be more specifically applied in this chapter to further inform discussion of microaggressions and mixed-type slurs as presented in the previous chapter. The two categories are as follows:

ENDORSEMENT OF HETERONORMATIVE OR
GENDER NORMATIVE CULTURE AND BEHAVIORS

Assumption of Sexual Pathology/Abnormality

Regarding the category of 1) endorsement of heteronormative or gender normative culture and behaviors, we can point to the existence of institutionalized heterosexism within major aspects of U.S. and other cultures. Beginning when we are young, we are exposed to films, commercials, greeting cards, and love songs that represent men and women together as romantic and sexual partners. While still in their early cognitive and social developmental years, children learn gender stereotypical roles for their sex, and they display gender conforming behavior as dictated by their culture (Fagot, Rodgers, & Leinbach, 2000). This is a part of social development, including among humans who eventually develop as gender nonconforming or sexually non-conforming from childhood (Rieger, Linsenmeier, Gygax, & Bailey, 2008). For persons who have cisgender privilege or heterosexual privilege, they may be unaware of the micro-aggressive nature of language usage and other assumptions that advance heteronormative attitudes or marginalize the identity and lives of LGBTQ persons.

The following statement conveys an underlying bias of endorsement of heteronormative culture and behaviors, which is evident in word choice:

> Our proposed new multicultural center on campus should be inclusive of all, including students who are leading alternative lifestyles.

A person who utters such a statement may not be aware of bias, particularly if the intent was to show support for LGBT students on campus. A close examination and analysis of the statement reveals its implication that a transgender identity or lesbian, gay, or bisexual identity equates to a lifestyle choice or deviant choice of behaviors and way of living. The example, without specifically stating such, implies that the speaker making the statement views LGBT students as expressing a chosen alternative lifestyle rather than perceiving the person as manifesting an identity. A key word in the statement is the word, "alternative"; this word can be analyzed with attention to the question: To what is an LGBT identity the alternative? Such phrasing as "alternative lifestyles" suggests that heterosexuality is perceived as a standard, norm, and expected identity. Any other orientation would thus by default be deemed deviant or pathological alternatives, as opposed to an identity status similar to a heterosexual identity. Upon hearing a speaker choose to use the words "alternative lifestyles," a person of LGBT identity may interpret this word choice as derogatory and offensive.

In the example given above, a speaker's positive intent, yet problematic word choice equates to researchers' highlight of the concepts of benevolent sexism and benevolent racism (Glick & Fiske, 1997; Ramasubramanian & Oliver, 2007). One might categorize the deliberate and problematic use of the words, "leading alternative lifestyles" (though the speaker's intention was to denote support for the LGBT students), as benevolent heterosexist bias due to its microaggressive heteronormative implication that LGBT students are people engaged in alternative lifestyles. The usage of this terminology of "leading alternative lifestyles" is also a good example of Croom's (2013) discussion of how to do things with slurs.

CULTURE AND CONTEXT

In some contexts, such as in one southern U.S. historically Black college and university (HBCU) context, Black LGBT students may not only be referred to as "leading alternative lifestyles," but they may also be referred to as "a homosexual," relative to being referenced as lesbian, gay, bisexual (LGB). Again, as in the case of the word "female" presented in the previous chapter, the word "homosexual" is not a taboo word. So, how might its usage qualify as a mixed type microaggressive slur? In the case of homosexual, both the evolution of usage of the term, and an HBCU southern cultural U.S. context are significant to the analysis of how the term is used, and its qualification as a mixed type slur.

In one of her early papers, psychologist Evelyn Hooker (1969) used the term "homosexual" throughout the paper. This was the norm when speaking of a gay man during the 1960s in the United States. However, decades later in a 1990s paper, Hooker's (1994) word choice had appropriately switched in her writings, from referring to the men in her studies as homosexual to referencing the men as gay. This represents the evolution of usage of the term, as it was influenced by significant progressive achievement within the nation, including up to the present (Byne, 2014).

In the field of psychology, when researchers began to display a serious interest in research and psychotherapy with gay men, same-sex attraction and orientation was viewed by a vocal camp of psychologists as a psychopathology. The use of the word homosexuality as a diagnosis was once included in early versions of the American Psychiatric Association's *Diagnostic and Statistical Manual of Mental Disorders* (DSM), (Dreshcher, 2010). Dreshcher (2010) has since outlined three categories of contemporary views in psychology about LGBT persons. These views are: 1) it is normal variation in sexuality, 2) it is pathology, and 3) it is immaturity of development. The pathological category is most relevant to the discussion of usage of the term homosexual in noun form, as may be uttered within some cultural contexts. Arguably, in some sociocultural contexts, the word homosexual may qualify as a mixed-type slur during contemporary times as indicated in the following examples:

> Some Greek organizations on campus are more okay with homosexuals than some of the other ones but like for my fraternity . . . uhmm, no!

> My view on homosexuals, is that what they do isn't going to send me to hell! And anyway, I don't view it as being any worse than any other sin. Sin is sin.

In both examples, the statements reflect emotionality as well as a descriptive nature of the persons being referenced. Further analysis, however, may inform what renders usage of the term biased and a mixed type microaggressive slur (Croom, 2014). Dreshcher (2010) references past and some present theories of pathology which represent adult LGB identity as a disease, being a condition that deviates from normal heterosexual development. Likewise, pathological theories state that having a transgender identity or gender queer identity and feelings are viewed as symptoms of a disease that could be addressed by mental health professionals. Dreshcher (2010) explains that pathological theorists attribute LGB identity to internal abnormalities or external pathogenic agents that may have occurred pre- or post-natal. Due to these former clinically based usages of the term homosexual, which conveys pathology or disease, organizations such as the Gay and Lesbian Alliance Against Defamation (GLAAD) publishes a media reference guide to delineate the offensive terms to be avoided in media references to LGBT persons (Gay and Lesbian Alliance Against Defamation, 2010).

Specifically, GLAAD (2010) states that usage of the word homosexual either as a noun or an adjective is to be avoided due to the clinical history of the word, and also its usage by anti-gay extremists to indicate that LGBT persons are diseased or pathological. Although persons using the term homosexual instead of the more contemporary and acceptable terms lesbian, gay, and bisexual (LGB) may not be familiar with the historical pathologically based usage of the word "homosexuality." In contemporary contexts, it is a loaded term and can qualify as a mixed type micro-aggressive bias in language use. GLAAD (2010) also notes for its readers that the Associated Press, *New York Times*, and the *Washington Post* prohibit journalists from using the term, "homosexual" because it is deemed offensive. The American Psychological Association (APA) also mandates that manuscript writers refrain from use of the word "homosexual," as descriptive of people, because it is offensive in current vernacular (American Psychological Association, 2010).

Prior to 1973, it was not only generally accepted that persons who are LGBT are disordered, but as well, LGBT persons may have been considered evil, bad, or sinful (Dreshcher, 2010; Byne, 2014). Such views are still present today (Reed & Johnson, 2010). Subsets of Black people in the United States within an historically or predominantly Black school or university context may have strong conservative religious values (Reed & Johnson, 2010), such that this may challenge them in their full and open engagement with advocacy and outreach to members of the LGBT community (Reed & Johnson, 2010; Lewis & Marshall, 2012).

Religion

Just as it may be difficult to disassociate the word "homosexuality" from its pathological connotation as a result of the word's history of use in psychiatry, it is logical to discuss religion when examining conscious and unconscious attitudes about LGBT persons. Religion may be significant in influencing word selection for some persons, when choosing to use the term homosexual instead of use of the label LGBT. Though the concept LGBT may not be completely unknown to persons in some regions who infrequently use it, it is plausible that usage of the label LGBT may not be deemed as culturally applicable, culturally familiar, or emotionally comfortable among some religious persons in a region of the southern United States who do not use LGBT, but instead may consistently still use homosexual.

Miller (2007) detailed the strong influence of Black churches in the history of Black people in the United States Black churches in the United States are revered for pursuit of equity in education for Black students from the antebellum period and throughout the period of establishing HBCUs. Promoting equity in the area of education is just one example of Black churches' involvement in fighting for social justice and civil rights throughout decades (Fulton, 2011). However, in addition to a positive history of accomplishments on behalf of Black people in the United States, there also exists religiously sanctioned homophobia within the history of this culture (Lewis & Marshall, 2012). Specifically, unless a Black church congregation clearly markets itself to be an open and affirming ministry, embedded in the church culture may be the perception that LGBT persons practice a kind of alternative "lifestyle" (Miller, 2007). Additionally, some members of the Black clergy have expressed that closeted LGBTQ persons are welcome in their churches, but direct and specific language of affirmation of LGBTQ persons in the church may largely be avoided (Barnes, 2013).

Cultural dynamics are related to the assertion that heterosexism is sanctioned in the Christian Bible. Miller (2007) referenced the often-cited biblical verses (Genesis 1–2, 19:1–9; Leviticus 18:22, 20:13; 1 Corinthians 6:9; Romans 1:26–27; and 1 Timothy 1:10) that are used within some churches as evidence that homophobia and heterosexism are scripturally normative. For persons of the southern United States who have developed in this geographic context and attended traditional Black churches of the southern U.S. region, their language and emotionality around their interpretation of the scriptures may be significant regarding word choice, even though they may know the meaning of concepts such as lesbian, gay, bisexual.

Research suggests there are complex effects of emotion on decision making and reasoning, with emotion sometimes hindering normatively correct thinking and sometimes promoting it (Blanchette & Richards, 2010). Emotionality connected to sin in southern U.S. contexts may influence the cognitive decision-making regarding word choice (i.e., homosexual) when speaking, even when one knows the other terms (i.e., gay or lesbian). Likewise, it is known that there are significant effects of emotion on reasoning style (Blanchette & Richards, 2010). Integral cognitive affect may be related to a greater usage of the term "homosexual" in lieu of using "LGBT" by some Black persons who are of a southern U.S. conservative religious environment. If within the culture or geographic region, LGBT persons have been repeatedly referred to as sinners, then this may create a negative feeling state within someone when speaking of LGBT persons within this cultural context.

An LGBT identity, particularly in many U.S. southern conservative religious contexts is cognitively (consciously or unconsciously) conditioned to the content of sin. Thus the word "homosexual," as it is heard in the context of some churches and communities may frequently be the word choice, rather than use of LGBT, which may be a less likely term heard in emotional and cultural connection to sin within Black churches. Some persons in a southern U.S. context may be accustomed to hearing the term "homosexual" in a religious context, relative to hearing the term LGBT within that same context. An emotional association of sin and homosexuality in church culture may influence decision-making regarding conscious or unconscious use of the word homosexuality. This usage may reflect implicit bias, rather than explicit intent to slur or offend. In psychology, research has revealed implicit bias can explain the prejudice in what humans see, do, say, and think (Eberhardt, 2019).

Schools that predominantly serve Black students within an HBCU context are prevalent in the southern regional area of the U.S. The southern United States has been delineated as the area of the United States that contains significant percentages of persons with strong and salient religious identities (Silk, 2005), and relatively less formal open and affirming discussions about LGBTQ inclusivity within the more traditional Black cultural spaces (Lewis & Marshall, 2012). Regarding the previous example,

> My view on homosexuals, is that what they do isn't going to send me to hell!
> And anyway, I don't view it as being any worse than any other sin. Sin is sin.

In mentioning "sin is sin," the regional culture may influence such cognition, emotionality, and word choice regarding the topic of LGBT identity and use of the term, "homosexuals." Similarly, for the earlier example referencing, "leading alternative lifestyles," a reference to "sin is sin" suggests an intention to convey a stance of perceived equity regarding the behavior of sinners. It can be interpreted to mean, if meting out punishments for behavior, LGBT persons would fair no worse than any other "sinner." For a gay person to be referenced in the year 2020 as homosexual, which historically and sometimes regionally connotes being mentally ill or a sinner, is reflective of a micro-aggressive mixed-type slur (Croom, 2014). As indicated by Tarakeshwar, Stanton, & Pargament (2003), religiosity deserves greater cultural analysis for its influence on the cognitions, emotions, and behaviors of individuals. In specific cultural contexts among some ethnic groups and regions in the southern United States, more empirical research is needed to build upon examples given here as common utterances in one U.S. southern regional setting.

Cultural Neuroscience: Disgust Based Inhumanity

Dr. Milton Diamond, Professor Emeritus of anatomy and reproductive biology at the University of Hawaii at Mānoa, once shared that diversity exists comfortably in nature, but is less embraced in society by human beings. So what might be the impact of this on the lives of a gender-nonconforming man or woman? What might society's relative discomfort with diversity mean for men, women, and intersexed persons who partner differently, identify themselves differently, and in other ways vary from societal expectations of gender binary categories or respectability politics? For example, the so called *ratchet* female discussed in the previous chapter, is a woman who varies from the historical traditional societal expectations of respectability for women. Could it be that such individuals evoke disgust responses from others?

Rozin & Haidt (2013) have detailed that disgust is an emotion that can be elicited by a wide range of stimuli. They propose that disgust can be understood as a reaction to stimuli and situations that pose threats. Disgust has evolved from primarily contamination sensitivity (i.e., vomit reflex to expel a toxic food or even the thought of ingesting something unpleasant) to also encompass disgust reactions to stimuli in the moral domain. Negative reactions to Black women deemed *ratchet* and/or to Black LGBT people for example, may fall under the categories of sex/mating and moral threat-based disgust (Tyber, Lieberman, Kurzban, & Descioli, 2009). For example, it is possible that a person is romantically and sexually attracted to women but has not conceived of a *ratchet* woman nor transwoman as a mate. Upon encountering such women, a person may feel aversive emotions. The *ratchet* woman may unconsciously pose a threat to a desire for maintaining conservative views of women. A transgender woman may pose a threat to body politic ideologies. Moral disgust may underlie the person's thoughts and behavior (Tyber et al., 2009).

Sensitivity to disgust and authoritarianism positively correlate with being opposed to the rights of transgender people. For people who jointly score highly on sensitivity to disgust and authoritarianism, they are more likely to be greatly opposed to transgender rights (Miller et al., 2017). These jointly high-scoring people have above average opposition to transgender body-centric rights such as a transgender person changing sex classification on a state-issued driver's license, or choosing a bathroom based on gender identity. Disgust sensitivity has also been related to anti-immigration reactions in people, based on resistance to foreign norms (Aaroe, Petersen, & Arceneaux, 2017).

Micro-aggressive questions have been uttered regarding transgender people. Statements may be heard such as, "Is that a he or a she?" This is an offensive mechanism. Famous personalities in media who have engaged jokes, slurs, and violent speech against transwomen for example, have evoked media outcry (Hawkins, 2017). Such use of language is powerful in its potential for further harm to Black transgender persons. Though Black transgender people are more accepted by their families than other demographics of transgender persons, they have the highest rates of maltreatment and endangered lives in society (Harrison-Quintana & Lettman-Hicks, 2011; Grant et al., 2011). It can be argued that intense feelings of race, gender, and perhaps sex-based disgust explain the severity of maltreatment of Black transgender women. Powerlessness, bias, and inhumane treatment enacted against Black transgender women, immigrants, lower income people, indigenous people, and other marginalized groups may be exacerbated by the normalization of slurs against these human beings. More functional magnetic resonance (fMRI) research is needed. Further exploration of disgust investigations may shed light on whether normalized implicit bias in language, such as use of slurs, may correlate with reduced empathy-associated firing of mirror neurons in the insula, even when exposed to inhumane treatment against marginalized human beings (Wicker et al., 2003).

Gender dysphoria (GDA) is a condition in which psychological suffering is not uncommon and may increase when the person cannot escape feeling the incongruence between experienced gender and the gender assigned at birth (Schneider, Spritzer, Soll, Fontanari, Carneiro, Tovar-Moll, . . . Lobato, 2017). In such cases, uninformed cisgender persons, could potentially exacerbate psychological challenges by using slurs against non-gender binary, gender-queer, and transgender persons. To cope with GDA, impacted persons may consult with their physicians and opt for gonadotropin releasing hormone analogs (GnRHa) to suppress the onset of puberty to relieve psychological suffering. Researchers have discovered, however, that while receiving GNRHa treatment, white matter of the brain, memory, and performance on cognitive tests have been shown to be compromised (Schneider et al., 2017). Thus, efforts to reduce psychological suffering for some (not all transgender persons take GRHa, nor suffer psychologically), unfortunately can have negative cognitive side-effects.

African-Centered Psychology

A key African-centered psychologist describes well-being as fundamentally connected to a grasp of the meaning of what it means to be human (Nobles, 2010). Such approaches highlight the significance and power of in-depth exploration of African healing traditions for the good of humanity. Bantu Kongo thought comprises cognitions that emphasize diverse forces and waves of energy surrounding humans and governing life (Nobles, 2010). Using this framework, Nobles has asked the question of how might decision-making and relationships be altered for the better if all living beings recognized their connection to all other living beings? This is an epistemology that recognizes the power of invisible life-spirit energies that perpetually and mutually exchange amongst human beings.

Under the African-centered psychology, all human beings are spirit regardless of race, social class, religion, gender, or romantic and sexual attractionality. Persons who possess such philosophy and belief are thought to operate at a higher consciousness according to African-centered psychology. As such, their ideology is described by Nobles as perceiving all human beings as instruments and containers of divine spirit. If a critical mass is reached of beings who view themselves and others in this way, it could have potentially widespread deep implications for healing -isms and phobias, such as transphobia and homophobia. Nobles (2010) described humans as spirits who are continually unfolding and inquiring into their own being, knowledge, experiences, and truth. For example, it is not unusual for transgender children to already have a true knowing of themselves as being transgender (Rae, Gulgoz, Durwood, DeMeules...et al., 2019). It is the antithesis of the African sense of well-being to harbor thoughts of negativity and enact violence towards such other spirit beings.

Spirit Beings: Questions for Neuroscience

In non-western cultures such as among the Dagara tribal people of Burkina Faso, people are not labeled as LGB or transgender (Somé, 2002). Instead such humans are viewed as spirit beings who are labeled gatekeepers of the portals between the physical and spiritual worlds. In the culture, gatekeepers maintain the peace and harmony among genders and the village. Nothing of significance happens in the culture without gatekeepers' guidance.

Mainstream scientists have engaged in-depth analysis of the culture-behavior-brain (CBB) loop regarding transgenderism (Mohammadi & Khaleghi, 2018). Specifically, they have asked if the brains of transgender humans are innately structurally and functionally different from cisgender people? Alternatively, they have asked, do the cultural life experiences of acknowledging and living as transgender eventually reshape the individuals' brains to be reflective of the cultural realities they live? In Dagara culture, such human beings would be regarded as having bodily vibrations that are different from others.

Wade Nobles has contributed an extensive body of work (Nobles, Baloyi, & Sodi, 2016; Nobles, 2015; Nobles, 2006; Nobles, 2010) to the discipline of African-centered/Black psychology (ACBP). However, the empirical data as evidence to support the statements that are central to ACBP regarding spirit are lacking, as evaluated under a western Eurocentric epistemology. Now, however, with recent newfound research interest in N, N-Dimethyltriptamine (DMT), an endogenous hallucinogen, insights to perception and consciousness as relevant to tenets of ACBP may be possible.

Researchers have discussed brain mapping of enzymes responsible for the biosynthesis of DMT and the presence and role of DMT in the pineal gland (Barker, 2018). Work is ongoing regarding new imaging studies of DMT, and discussion of new routes of administration beyond vaping and oral ingestion. However, it is known already that vaporized DMT is highly psychoactive. Using advanced brain imaging and molecular biology, researchers may be able to gain a better understanding of the common biochemistry that creates the mind. For example, Brazilian scholars have detailed that hallucinogens, primarily via serotonergic receptors, promote self-awareness and positive mood through modulating effects in the fronto-temporo-parieto-occipital cortex (dos Santos, Osório, Crippa & Hallak, 2016).

Within ACBP, the emphasis is on spirit and healing. Discoveries of the biological and physiological reward and motivational mechanisms associated with the limbic system are another avenue for advancing a cultural neuroscience of compassion, love, and collectivism under an African-centered framework of spiritual connectedness. The high amplitude synchronized gamma waves, as measured by electroencephalogram (EEG) during deep meditative states has been mentioned as relevant for gaining further knowledge into spirituality and the brain (Esch & Stefano, 2011).

To learn more about the role of endogenous DMT requires new direction and new experiments. The natural role of endogenous hallucinogens must be better understood. Investigating DMT as a therapeutic is of interest in relationship to this chapter's evidence of the denial of LGBT persons' spirit beingness; such interest parallels investigations of DMT's capacities as a neurotransmitter (Barker, 2018). I acknowledge too that a significant role of DMT in higher consciousness and spirituality has been refuted by other scientists (Nichols, 2018), who maintain that the amount of DMT produced in the pineal gland is too low to have any significant therapeutic psychospiritual impact. Such refutation among mainstream scientists is not unusual, because their perspective is that there are distinct and separate intellectual spaces of discourse for spirituality and science. There still is not enough empirical study of these matters.

Non-mainstream psychologists and systems' theorists, however, advocate that religion/spirituality and science are different sides of the same coin, making it impossible to find answers to important questions of life without the two relying upon one another (Nobles, 2006; Laszlo, 2014). Ancient Egyptians and Indian philosophies wrote of an illumination of spiritual intelligence which manifests as higher consciousness. The higher consciousness spiritual intelligence recognizes the secondary significance of physical matter to the primacy of time and space in the cosmos (Laszlo, 2014). Such perspective on the universe is that physical beings exist within a vast cosmos in which all living matter is connected across space and time.

Conclusion

Women, low-income persons, people of color, and sexual and gender minorities (as well as those having intersections of each of these identities) no longer experience the same invisibility as in past decades. Thus increasingly, these groups' more mainstreamed presence will likely continue to affect emotions and language directed towards them in societies. There is also potential for advancing empirical investigations inclusive of LGBTQ persons. This reflects the ongoing need for social justice on behalf of those who have experienced a history of stigmatization, bias, and inhumane treatment such as verbal and physical abuse. There is a need for greater research on how slurs and other offensive mechanisms of language and emotion-based targeting are processed in the brain of privileged offenders, possibly leading to bias and maltreatment of marginalized groups. Hate speech and actions may stem from socialized disgust sensitivity reactions in the brain which might originate with the predictive brain's socialization and social cognitions associated with the dehumanization of others. There are consequences for the negative language and behavior directed at others, because we also risk dehumanizing ourselves by dehumanizing others (Kouchaki, Dobson, &Waytz, 2018).

A consciousness which stems from a knowledge and appreciation of non-western beliefs such as the oneness of science and spirit, could heal minds experiencing socio-functional threat that has been shown to produce prejudice towards transgender people (Buck & Nedvin, 2017); the same can be said for eliminating disgust, hatred, or bewilderment regarding the existence of transgender humans. The evolution of spiritual intelligence beginning at a neurobiological level could result in an extinction of negative emotionality and actions directed at transgender and LGB persons. Currently there is limited empirically based scientific answers about the role of mirror neurons in showing compassion, exchange between prefrontal and limbic areas to promote positive emotionality, and the science of neurobiology that underlies compassion, love for the world, and love for others (Esch & Stefano, 2011).

Chapter Seven

Collectivist and Individualist Brains

In December 2017, *The Chronicle of Higher Education* published a story on Kennett, Missouri, entitled "A Dying Town" (Brown & Fishcher, 2017). Throughout the story, the authors provide statistics to highlight the poverty among the residents of Kennett. The authors state the lack of higher education in the town (1 in 10 adults in Kennett have a college degree) poses a public health crisis. The journalists advocate as much for education as for health. The statistics presented in the article reflect that men with a high school education or less are the most susceptible to chronic illness and death. The dire straits of several residents are presented; the dismal life of poverty and chronic illness is detailed for one couple trapped in a cycle of suboptimal living including poor diet, frequent doctor's visits, daily medications, and chronic illness. Would many people reading the article feel empathy for the couple, or would they read the story and feel nothing, or maybe even feel condemnation? What might explain differences in moral reasoning, empathy, or feeling connected to others such as those discussed in "A Dying Town?"

INDIVIDUALISM AND COLLECTIVISM

Researchers largely agree that culture is a complex term, and as such, there have been multiple definitions (Berger, 2000). Throughout this chapter, using the various definitions of meaning indicated by multiple others, I will refer to culture to mean the values, beliefs, customs, and practices of a group of people that have been handed down from generation to generation, often to aid in the group's survival. For the descendants of enslaved Africans, several of their sustained values, beliefs, customs, and practices have been identified as evidence of Black people's cultural similarities across the

African Diaspora despite their forced physical displacement from places of origin (Irobi, 2007).

Researchers first studied a cultural dimension labeled as individualism-collectivism (Hofstede, 1980), by measuring the frequency of existence of two components of individualism assessed across cultures: self-reliance and separation from in-groups within cultures. They also assessed the degree of existence of collectivism across various cultures: family integrity and inter-dependence with sociability (Hofstede, 1980). The researchers concluded that using these four factors allowed for assessment of individualism and collectivism both within and across cultures, with evidence of a convergence of the four, even when using different methods for measuring.

Individualism has been given various names by different researchers, but consistently is reflective of individual achievement, competition, perceived loneliness, and putting one's own personal goals and interests above what might be best for a group (Triandis, Bontempo, Betancourt, Verma, 1986). Researchers have stated that the United States and other English-speaking countries tend to show higher levels of individualism, relative to non-western nations such as Japan, where English is not the primary language. Collecti-vism on the other hand, has been stated as reflective of cultures in which cooperation, sociability, and feelings and thoughts of connection to others are important. For the purposes of this chapter, a discussion of the connection between culture, social cognitive neuroscience, and social behavior is cen-tral, particularly as related to marginalized populations of the world relative to those having power and influence.

Some researchers challenge the notion that individualism and collecti-vism are rooted in a culture or country; they view such labeling as evoking cultural stereotypes (Knyazeva, Savostyanova, Bocharova, & Merkulovaa, 2018). This raises for consideration, the notion that individuals from the same culture may vary in their degree of individualism or collectivism. For example, in a diverse nation such as the United States, in which there are many types of Americans, when the United States is consistently regarded as individualistic in terms of its people's behavior, which Americans are being viewed as the standard? The label of individualistic, as attributed to U.S. culture is perhaps rooted in a White supremacist, capitalist, heterosexist, patriarchal worldview that does not include the histories and experiences of diverse ethnic/cultural groups and lower social class statuses. A reliance upon a western grand narrative as a norm within many disciplines is proble-matic because the western grand narrative is grounded in beliefs that privi-lege difference, aristocracy, elitism, classism, racism, sexism, genetic inferi-ority and caste attribution (Nobles, Baloyi, & Sobi, 2016).

The construct of a self-construal that is either independent or interdepen-dent, based on the country being in the west or in the east can be misleading. For example, when the self-construal is labeled as independent for

Americans and Europeans and more interdependent for East Asians, the most marginalized or disenfranchised residents of the United States and Europe have not been well-represented in the studies on which such findings and statements are based (Markus & Kitayama, 1991). Most research in traditional western psychology has focused on White undergraduate psychology students and the numerically minority persons of the world, i.e., White, rather than including the majority persons of the world who do not identify as White. This has prompted non-western scholars to deconstruct major social science theories that have been the basis for findings deemed universal (Dasen, 2012).

The Evolution of "Social Expertise

It has been written and accepted that human sociality or relatedness is so intrinsic to human nature, that sociality even shapes development of the brain (Dunbar & Shultz, 2007). Researchers who have addressed the intrinsic nature of sociality have described an evolution of brain development that promotes pair bonding. There are long-term benefits for individuals who form pair bonds because this leads to individuals coupling to produce families, leading to the eventual formation of communities. This view is that the promotion of healthy and stable communities has the potential to trickle down to be a benefit to the individuals who make up the community (Dunbar & Shultz, 2007). Boyd (2006) described communities in which those who are ill, hungry, and disabled are cared for, and social lives are governed by a moral system and sanctions against social violations. Boyd also, however, acknowledges that among some primate species (humans included) the cooperation might be more limited to one's relatives or other subset of the larger group.

Throughout his piece, Boyd (2006) expounds upon the work of a fellow researcher, Bowles, as a means of explaining why humans display overall group level prosocial cooperative behavior regardless of individual level competition. A benefit of relatives' collective dominance of out-group members is explained by the drive to be competitive across groups. The more dominant group, Boyd explains, values competition and successful takeover of another outside group. He used this to explain that though relatives may compete with one another, their goal is to reap the collective benefits from their families' cooperation and collectivism, united to conquer and control the resources of weaker outside members. A problematic aspect of what Boyd describes, lies in the disenfranchisement and power grab motivation at the center of the description. Competition amongst relatives is acceptable, if the relatives understand the larger goal of unification for the purpose of domination and exploitation of outsiders and others' territories. The behavior and thinking is in the interest of the in-group's collective good.

Wilson (1993) warned of Eurocentric psychiatry/psychology and Euro-centric histories that are written in what appear to be a benign apolitical manner, even as they promote an ideology of imperialism. Evolutionary psychology is a good example of a concentration in Eurocentric psychology in which researchers present their theories in apolitical ways. One example of this from Byrne & Whiten (1986) states that a greater magnitude of social complexities is necessary for humans; humans' need to engage in social complexity, is stated as a potential reason for the larger brain mass develop-ment of humans relative to that of non-humans. However, Byrne & Whiten make this statement as though such social complexity-based brain develop-ment is not only adaptive but has equitable positive outcomes for all humans. This ideally should be true for all humans under ideal social conditions. However, the examples of social complexities highlighted by Byrne & Whit-en (1986), reflect a clear bias regarding who primarily engages the domineer-ing behaviors to the collective benefit of their in-group.

From their title alone, Byrne & Whiten's (1988) political worldview is evident, as they used the term "Machiavellian intelligence" in their book's title. Social expertise is highlighted in the book and defined as a beneficial set of cognitive processes that enables social manipulation of others who are viewed as presenting a problem. In the book, interdisciplinary and interna-tional Eurocentric scholars present detailed analysis of the social evolution of the brain, using their Machiavellian intelligence hypothesis.

The hypothesis asserts that humans' large brains and distinctive mental capabilities are a result of evolution. The assertion of Eurocentric scholars is that humans evolved large brains over time via engagement in intense social competition. They contend that human social competitors, over time, devel-oped sophisticated Machiavellian strategies to achieve higher social and re-productive success beyond their competitors. It is noteworthy to read Euro-centric theories that are written in a depoliticized manner, when asserting that naturally selected forces evolved as effective strategies for achieving social success. The examples given of social success include deception, manipula-tion, alliance formation, and exploitation of the expertise of others (Gavrilets & Vose, 2006). The effective strategies for achieving social success are examples of behaviors reflective of the western grand narrative and sub-optimal worldview (Nobles, Baloyi, & Sobi, 2016; Myers, 1993) that has historically led to the systematic disenfranchisement of large numbers of people internationally. Exploitation of the expertise of others is evident in the history of enslaved Africans.

Enslaved Africans' skills in planting, carpentry, shoemaking, basket weaving, and brick masonry were exploited for their owners' own success (Joyner, 1984). This behavior represents oppression and disenfranchisement by slaveholders. However, as described in the literature, Eurocentric scholars might merely categorize these tactics among former slaveholders as Machiavellian intelligence or social expertise.

A problem exists, though, in classifying this Machiavellian intelligence as solely individualistic behavior, based on its behavior being representative of a Eurocentric worldview. Although the Machiavellian hypothesis focuses on behavioral priorities that fall under a Eurocentric western grand narrative worldview, regarded as both sub-optimal and individualistic in African-centered psychology, such behaviors also manifest as collectivist practices of elitist, racist, sexist in-groups who exploit, disparage, deceive, and manipulate out-groups of powerless and oppressed people.

The critical thinker might ask the question of why researchers would deem it significant to study and then inform readers of the scientific origins and purpose of using a type of "social expertise" called tactical deception? Whiten & Byrne (1988), identify tactical deception as that which occurs when an individual can use an honest act from his normal cultural behavioral patterns in a different context, to mislead familiar individuals. The researchers emphasize there are different classes of tactical deception that can be used for different purposes. Irrespective of the classification of the deception, it is necessary that the deceiver know the features of others' state of mind (Whiten & Byrne, 1988). The researchers state the deceivers must be able to act as "natural psychologists" to be able to take full advantage of the to-be-deceived. When viewing this literature from an African-centered worldview, it is evident that the research literature on tactical deception has been presented as an apolitical investigation into the social cognition of primates. A close examination of what it is, how it is used, and why, reveals it as a practice that is not solely for use in warfare against enemies, nor is unquestionably an example of evolved intelligence; it is relevant to acts of inhumanity, power, and abuse.

For countries such as the United States that are deemed individualistic, this label of individualism may only apply to a certain extent. Among individuals in such a culture, there is competition, but in terms of the maintenance of social ills such as White supremacy and patriarchy, these systems are maintained through overall collectivism within the ruling class culture of White males at large (Liu, 2017). A vivid example of this exists in the relationship between two U.S. public figures, Senator Ted Cruz of Texas, and Donald J. Trump, 45th president of the United States. When these two men were embattled in a Republican primary to become their party's nominee for president, they were fierce competitors. They engaged in name calling and accusations of each other. They maligned one another's character, and both tried to convince voters that the other was incompetent and thus not qualified to lead their party. This fierce competitiveness subsided once Trump became president, and Cruz was in the position of being an incumbent senator, desiring to keep his position and their political party's majority seats in Congress. Trump then became a supporter of Cruz and planned rallies to get out the vote to help Cruz and their political party to win the mid-term elections (Chaitin, 2018). Collective party over the individual personal is exemplified here. Trump and Cruz put their individual competition or dislike of one another aside for the good of their collective political agendas. Thus, the western grand narrative is maintained through this sort of alliance formation which advances the collective power structure. In this example, Cruz and Trump cannot be said to be exclusively individualistic in their way of being, as resulting from their national culture.

Relevance of the Medial Prefrontal Cortex and Collectivism

Collectivism has been investigated as an independent variable that may impact social cognition. Researchers have used sophisticated equipment and techniques to reveal there is an area of the brain, the medial prefrontal cortex (MPFC), that at rest influences the degree of collectivism's impact on social cognition (Knyazev, Savostyanov, Bocharov & Merkulova, 2018). The researchers referenced several brain areas as being significant to empathy, moral reasoning, processing of emotions, and decision-making, with differential outcomes indicated via functional magnetic resonance imaging (fMRI). Those who are collectivist showed different connectivity between the MPFC and other cortical areas, relative to those who were individualistic. The implication is that human brains may reveal who is more likely to think about others and who is more likely to be self-centered in thinking.

A close reading of one study revealed, however, that the others who were being referenced and recalled were relatives of the research participants. This represents a weakness of generalizability of the findings to situations where people are not thinking of relatives and friends, versus unrelated others (Knyazev, Savostyanov, Bocharov & Merkulova, 2018). Thus, the bent of this science still reflects the self-referential nature of the findings, even as such findings are being deemed reflective of collectivism.

The Politics in the Science

The researchers of the previously described MPFC studies depoliticized the findings by failing to study diverse research participants' knowledge and understanding of oppression, White supremacy, and disenfranchisement as they manifest in relationships. Highlighting this may reveal further differences in types of memories retrieved, and the reasoning regarding moral issues and types of social motives. Consumers of scientific research who may be less knowledgeable of power, privilege, Eurocentrism, and the biosocial nature of the brain, may read depoliticized work as purely scientific findings that have no socio-political or social justice connections.

A deeper more thorough investigation using qualitative analysis might provide further information regarding how often identified collectivists think of other people who are not members of their in-group (e.g., same social class, race, power status). For example, researchers in one study, stated most of the participants in their study were White females. They used age and sex as nuisance co-variants with collectivism. Yet culture and social class as points of consideration for future studies were not mentioned. The findings of the study were presented as both apolitical and universal, even though the findings were biased based upon testing middle-class majority White Russian women who were likely thinking about their relatives or other personal relationships during social cognition. How generalizable are these results?

Selfishness, Power, and the Brain

For humans who support and participate in inhumane behavior and selfish ways, could it be that something has gone awry in these humans' MPFC connectivity capacity in the cortical regions that are related to reasoning, morality, and empathy? Alternatively, researchers might investigate how neural firing in such persons has been differentially conditioned, impacting an area known as the DMN (default mode network). In the subcortex, the DMN is composed of several connected areas of the cortex in the cingulate, prefrontal, and parietal areas of the brain. The DMN areas remain active when people are engaged in goal-directed self-referential thoughts, as well as during social cognition (Gobbini et al., 2007; Mitchell, Banaji & Macrae, 2005). Thus, the DMN is relevant to the social expertise that Eurocentric scholars entitled Machiavellian intelligence; they identified this intelligence as deception, manipulation, alliance formation, and exploitation of the expertise of others (Gavrilets & Vose, 2006). Brain-based evidence informs the motives of some people who act in their own self-interest to the disregard of others. Such persons may be consistently societally reinforced due to their social power and privilege, and display more approach-motivated behaviors (Boksem, Tops, Wester, Meijman, & Lorist, 2006; Boksem et al, 2012).

Left Prefrontal Cortex and Social Power

Keltner, Gruenfeld, & Anderson (2003), has defined social power as an individual's relative capacity to modify others' states by providing or withholding resources or administering punishments. Myers (1993) sheds light on sub-optimal psychology common in Eurocentrism, and associated behaviors related to feeling socially powerful. It is telling however, that the social injustice implications of enacting social power against marginalized people was not included in the brain research, even though it is directly relevant.

Boksem et al. (2012) reported findings of EEG based asymmetry of the frontal lobes among undergraduate research participants. Research participants were primed to recall themselves in high social power situations versus primed to recall themselves in low social power situations. In the study, the researchers stated only right-handed participants were used in the study (to control for the naturally weaker left-brain activity among left-handers). They also inform readers that 15 of the 36 undergraduates of the study were males. What is never mentioned in the study, however, is the ethnicity nor social class of the participants. In such a research study that focuses on how social power manifests in the brain and leads to approach motivation, the omission of reference to the social class of the participants is mentioned as common in hegemonic research (Adams, Dobles, Gómez, Kurtiş, & Molina, 2015). Henrich, Heine, & Norenzayan (2010) described such psychological science as being WEIRD (western, educated, industrial, rich, democratic). WEIRD societies comprise 80 percent of research participants, but only 12 percent of the world's population.

The Boksem et al. (2012) social power brain research was conducted at Tilsburgh University, in the south of the Netherlands. The primary author's university website details its percentages of international, undergraduate, and graduate students; yet the authors' reference to financial need, social class, and ethnicity cannot expressly be found in the research article nor on the university's website. Thus, the researchers concluded that social power is positively correlated with left pre-frontal cortex and approach motivation in a select group of likely privileged participants. The researchers also state that the accompanying feelings of approach motivation may be positive or negative. Thus, a person who is high in social power may display approach motivation in connection with joy and happiness or may display approach motivation connected to negative emotions such as anger. The following is an example of negative mood- based approach motivation from the confirmation hearing of now U.S. Supreme Court judge, Brett Kavanaugh.

> Opponents of Brett Kavanaugh saw his performance last Thursday as an unhinged, petulant tantrum, while his supporters saw a display of wholly-justified, righteous anger, when he denounced what he called "this grotesque character assassination." (Sykes, 2018)

Sykes argues that Kavanaugh was justified in his anger at being accused of rape, assault, and blacking out due to heavy drinking. However, Sykes is critical of the unrestrained way that the anger was displayed. While watching the Brett Kavanaugh Senate confirmation hearing in October 2018, which was continuously mired in controversy, one may have wondered why Kavanaugh did not withdraw from consideration for nomination to the U.S. Supreme Court, when events did not go as he expected. The proceedings became heated and partisan, though this is not how the process should have been conducted. Kavanaugh seemingly could not hold back his display of anger and frustration.

Brain science provides insight to Kavanaugh's behavior. According to his race, class, and gender classification it is not surprising he would continue to pursue his goal-directed behavior towards higher social power and status (U.S. Supreme Court Judge), despite experiencing threatening or unexpected changes in his environment (Corbetta & Shulman, 2002). Boksem et al. (2012) concluded that the pathway from the limbic system to the left dorso-lateral prefrontal cortex for people high in social power is primarily the basis for approach motivation in such individuals. A person high in social power is less distracted by changes in the environment, such as unanticipated opponents or enemies attempting to thwart one's goal-directed behavior. A person high in social power such as Kavanaugh is privileged to be able to stay focused on his pre-determined plan, blocking out distractions. Persons such as Brett Kavanaugh, being high in social power, are privileged enough in social power to be proactive rather than avoidant, and according to the research, their brains have been socially influenced to represent a pattern of such approach motivation. The opposite is true for people low in social power who monitor their environments for the signs of threat, control, and punishment from people in power. The socially powerless have been socialized to be more reactive than proactive; top-down regulatory processes of their social brains can result in avoidance motivation (Tucker & Williamson, 1984); the behavioral inhibitory reactivity of the socially powerless continues to benefit those in power.

Regarding Kavanaugh, one could argue that his individualistic, western grand narrative–influenced brain explains his goal-directed behavior, yet his behavior also represents the collective socially powerful group's brain-based goal-directed, frequently rewarded behavior (Carver & White, 1994). In spite of the animosity and challenging experience that was Kavanaugh's confirmation process, on October 6, 2018, Brett Kavanaugh was sworn in as the United States' 114th Supreme Court Judge (Naylor, 2018). The Senate vote was a narrow 50–48 in favor of his confirmation. At the age of 53, he was rewarded with another significant goal-directed behavior in his life, while already living as a man in high social power, with accompanying brain and behavior that have been shaped by socially privileged status. There is brain-based evidence that this positive reinforcement will continue to shape his future decision-making and relevant behaviors (Elliott, Dolan, & Frith, 2000).

Cultural Neuroscience of Person Perception

All humans have the same anatomical brain parts and structural layout. Therefore, this chapter remains focused on how culture influences humans' brain-based perception and behavior, rather than on differences across humans in neural composition. In mainstream traditional scientific research, researchers have historically been reluctant to take an interest in culture as more than random noise in the research studies of the brain; increasingly though, researchers have begun to highlight, the role of culture in the brain's processing of emotional and cognitive information (Freeman, Rule, & Ambady, 2009). A question inspired by cultural neuroscience is how do people of varying cultural and status backgrounds perceive the world and people around them? For example, at the beginning of this chapter, impoverished people from Kennett, Missouri, are mentioned. Is it possible that people from different cultures and worldviews might perceive the Kennett residents differently, thereby behaving differently towards them because of how their brains' process information about people in poverty?

Affordance value research reveals that the answer to the previous question might be yes; perceptions of stimuli may vary culturally (Kitayama, Duffy, Kawamura, & Larsen, 2003). People of different sociocultural experiences might perceive the Kennett residents differently. The research on affordance value explains that humans perceive stimuli based on what the stimuli may afford the perceiver. The perceiver's cultural experiences and values influences how stimuli within the environment are perceived; questions of value become important due to how much someone or something is perceived to be of benefit to the perceiver, according to his or her cultural worldview. It is worth noting here again, that original historical writings on affordance value were written as apolitical and benign, primarily focusing on physical objects and only slight references to humans as opposed to animal behavior (Gibson, 1979). Yet, as with the writing on Machiavellian intelligence, a critical read of this literature reveals how it also informs understandings of bias against marginalized groups who may be perceived as low affordance value objects rather than as human beings.

In her book, *Plantation Memories*, the Afro-Portuguese scholar Grada Kilomba discusses White Europeans' perceptions of Blacks in Europe; through interviews with Black German women, Kilomba highlights the manner in which Black people are perceived as objects rather than human subjects (Kilomba, 2010). Such othering appears connected to a low affordance value of the affected, as inferred from how they are treated by those in power.

The following is an example of othering from the nation of Brazil. Black Brazilians who currently live in rural settlement areas are referred to as *quilombolas*; the quilombola residents are descendants of formerly enslaved

Africans who escaped from slavery. The Worker's Party of Brazil though imperfect, when in leadership, was open to dialogue with the residents of the *quilombos*; the former president of Brazil, Luiz Inácio Lula (da Silva) supported progress for the residents, such as providing running water and electricity in the case of one *quilombo*, *Quilombo Primavera* (Watson, 2018).

As well, in the year 2003, President Lula's administration specifically enacted government provision for the nation's residents of the *quilombos* by referencing the International Organization of Labor (ILO) Convention 169 for Indigenous and Tribal Peoples. This was necessary as the *quilombolas* needed some model upon which policy could be established to provide them with protection, and right to self-identify, including living in accordance with a salient African identity. Lula's administration acknowledged the salient Africanness that is the basis for *quilombolas'* traditions, authenticity, and need for land preservation rights (Farfán-Santos, 2011).

However, the 2018-elected Brazilian president Bolsonaro, has made public comments stating the residents of the *quilombos* are not even fit for procreation (Watson, 2018). A *Quilombo Primavera* resident stated, such language reflects that Bolsonaro views the residents of *quilombos* as animals. Bolsonaro has also described residents of *quilombos* as lazy. The tribalization by the Brazilian government's *quilombo* law of Brazil's Black *quilombo* communities has led to stereotyping, discrimination, and violence enacted to remove the Black people from their land (Farfán-Santos, 2011).

Under Brazil's newly elected President Bolsonaro, anxiety, sadness, and fear among these poorest citizens are heightened. The history of the oppression and disenfranchisement is such that the country's residents of the *quilombos* do not necessarily have deeds of title to the land on which they and their ancestors reside. This is because the original inhabitants of the land were formerly enslaved people who escaped to isolated rural areas, in which they could hide and establish themselves as a community away from slavery. Thus, the lands occupied may have never been officially deeded as their own. Today, their ownership of the lands are disputed, and there are those who assert that few of the people living in *quilombos* are actual descendants of the formerly enslaved; this has been reported as another means being used to justify removal of the people from the lands (Farfán-Santos. 2011). This ongoing crisis reflects the affordance value and person perception of the residents of *quilombos*.

Person characteristics include gender, race, ethnicity, age, cultural membership, emotional status, and social status (Freeman, Rule, & Ambady, 2009); the responses of a perceiver will vary, based upon whether the perceived person is of the same culture or not. Even basic emotions such as fear, are not equally perceived when manifesting from outside of the perceiver's own culture; researchers have written that acting in response to perceived fear in another, likely has higher affordance value when it is a fearful member of one's own cultural group (Weisbuch & Ambady, 2008; Phelps & LeDoux, 2005). Further research is needed on human behavior such as inhumanity towards one's own culture, once that person is perceived as an enemy.

On October 2, 2018, Saudi Arabian born, U.S. resident and *Washington Post* journalist, Jamal Kashoggi disappeared from the Saudi Consulate in Turkey. Kashoggi was known for writing critical opinion articles against Saudi leadership in the *Washington Post*. Crown Saudi Prince Mohammed bin Salman was later revealed to be behind the killing of Mr. Kashoggi; Mohammed bin Salman was revealed to have perceived Kashoggi to be a member of a dangerous Islamist group known as the Muslim Brotherhood (Kirkpatrick & Hubbard, 2018). Jamal Khashoggi's body was "dissolved" in acid after he was murdered and dismembered inside the Saudi Arabian consulate in Istanbul, according to a Turkish official. Specifically, it is believed he was strangled and then dismembered so the body would be more easily destroyed with acid, ensuring no remains would be found (Agence France-Press, 2018).

One month following Kashoggi's murder, and the internationally accepted knowledge that Mohammed bin Salman was behind the murder, bin Salman is still in power and maintains relations with both U.S. and European government officials. Thus, the minds of eastern and western acculturated men have synced and aligned for the maintenance of power, dominance, and capitalism. This again reflects how actions are influenced by the affordance value of people and other stimuli, under the worldview of a western grand narrative.

In contexts in which individuals have been culturally conditioned towards dominance and independence, their brains' mesolimbic reward systems have also been culturally shaped to react to environmental stimuli that represents aggression, dominance, and independence. Therefore, a U.S. acculturated leader such as Donald Trump might find it rewarding or pleasurable to be associated with other powerful, aggressive, and dominant leaders such as Mohammed bin Salman or North Korea's Kim Jung-un. This is despite that Trump is of a western culture and they are not. Likewise, all the men's brain-based approach-motivated behaviors are reflective of the motivations of people who have high social power (Galinsky, Gruenfeld, & Magee, 2003). People of the same culture may behave inhumanely towards one another, if intracultural person characteristics are perceived negatively, such as being of lowered status or low social power.

Fascism is an ideology based on power and loyalty; Stanley (2018) has described it as based in hypermasculinity and hyper-patriarchy with one usually male nationalist leader maintaining it. Stanley (2018) also identified 10 pillars of fascism:

mythic past, a great mythic past to which the leader harkens back

propaganda

anti-intellectualism

unreality

hierarchy

victimhood

law and order

Sodom and Gomorrah—urban people sin; rural people are godly

Arbeit macht frei—work shall make you free. The out-group is lazy.

Rather than focusing much of the cross-cultural research on whether an individual has been socialized in an individualist or collective culture, it is also informative to expand the brain research on social power versus powerlessness to learn more across a wider range of cultural contexts. Fascist personalities and their behavior have relevance to developing research in social neuroscience which has examined neurological associations between dehumanization and human rights abuses (Murrow & Murrow, 2015). There is evidence that socially powerful humans are not only more approach motivated, but also may be less capable of showing humanity and empathy for others (Galinsky, Magee, Inesi, & Gruenfeld, 2006; Hogeveen, Inzlicht, & Obhi, 2014).

Conclusion

There is limited universalism of processing and its resulting perception that stems directly from solely the neural components of the brain. Thus, it is misguided to broadly and simplistically ground studies in cultural neuroscience on individualist compared to collectivist cultures. There is complexity regarding how the human brain processes stimuli and impacts human behavior. The world's disenfranchised are susceptible to the social manipulation of some in power, whose brains are socioculturally conditioned to prompt motivation towards dominance, disenfranchising, and in some cases murder. Their mesolimbic reward systems are culturally conditioned to activate and release pleasurable chemicals that are reinforcing during approach-motivated actions. Some people of low social status such as those mentioned at the beginning of this chapter and those living under dictators or fascists, have social experiences that are similar regarding their brains' adaptive reactions to low social power and avoidance motivation. Those of higher social status often behave similarly to one another based on their brains' histories of operating in a culture of privilege and power. In-group members who are of privileged statuses are more likely to have similarly operating cortical and subcortical responses to stimuli, including responses such as use of tactical deception towards other humans not perceived to be of their in-group. Though cultural neuroscience is still a relatively new specialty of study, it may already be off to a poor start by avoiding socio-political and controversial subjects and their implications. It is important to decolonize cultural neuroscience while still in the early stages of the field's development. In discussing affordance value and person characteristics as relevant to a cultural neuroscience of person perception, this has implications for understanding powerful humans' motivation to remove Black Brazilians from *quilombos*, motivations to continuously support offshore drilling, removal of national park land reserves, and ongoing targeting of neighborhoods for gentrification displacing longtime residents. Not only must the science incorporate more socio-political integration with neuroscience, but likewise marginalized groups cannot afford to be ignored in research in neuroscience, cultural neuroscience, and biopsychology done by responsible researchers. These fields have historically been comprised of lengthy texts which on the surface appear to be apolitical yet may contain racist, classist, and sexist research. Such works have the potential to continue to inform the thinking of "medical men" and proletariat class individuals who can use the information to enhance problematic behavior such as tactical deception that has been heralded as a form of intelligence according to a Eurocentric worldview.

Chapter Eight

Minding Perceptions of Native People

It is not a crime for people to peacefully assemble in resistance to social injustice. Yet, even when dehumanized people peacefully protest, their oppressor may command dogs to attack them; security officers may pepperspray the oppressed, even as the they engage in peaceful protest. When a people are dehumanized, their ancestors may be deemed meaningless. This is relevant to how indigenous peoples' sacred burial grounds and artifacts could be desecrated with no empathy nor regard during indigenous peoples' fight against the Dakota Access Pipeline at Standing Rock in the United States

Dave Archambault II, chairman of the Standing Rock Sioux Tribe described the conflict as being similar to a perpetrator committing a crime against an innocent person (ABC News, 2016). When money and profit are prioritized over human beings, then empathy for the people is unlikely to exist (Harte, 2016). The disparity and disregard for marginalized people are also evident in the words of Alicia Garza when she expressed that White privileged persons can behave with impunity, while the same is not afforded to Native people:

> If you're white, you can occupy federal property . . . and get found not guilty. No teargas, no tanks, no rubber bullets. If you're indigenous and fighting to protect our earth, and the water we depend on to survive, you get tear gassed, media blackouts, tanks and all that. (Eversley, 2016)

Energy Transfer Partners is a U.S. company headquartered in Dallas, Texas. The company engages in natural gas and propane pipeline transport. Instead of knowledge of and respect for ancestral veneration and Native cultures, a representative of *Energy Transfer Partners* reduced the Standing Rock Sioux tribe and allies' position as being merely a narrow and extreme political constituency (Business Wire, 2016).

On January 24, 2017, newly elected U.S. president Donald Trump signed a presidential memorandum to advance the construction of the Dakota Access Pipeline despite widespread opposition and resistance to its construction leading up to his election in 2016. The swiftness of his action is to be noted. He had been inaugurated the same week. The swift presidential action despite many months of resistance from the Standing Rock Sioux tribe and their allies belies a dismissal of the significance and seriousness of the indigenous peoples' culture. Likewise, evidence of such disregard is further provided by report that young White "protestors" increasingly entered the space of the pipeline resistance movement; however they treated it like a party such as a Burning Man festival (Dowd, 2016). This behavior from young White privileged persons contributed to millions of dollars required for clean-up of debris at the site, abandoned dogs, abandoned cars, and human waste following the end of the occupation (Richardson, 2017; Haney, 2017). Psychologically, what would cause non-indigenous people to go to the area for objectives other than remaining focused on the matter at hand, which was protesting the construction of a pipeline being constructed in a sacred sovereign area? Could the inappropriate festival-like behavior have been related to their misperceptions of indigenous people and the related cultural significance of the space?

CULTURE, BRAIN, AND PERSON PERCEPTION

Scholars in the nascent field of cultural neuroscience (CN) have addressed the methods used and variables commonly investigated in the field. CN examines the interplay of neuroscience and cultural psychology when examining thoughts, emotions, and behavior; it is understood that culture and neuroscience have reciprocal influences (Ames & Fiske, 2010). The impact of culture on genetic expression, chemical release, and brain responses is examined in the field. The field also addresses that humans' neural processing has an impact on society and culture. In CN, studies are also conducted in areas of cognition regarding person-perception, which may inform about how Native people are perceived by out-group members, such that young White outsiders would throw a wild party in a sacred Native space.

Freeman, Rule, & Ambady (2009), presented a review of studies regarding culture's ability to shape processes of social perception. Specifically, individuals' cultures influence their social perception-based outcomes and the neural activity that mediates the outcomes. For example, individuals who are of the same culture have demonstrated being more adept at accurately perceiving the emotions of members of their own culture rather than those outside of the culture (Weisbuch & Ambady, 2008). Other research has highlighted fear-based responses (among Black and White participants) in the amygdala to Black faces. Researchers explained this finding as reflecting culturally ingrained attitudes of bias against Black people as a marginalized outgroup (Lieberman et al., 2005).

Freeman, Rule, & Ambady, 2009 extensively detail the literature regarding social perceptions as affected by the social affordance value judgments of the people encountered in the socio-cultural environment. They reported that the visual construal of a group of people is influenced by characteristics of the group such as gender, race, ethnicity, age, social status, and cultural membership. Thus, being of oppressed outgroup status can result in such oppressed groups receiving negative types of evaluations, judgments, and interpersonal engagement. Such negative evaluations and judgments may be linked to historical and contemporary interpersonal engagement with and regard for indigenous or First Nation peoples living in various geographic spaces.

Attitudes about and Treatment of Indigenous People

Hilton (2011) uses the framework of Frantz Fanon to explicate the mental health challenges of Native Americans in the United States In doing so, Hilton focuses on Fanon's writings on the psychology of oppression, wherein Fanon thoroughly addressed colonizers' perceptions of the oppressed. Hilton summarizes that, at various times throughout history, Native people have been perceived as evil, savage, and therefore deserving of paternalistic treatment from their oppressors. Hilton provides a thorough account of oppressors' negative perceptions of indigenous people and their horrific treatment experienced across time. Hilton's perspective centers on Native Americans' lack of psychological well-being because of such oppression.

Subsequent to presenting the accurate history of the maltreatment of Native people, Hilton's account unfortunately, primarily reflects a doom and gloom narrative of Native people. His focus is on substance abuse, anxiety, mood disorders, and suicide among the various tribes. He references these pathological outcomes as stemming from internal unresolved conflict rooted in Native American's psychological oppression. Other scholars, take a different approach, by instead focusing attention on the minds of the oppressor, who have enacted the injustices against Native people.

Poussaint (2002) for example, takes the approach of interrogating the mental health of the racist oppressor rather than the oppressed. Poussaint's argument is that extreme racism is a mental health problem in need of recognition by the American Psychiatric Association. He designates extreme racism as a delusional symptom of psychosis. Poussaint describes extreme racism as a subtype of delusional disorder, which he labeled prejudice type delusion.

Prejudice type delusion has a theme. A person with extreme prejudice type delusion, would perceive Native Americans, for example, as collectively possessing unusual and significant characteristics. Xenophobia warrants further examination in the person perception literature as it relates to the activity of the hormone, oxytocin. There is existing research evidence that oxytocin release during associative learning through pairing with charitable social cues helps counter the effects of xenophobia and enhances altruism towards people perceived as members of a strange or foreign out-group (Marsh, Scheele, Feinstein, Gerhardt, . . . et al., 2017).

Delusional perceptions of Native people by their oppressors historically have been characterized as negative or pejorative. Poussaint (2002) discusses the grandiose nature of the content of such racist delusions. Prejudice subtype delusion, when extreme, may result in acting out behaviors such as murder of members of the despised group. Hilton (2011) appropriately referenced Fanon's work as relevant to deconstructing the terrorism repeatedly enacted against Native Americans.

Donald Trump's swift disregard of U.S. Native peoples' land and culture in 2017 can be compared to Andrew Jackson's racism while president in 1830. Jackson, too, acted swiftly when deciding to remove Native people from their land, authorizing the forcible removal of Native people at gunpoint. In the 19th century, Native people died in the forced removal from their U.S. southeast land to west of the Mississippi River in what eventually became known as The Trail of Tears. Currently, images and language, advertising, children's books, sports, and art continue to permeate U.S. culture with normalized stereotyping of Native Americans (Hirschfelder & Molin, 2018). These are examples of what the human brain may absorb for many decades across most humans' lifespan.

Terrorism and threat of murder of tribes of native people is not limited to the United States. Even as recently as 2018, uncontacted tribes of native people were disregarded and killed for their resource rich land in Brazil (Watson, 2018). In Brazil, under President Jair Bolsanoro, native uncontacted tribes living in the Amazon forest have been dehumanized and viewed merely as disposable nuisances. Yet, the amount of media coverage that is given to the global violence and disregard of indigenous people is relatively limited.

The native Yanomami people live at the largest area of primary rainforest in Brazil, representing a portion of the Brazilian border with Venezuela. It is estimated that there are approximately 32,000 Yanomami (Watson, 2018). The Yanomami have been illegally invaded by goldminers seeking to pillage their land for resources, with no regard for how their pillaging brings disease and death to the Yanomami people. There have been reports that some previously uncontacted Yanomami have been outright murdered.

The Brazilian president, Bolsonaro, has publicly stated on record he regrets indigenous people of the Amazon were not murdered as widely as was done by cavalry in U.S. history. Commencing his administration, Bolsonaro appointed a known anti-indigenous people evangelist, Damares Alves, as his human rights minister (Watson, 2018). Alves has stated that the uncontacted native people will be brought out, which is code for they will be disallowed to remain legally protected on their respected land. Subsequently, it is expected that the native people's land and resources will be taken from them for greed/profit. Based upon his words and actions, Bolsonaro disregards the lives of the native people living in the Amazon. The following is a quote from Jair Bolsonoro:

> There is no indigenous territory where there aren't minerals. Gold, tin and magnesium are in these lands, especially the Amazon, the richest area in the world. I'm not getting into this nonsense of defending land for Indians. (Watson, 2018)

Nobles (2015) would classify the above quote from Bolsonaro as representative of the western grand narrative which incorporates the prioritization of money, greed, profit, and materialism. However, also underlying Bolsonaro's words is a sentiment that aligns with Poussaint (2002) and Hilton's (2011) descriptions of oppressors' racist-based cognitions regarding people they view as inferior to themselves. As well, Bolsonaro's words represent descriptions by Freeman, Rule, & Ambady (2009) of judgment affordance value attributed to the perceived out-group's marginalized status characteristics.

Since Bolsonaro came into power as the president of Brazil, invasions of indigenous people's lands in the Amazon increased by 150 percent in the country (Tomassoni, 2019). The increase is attributable to the right-wing president's outspoken disregard for the culture and inhumanity of the indigenous people of Brazil. Because of his presidency, Brazil has seen the largest attack on the Amazon in thirty years. Bolsonaro's commitment to the western grand narrative of capitalist greed is evident in his push for commercial mining and farming on the land of the indigenous Waiapi people in Amapa state, Brazil. By Brazilian Constitution, since 1988 the land was legally reserved for the indigenous people.

Tomassoni (2019) reported there was security for the indigenous people throughout Brazilian history, when they were able to remain isolated from other human contact until a measles outbreak occurred in the 1970s. Currently, the numbers of indigenous Waiapi people are low because of the exposure to the infectious disease. The outbreak was spread by illegal minors who came onto their land in search of gold. Now in 2019, again armed (automatic weapons and shotguns) illegal gold miners have invaded the Waiapi community. The illegal miners murdered chief Emyra Waiapi, 68, in Brazil's northern Amazon. His body was discovered with several stab wounds, including to his genitals. Although the murder was reported by several of the group's leaders and indigenous rights activists, Bolsonaro is quoted as saying,

> There is no strong indication that this Indian was killed there (Tomassoni, 2019)

Debating Racism/Out-group Bias as Illness

A debate exists in the dichotomy of viewing White supremacist-based oppression as mentally disordered, i.e., Poussaint (2002) versus viewing racist ideology and its resulting behaviors as socio-politically based, rather than mental illness (Gilman & Thomas, 2016). In relating this dichotomy to persons such as Bolsonaro regarding the Yanomami people and other indigenous uncontacted Native tribes, the following question becomes important: Is Bolsonaro's racism an indication of mental illness, or is he a bad person acting out of socio-political economic capitalist interests, or both? Gilman & Thomas (2016) pose two questions related to this question:

> How did prejudice, racism, and antisemitism become markers of insanity?

> Are racists crazy?

The authors' position focuses on the intellectual history of shifting views on the meaning of race across the centuries. Gilman & Thomas lean heavily towards the shifting socio-political, economic, and cultural explanations of racist ideology, irrespective of the extreme nature of the racist views and practices. They reject notions that thinking and behaving as a racist are signs of mental illness. In their position, it is evident they reject a movement towards an American Psychiatric Association *Diagnostic and Statistical Manual of Disorder (DSM)* classification of extreme racism as a type of delusional pathology as suggested by Poussaint (2002). They make a valid point for consideration, that such a diagnosis could absolve hate crime offenders of culpability based on the medicalization of their behavior.

Gilman & Thomas (2016) are among scholars who have critically interrogated the findings of an empirical study of the drug propranolol, which was shown to reduce implicit race-bias in a sample of White-identified mostly British study participants (Terbeck, Kahane, McTavish, & Savulescu, 2012). Researchers used the pharmacological intervention as a means of potentially effecting implicit race-based emotional reactions via the drug's impact on the noradrenaline pathway. β-adrenergic receptors have been found to be involved in memories and perceptions of an emotional nature (Cahill, Prins, Weber, & McGaugh, 1994).

Pharmacological interventions offer another way to study the causal role of emotional processes in implicit bias, and noradrenaline pathways involving β-adrenergic receptors are known to play a role in emotional memory and emotional perception (Cahill et al., 1994; Harmer et al., 2001) as judged by the effects of the non-selective β-adrenoceptor antagonist, propranolol. Besides its well-established effect on emotional memory via reduction in emotional conditioning (Chamberlaine et al., 2006), functional neuroimaging studies have also shown that propranolol leads to a reduction in amygdala responses to both facial expressions and visual emotional stimuli (Hurlemann et al., 2010; van Stegeren et al., 2005).

Thus, use of propranolol to block the β-adrenergic receptors could also reduce emotional/stress-based reactions by reducing autonomic system flight or fight type reactions. Functional neuroimaging research, introduced propranolol as an independent variable. Through this research it has been revealed that propranolol has the ability to reduce fear-based responses in the amygdala to facial expressions (Hurlemann et al., 2010).

In a study by Terbeck, Kahane, McTavish & Savulescu (2012) a single dose administration of propranolol was used in a randomized, double-blind experimental study; thus participants nor researchers knew who was receiving the propranolol dose. Who received it was also randomly determined. The reduction in implicit attitudes of race bias found in the study opens the door for further research on neurobiological mechanisms (central nervous system-amygdala and peripheral nervous system) that may underlie racial and other out-group targeted prejudicial thoughts and behavior. The findings were laboratory based. Yet there are implications for this sort of research for cases of xenophobic disdain and disregard that may implicitly impact policy, authorizations, and government-sanctioned desecration of lands, such as in the Dakota Pipeline decisions. The implicit bias research using propranolol is intriguing because covert forms of White supremacy may be unconscious while still being pervasive and insidious.

However, the propanolol effect had no impact on explicit racial bias, which is a different challenge. Gilman & Thomas (2106) wish to avoid the medicalization and excusing of racist-based crimes, so they negate the notion of racists being pathological or mentally ill. Yet what has not been thoroughly examined is the perspective of cultural neuroscience (CN), which emphasizes the interplay of nature and nurture (Sasaki & Kim, 2016) regarding cognitive, emotional, and behavioral outcomes. Within the framework of a cultural neuroscience approach, there is room for consideration of the interplay of differential illness susceptibility and socio-political and economic influences. Note one of many definitions of culture below as described by Schwartz:

> Culture consists of the derivatives of experience, more or less organized, learned or created by the individuals of a population, including those images or encodements and their interpretations (meanings) transmitted from past generations, from contemporaries, or formed by individuals themselves. (Avruch, 1998, pg.17 as cited in Spencer-Oatey, 2012)

The American Psychological Association Resolution

Long-standing experiences in a culture that dehumanizes First Nations people, and miseducates about the people, have the potential to affect how they are perceived; such a possibility is described within the cultural neuroscience of person perception literature and conscious awareness of feelings (Freeman, Rule, & Ambady, 2009; Craig, 2009). In summer of 2005, the American Psychological Association's (APA) council of representatives adopted the resolution recommending immediate cessation of use of Native American mascots, symbols, images, and personalities by schools, colleges, universities, athletic teams, and organizations (APA, 2005). The specificity of the resolution revealed the wide-ranging categories in need of discontinuation by the resolution. The language written to cover organizations and educational institutions, symbols and images, and professional mascots and logos was an indictment of sub-optimal cultural norms. The 2005 APA resolution was adopted because the use of the symbols, images, and mascots were deemed to:

> undermine the educational experiences of members of all communities
> establish an unwelcome and hostile learning environment for American Indian students
> negatively impact the self-esteem of American Indian children
> undermine the ability of American Indian Nations to accurately and respectfully portray their own images and culture
> violate the civil rights of American Indian people (APA, 2005).

It is worthy of note that while collegiate and professional athletic teams had earlier experienced some degree of restrictions placed on the use of Native American mascots and logos, such usage in middle and high schools has been historically less regulated (APA, 2005). The likely consequences of this are grave, as the secondary school-aged students are at risk of becoming desensitized to covert White supremacy by experiencing it as normative everyday experience, what some researchers reference as "new racism" (Kohli, Pizarro, & Nevárez, 2017).

Campbell (September, 2018) produced a controversial report on a video game called *This Land is My Land,* described as a stealth open-world game set in the late 19th-century frontier, operating from the perspective of a Native American defending his land against White settlers. Yet, controversy and racism remain intact in the characteristics of the game. Tribes as diverse as Chickasaw, Cherokee, Lakota, Cheyenne, Apaches, Navajo, Shawnee, Shoshone, Mohawk, and Utes are represented in the game, but portrayed by the same singular Native American character. This has been criticized for its racist stereotyping of Native Americans; these tribes are not homogenous any more than all Europeans, Asians, or Africans are homogenous. Critical analysis of such video games is warranted. Should adolescents take a strong interest in games such as *This Land is My Land*, research has shown that areas of their brains can become negatively impacted if excessive gaming is practiced (Wei, Zhang, Turel, Bechara, & He, 2017). Relevant to the brain as a biosocial organ, bilateral damage to the insula has been linked to the inability to show compassion for others in studies of gaming-based screen time usage (Zhou et al., 2011; Weng et al., 2013; Yuan et al., 2011). A compounded issue of concern is how indigenous peoples are depicted in the games. The popularity of such games as cultural phenomenon is evident and has the potential to influence the psychology of person perception and reactions in the real world to already marginalized groups.

Insula

In the 18th century, the insula was referenced as an island of the cortex, but subsequently the insula disappeared from targeted study until near the end of the 20th century (Namkung et al., 2017). The insular region of the cortex has anterior (AI) and posterior (PI) areas that connect with the limbic system (anterior insula) and brain stem and spinal cord (posterior insula). As well, the insula is located at a point of connection to the frontal, parietal, and temporal opercula of the cortex. This renders the insula a critical area for current and future research, due to its potential to expand the literature on emotions in basic and clinical neuroscience (Namkung et al., 2017).

The anterior and posterior areas of the insula warrant further exploration in cultural neuroscience. Research questions regarding the cultural neuroscience of person perception specifically related to ethnicity, race, class, geography, LGBTQ persons are lacking. Yet we know that the anterior insula via its projections from the limbic system is involved in explicit subjective emotionality. Thus, after exposure to both positive and negative stimuli associated with Native Americans, it may be possible to capture reactions in non-Native participants' anterior insula. Research participants may then report their subjective explicit emotional reactions.

The more researchers learn about such socio-cultural neural reactions, they can begin to strategize methods using advanced technologies to extinguish emotional reactions indicative of such problematic conditioning as positive emotionality to images of racist mascots of Native Americans. These are stable perceptions of Native people that seem to be normalized. Perhaps it will be possible to note within the brain's neural network when a shift occurs away from such sub-optimal perceptions to more optimal, accurate, humanistic, and empathic perceptions of persons outside one's own cultural group. Reports of beliefs and knowledge of Native people can be the impetus for more studies.

Reclaiming Native Truth Report

Research is lacking that is inclusive of Native Americans as research participants; however, quality information does exist from which to develop further empirical research based on what non-Native people believe about Native Americans (Reclaiming Native Truth, 2018). The Reclaiming Native Truth (RNT) report released in June of 2018, is a thorough report from four research teams that used multiple research methods with a narrative change strategic approach to initiate a social justice movement on behalf of Native Americans in the United States. The project aimed to understand U.S. citizens' knowledge and beliefs regarding Native Americans. The approach acknowledges the transformative power of narratives and storytelling to challenge hegemony.

How Native Americans are viewed, depicted, and discussed historically within the dominant culture have negatively impacted the political possibility for social justice movements on behalf of the 573 federally recognized Native American tribes that are eligible for funding and services from the Bureau of Indian Affairs (BIA). The RNT report addressed the following research questions:

What are the dominant stories, or narratives, about Native peoples in North America?
Who holds these views?
How do these views affect public perception, public support, and public policy?
What can be done to educate people about Indian Country?
What can be done to counter the negative stereotypes, myths, and stories about Native peoples that are present in the media, among policymakers, and among the general public?

To obtain the data of the RNT report, 13 cities were sampled from the north, south, east, and west of the United States. Across four research teams, varying methodologies were used to include focus groups, surveys, in-depth interviews, message testing discussion groups, and analysis of social media posts. The respondents varied in socioeconomic status, race, region of the country, gender, and age. Given the diversity of the respondents, the RNT report provides a wide and representative sample of what people think they know about Native Americans, as well as what beliefs they have about Native Americans and Native concerns. The RNT report highlights learning more about views and perceptions, particularly the stereotypes, bias, miseducation, and racist beliefs that motivate attacks against Native people; it is expected that knowing this information can inform public policy and lead to changing the narrative. The results of the RNT report revealed themes such as a tendency to 1) promote stereotypes of Native people rather than non-pathological everyday life realities, 2) focus on deficits rather than strengths, 3) beliefs in the homogeneity of Native Americans, 4) lack of understanding of sovereignty, 5) bias, based on region of the respondents 6) simultaneously holding both positive and negative stereotypes of Native Americans, 7) incongruence between reported respect for positive Native American values and representations of these positive values.

Overall the RNT report provides hope for improvement regarding perceptions and treatment of Native Americans. For example, almost half of U.S. participants reported what they were taught in schools about Native Americans was incorrect; 72 percent stated it necessary to significantly change what is taught in schools about Native American cultures and history. This is perhaps one of the most critical findings from the survey research because the percentage is very high. Therefore, to what is this to be attributed? Seventy-two percent of participants reporting miseducation represents a pervasive problem within the educational systems of the United States. A follow-up study of U.S. educators, policy makers, and curriculum and instruction professionals could possibly shed light on this finding.

The RNT report also featured some promising results. After persons hear accurate history, most Americans believed more assistance is needed to fight the injustices against Native Americans. The authors of the RNT report stated that duality of consequences exist regarding some of their findings. For example, connection, fairness, and patriotism of respondents appeared among the themes as reporting positive information about Native Americans. Each of these are values that could contribute to positive narrative change regarding perceptions of and treatment of Native Americans; yet dual meanings of these values make them also a challenge to progress. The RNT report mentions participants' internal motivations to be fair, unbiased, and nonracist as beneficial to support for Native issues. Yet, a focus on fairness as a value also correlated with lack of support for sovereignty for Native tribes. In the report, it is reported that this is based in beliefs that sovereignty for Native people is unfair. As well, this viewpoint existed with another belief that it is not fair for the government to violate laws and treaties made with Native Americans. In cultural neuroscience research, how might this duality manifest in the brain? These are research questions worthy of pursuing.

The duality was also exemplified by stated values of patriotism and masculinity that emerged in the RNT report. Participants high in patriotism and masculinity showed support for sovereignty for Native Americans; yet being masculine also related to support for racist mascots in the athletic mascot debate. The finding of support for the racist mascots remains troubling; Why, from a brain and cognitive perspective, is this such a stubborn, persistent commitment? The person perception research findings suggest that the commitment and fondness for racist images of Native Americans, (particularly as logos for athletic teams), reflects a stability of person perception of Native Americans.

Stable false images of Native Americans have been seemingly imprinted in the brain and may be relevant to research that has revealed there are brain regions that support the acquisition of prejudice (Spiers, et al., 2017). How then, can neuroscientists test for existence of this persistent socio-culturally imprinted image within the human neural network? Such images of Native Americans as mascots have been rendered seemingly innocuous as imagery for display in sports and advertisement; even 9 out of 10 Native people have reported elsewhere that they are not bothered by racist names of athletic teams such as Redskins (Cox, Bui, & Brown, 2016). A survey was given to over 500 Native Americans representative of all 50 states and the District of Columbia. The neutrality of feelings among surveyed Native Americans regarding the name of the Washington professional football team has remained relatively stable since 2004 when Native Americans were previously surveyed on the issue. There has been consistency of Native American response to the survey irrespective of income, education, age, political party, or proximity to reservations.

In the RNT report, the positive statements mentioned by the survey participants about Native Americans were the values attributed to Native Americans, such as their unity and collectivism. However, survey respondents also reported support for the idea of a melting pot culture, rather than an appreciation of diversity. Thus, these beliefs align with the homogenization of Native peoples, and an expectation that Native Americans should blend into *American* culture.

If gamers starting at an early age are chronically exposed to racist symbols, images, and mascots, the potential negative impact is logical. Therefore, games such as *This Land is My Land*, which depicts all Native American tribes in one stock character are problematic, as they reinforce the already miseducation and misperceptions. This can be related to the RNT findings which revealed that support of policy to ban use of racist mascots is still not looked upon favorably by substantial numbers of respondents in the United States The less-regulated (relative to professional sports) secondary school athletic programs' usage of racist Native American symbolic mascots have consequences beyond what is stated in the American Psychological Association's resolution (APA, 2005). There is further knowledge to be gained that could perhaps promote narrative change and empathy for Native American causes; exploring the research of the neuroscience of empathy is therefore relevant to this social problem.

Neuroscience of Empathy

Experience sharing and mentalizing are two neural systems active in the experience of empathy. They engage two disparate neural pathways; however, the goal is the same for both. The goal is understanding and responding to another's internal state. Zaki & Ochsner (2012) are critical of early phase brain studies of empathy that rely too heavily, in their view, on presentation of overly simplistic stimuli taken out of context, and which used a bottom-up approach rather than a contextualized examination of the processing of stimuli in the brain. As such, Zaki & Ochsner, question whether relying upon behavioral reactions to isolated stimuli, rather than gestalt contextualized processing, is valid for understanding the complexity of empathy in humans.

A pitfall they describe is a lack of adequate generalization and connection of neuroscientific models of empathy to the data obtained from behavioral studies in psychology. Such findings, which they question, are those from studies regarding the insula's role in empathy. Zaki and Ochner's recommendations for improved brain research methodologies are methodologies that focus on the study of empathy via engaging contextualized real-world social settings, known as the naturalism approach. Naturalistic social cognitive methodologies are becoming more prevalent in research on empathy and are relevant to this chapter's content due to their promise of expanding upon the findings of the RNT (2018) report. For example, future research participants should have opportunities to engage their neural systems via experience sharing and mentalizing engagement within a specific Native American cultural immersion. This would involve yet another methodology to supplement the varying methodologies used within the RNT report. Experience sharing and mentalizing may behave as coactive neural systems in the face of the experiences of Native Americans. Relevant complex social and cultural cues could be examined.

It is worth exploring the impact, on perceivers, of videos of Native Americans describing autobiographical experiences, including everyday cultural life events. It is also worthwhile to assess the impact of experiences such as engagement with Native American human beings in live tasks. Examples of live task engagement are organizing for change meetings, and participation in protests such as the Dakota Access Pipeline (NoDAPL) standoff. This work might include pre- and post-quantitative and qualitative measures.

NoDAPL Movement and Lessons Learned

RNT (2018) quoted the Standing Rock Sioux Tribe's attorney, Jan Hasselman, as saying that over the last three decades, nothing pierced the broader public's consciousness and raised awareness of experiences inside Indian country more than the NODAPL movement. The movement was from August 2016 through February 2017. Residents of the United States and around the world were privy to the powerful story of social injustice as told through indigenous people, social media posts, independent media, citizen journalists, celebrities, and eventually mainstream media outlets. The setting was Cannonball, North Dakota. Several thousand people allied with the Standing Rock Sioux Tribe against settler capitalist oppressors aiming to complete construction of an oil pipeline that would negatively impact the tribe's drinking water and violate historical treaties regarding the tribes' lands.

The social media data from the RNT (2018) report, found that Standing Rock made a lasting impression on the U.S. public. Most focus group participants referenced Standing Rock when making comments about Native Americans; they also voiced support for the Souix tribe's stance to defend its rights to its land and water. The support came from people across race, geographic location, gender, and political affiliation. The RNT report concluded that the movement at Standing Rock was successful for four reasons: 1) the movement was grassroots and led by the tribal nation, 2) organic and culturally authentic messaging, 3) historically large successful unification of tribal nations 4) power of social media, alternative media, mainstream media, and celebrity advocacy. The greatness of the Standing Rock movement is attributed to the disruption of false narratives about Native Americans. Native Americans are often viewed as historical peoples rather than present-day peoples of numerous tribes possessing strong values, pride, and self-advocacy. The report ends with a strong message to maintain the momentum of the movement. A new frontier for continuing the Standing Rock momentum may also incorporate race relational formations with other oppressed groups.

Molina, HoSang, & Gutiérrez (2019) edited a volume of essays from interdisciplinary scholars representing African American, Chicano/Latino, Asian American, and Native American studies. The volume aligns with an African-centered psychological approach of *Ubuntu* (I am because we are) to highlight the collective racialization that results in the formation of subordinated oppressed groups. An expected impact of the volume upon readers is an enhanced ability to perceive and interrogate similarities and differences across subordinated peoples, pertaining to the social constructive process of othering in a context of White supremacy.

Conclusion

In the African-centered/Black psychology (ACBP) approach, the question is raised of what does it mean to be human (Nobles, 2006)? While the Molina, HoSang, & Gutiérrez (2019) collection does not pose this explicit question, they do draw connections among subordinated groups to shed light on the fact that such majority-minority groups have been both included and disenfranchised differently and similarly across time periods and regions based on racist, classist, and ethnically based stereotypes and dehumanization. Groups are discussed in the Molina, HoSang, & Gutiérrez (2019) collection, not just from the perspective of racial classification but as well, the interactive dynamics of religion (e.g. Muslim), culture, refugee, and immigration status. Native American experiences are included in the volume and presented comparatively to experiences of African Americans and Palestinians across time. Finally, such a framework of relational formation of race has the potential to expand research questions and pursuits in cultural neuroscience. It can inform methods for assessing complex neural activation patterns as influenced by all marginalized groups' both common and unique cultural experiences with othering, white gaze, and xenophobia.

Chapter Nine

Killing Loneliness, Saving Humanity

On Wednesday night November 7, 2018, in Thousand Oaks, California, a lone gunman approached a security guard at the Borderline Bar and Grill and shot the guard with a Glock .45-caliber handgun. The gunman then proceeded into the establishment and shot a person at the cash register, followed by shooting several patrons who were dancing or playing pool. By the time the gunshots ceased, 12 people had been killed before the gunman fatally shot himself in the head. A former roommate of the gunman described him as a weird, aggressive, anti-social loner (Woodyard & della Cava, 2018).

Harvey Weinstein may have been a budding abuser and sexual predator long before he became successful in the film industry (Johnson & Galloway, 2018). Today he is known as the disgraced movie producer charged with rape, physical intimidation, and abuse of employees and actresses. Weinstein's exposure led to a subsequent string of powerful men being taken down under the #metoo sexual harassment and sexual assault movement (Gonzalez, France, & Melas, 2018). Research of Weinstein's formative years via interviews with his friends and associates references Weinstein as having rough looks, a browbeating mother, and an ineffectual father (Johnson & Galloway, 2018).

The complexity of Weinstein's profile and human development is evidenced by his transformation from an often-charming young artsy guy, who was not a part of the popular crowd, to becoming a guy with an explosive personality prone to using strong-arm tactics and womanizing to demonstrate his importance, and to demonstrate success with women. A former friend described Weinstein as changing into a "schmuck," eventually treating former friends like *shit*, once Weinstein's life began to change (Johnson & Galloway, 2018). The social power Weinstein eventually obtained may have exacerbated an angry nature; research has revealed men may underestimate their power in relationships with women, thereby leading to increased sexist hostility in their interactions with women thought to be threatening to their male power inside the relationship (Cross, Overall, & Low, 2018). Although the research findings regarding sexist hostility are based on couples in romantic relationships, rather than work situations or industry, the research is nonetheless informative regarding the Weinstein scandal. Some victimized actresses reported feeling initially motivated to socially engage with Weinstein because of upcoming movie roles or other film industry business discussions which turned into sexual assault (BBC News, 2018). This can be compared to a man or woman demonstrating approach motivation in a romantic relationship, because the partner controls access to desired resources or opportunities. This represents a power dynamic.

To date, Weinstein has six felony charges as relates to three women. These six charges include predatory assault, criminal sexual act in first degree, first-degree rape, and third-degree rape; the relevant years of the incidents are 2004, 2006, and 2013. The series of accusations and charges against him resulted in Weinstein being fired, dismissed from the motion picture academy of arts and sciences, ousted from the public eye, and estranged from his family and friends (Gonzalez, France, & Melas, 2018; Johnson & Galloway, 2018).

This chapter's objective is not to evoke empathy for mass shooters and otherwise violent or predatory men. Instead, the cultural neuroscience and biosocial research of the brain will be presented to address social pain such as feelings of isolation. An adoption of sub-optimal learned behaviors to feel relief has been particularly evident in cases of male-identified persons who have committed violent crimes. Here, the discussion of men and hegemonic masculinity is in order, as relates to men's gender role trauma and intersection with White privilege and loneliness.

Case studies of various violent, sexually predatory, and aggressive men will be highlighted in conjunction with relevant brain research that is reflective of the acculturation that leads to sub-optimal behaviors for some men. Adopting the western grand narrative may lead some men to a style of masculinity that represents a Eurocentric worldview of dominance, power, and violence.

In November 2018, the number of mass shootings in the United States for that year reached 307. Using data provided by the online source, *Gun Violence Archive*, it is noteworthy that mainstream attention to shootings occurs when there are five or more fatalities (not including the shooter). It is also notable that criminal perpetrators and their victims may differ in media coverage received based on race and gender (Paulsen, 2003).

In September 2018, a 54-year-old man fatally shot his wife and four other people in Bakersfield, California. The incident is listed with *Gun Violence Archive* as being in the domestic violence category. In a separate incident across country the following week, in Aberdeen Maryland, a 26-year-old masculine-presenting, gender queer person, fatally shot three people and injured three. The Maryland shooting was identified as a workplace shooting committed by a possibly disgruntled employee. The two shooters were identified as Latino (California) and Black (Maryland); the shooters committed suicide by eventually turning the gun on themselves. A friend of the Maryland shooter said S. M. (initials of the shooter) sometimes felt as if the world was against him but was not an angry person despite feelings of alienation. The same friend also referred to S.M., as a person likely under emotional distress who chose murder and suicide as a last straw (Reed & Duncan, 2018). The California perpetrator's neighbor told reporters that she saw him the week prior, when he gave her his regards on the death of her husband. During that conversation, the neighbor reported the perpetrator broke down crying because of his wife leaving him; the report states he believed his wife to be cheating (Bonvillian, 2018).

Comparative analytical differences in the details provided for incidents of violence, and the breadth of media coverage, may be explained by discussions of the cultural other and perceptions of who is perceived as an object versus who is perceived as a human subject (Ani, 1994; Kilomba, 2010). As example, an incident occurred in the U.S. state of Kentucky in October of 2018, in which a 51-year-old White male with a history of violence, murdered two Black shoppers at a Kroger grocery store. When another White male witness was confronted with the White male gunman in the parking lot of the store, the shooter said to the armed witness,

Don't shoot me. I won't shoot you. Whites don't shoot Whites. (Novelly, 2018)

Yet, this detail of the incident was not widely discussed or analyzed in national mainstream media outlets.

WESTERN GRAND NARRATIVE'S MASCULINE IDEOLOGY

Gender role expectations among men have been examined for how they impact men socially, behaviorally, and emotionally, specifically examining gender role dysfunction, gender role trauma, and gender role discrepancy as significant to men's psychological well-being (Blazina, Eddins, Burridge, & Settle, 2007). Blazina et al., (2007) present that the developing boy or adult male who believes that he cannot fulfill the behavioral expectations set for men in his culture, may feel low self-esteem because of the low self-efficacy regarding his ability to successfully perform the "ideal" masculinity. For the boy or man who accepts himself as a human, and who does not have to live up to a Eurocentric patriarchal, socialized masculine ideal, the prognosis for his well-being could perhaps be more optimal (Myers et al., 2018).

However, the man or boy who adjusts his behavior to fit the ideal masculine socialization could be wounded from long-term performance of this idealized masculinity. The long-term stress of this performance could also lead to gender role dysfunction in which the men are not only emotionally wounded but could exhibit negative effects such as muted emotional expression or persistent aggressive sexual predatory motives (Blazina, Eddins, Burridge, & Settle, 2007). This unhealthy masculine socialization and ideology can be related to the behaviors of Weinstein mentioned earlier, and comedian Bill Cosby, who was also convicted and sentenced for sexual assault (Dekok, 2018).

Male Socialization and Cultural Neuroscience

Researchers have deemed the measurement of masculinity to be important. They have devised scales to assess masculinity and male role norms (Brannon, 1985; Thompson & Pleck, 1986). It is notable that both scales assess attitudes regarding traditional values and expectations for male expression. To a lesser degree, the various cultures of male socialization have not been analyzed for how they influence the brain and its corresponding emotions and behavior. Yet, attitudes revealed through scales such as the male role norms scale may be particularly informative as related to cultural neuroscience, due to the scale's assessment of attitudes such as socialized toughness, anti-femininity, and status; these attitudes have been revealed as related to loneliness (Blazina, Eddins, Burridge, & Settle, 2007).

Loneliness is an aversive emotional state and is represented in mouse studies of the brain as social isolation; a brain area that corresponds to social isolation likely has evolutionary motivational value to meet a fundamental human need for interpersonal attachment (Baumeister & Leary, 1995). Researchers have found men are likely to experience loneliness, the more they ascribe to masculine role norms such as maintaining an attitude that they must conceal emotions to avoid feelings of vulnerability. Such men are motivated to show mental and physical toughness through self-reliance (Blazina, Eddins, Burridge, & Settle, 2007). As well, some such men demonstrate a conflicted and fragile sense of their masculine selves, hiding parts of themselves from others; or alternatively, they may look to others to help them manage and cope with their negative emotions. Recall the behavior of Weinstein choosing to flaunt being a womanizer, as a means of proving his success as a man, thereby using a traditional masculine role norm and ideology. Therefore, various dysfunctional dependent, excessive, or threatening behaviors are possible from men such as Weinstein or Cosby, perhaps stemming from a fragile sense of the masculine self.

The Dorsal Raphe Nucleus

April 20, 1999, was the deadly school shooting at Columbine High School in Littleton, Colorado. In total, 12 students and 1 teacher were murdered, and 24 others injured. The mother of one of the two shooters shared in her memoir that her son had written in his journal that he was in agony, cutting himself, and desirous of a gun so he could end his life (Klebold, 2017). The mother is to be commended for discussing the importance of brain health as it relates to her son's murder-suicide in Colorado. She revealed in the memoir his motivation was as much about wanting to die as it was about murder. Several statements made in the mother's book regarding her son's mind is related to the literature about the dysfunction of toxic forms of masculine socialization (Barker, 2005). It is noteworthy that Klebold's son became shy into adolescence, and became moodier and irritable during the months leading up to committing the mass murder-suicide. Ms. Klebold also stated that as a child, her son was shy, easily embarrassed, tearful, and hard on himself. As a teenager, he talked about looking weird and began to lose interest in getting good grades. She has also stated he eventually built his own computer and began spending more time in his room; though these are not independently, signs of violent mass murderer tendencies, these are indicators of her sons increasing social withdrawal.

Klebold's son had written in his journal that he acknowledged having good parents, a nice home, a couple of close friends, but no girls in his life. This may suggests his masculine sense of self included the desire to achieve a certain level of success with girls, and desire for other interpersonal experiences that would enable him to self-perceive as more accepted and less isolated. The mother revealed in her book that her son wrote about wanting to be accepted and had even written a list of names of people he loved, but who he believed would never love him reciprocally. These are but a few examples of a self-loathing that can accompany feelings of social isolation.

Klebold's son's behavior aligns with literature suggesting that on-going, in-depth research is needed to investigate males with a fragile masculine self who may display a neurotic triad of responses such as 1) moving against others in an aggressive manner, 2) moving away from others as in loneliness, and 3) moving towards others in a type of overly dependent manner (Mahalik et al., 1998). In the case of Klebold's son, he displayed a combination of all three: 1) the violence of moving against others to murder his schoolmates, 2) the social isolation of moving away from his peers, and 3) the moving towards dependence via his co-dependency with a disturbed friend, the other White male shooter in the incident.

Although Ms. Klebold's book also aims to humanize her son by highlighting brain health and mental illness, readers will not receive, via her book, a cultural neuroscience perspective on the inhumane behavior of her son. Understanding the socialization of the fragile masculine self that could precipitate violence is critical (Hong, 2000; Kimmel & Mahler, 2003). A cultural neuroscientific explanation of this can be further understood via studying the role of the dorsal raphe nucleus and its under-examined dopaminergic neurons (Matthews et al., 2016).

Sitting atop of the human spinal cord is an area of the central nervous system labeled the brainstem. This area of the central nervous system is comprised of three major parts: the pons, the medulla oblongata, and the reticular formation. For purposes here, the reticular formation warrants further description. The reticular formation is comprised of a series of nuclei with various projections into the subcortical and cortical areas of the brain; collectively the nuclei are labeled raphe nuclei. The raphe nuclei deploy several neurotransmitters through neural pathways to help regulate emotions, cognition, and behavior. Though dopamine is frequently discussed for its role in reward and pleasure in the brain, it has not been as often studied in relationship to social isolation and activity of the dorsal raphe neurons. Its role is applicable to the cases of inhumanity of this chapter, because there is existing research to inform the connection of the dorsal raphe nucleus to an aversive emotional state (Matthews et al., 2016; Cacioppo, Capitanio, & Cacioppo, 2014).

There are several dopamine (DA) neurons that are functionally distinct. Some researchers have taken an interest in a subpopulation of DA neurons that are a part of the dorsal raphe nucleus (DRN). In investigating these neurons, a team of researchers have discovered a neural basis for a kind of "loneliness-like" feeling (Matthews et al., 2016). Using light to stimulate the activity of dopamine neurons of the dorsal raphe nucleus, researchers observed that such neurons became potentiated (primed to fire signals) as a result of the organism being socially isolated. There was a rebound effect in the firing of DA DRN cells following periods of isolation, once the animal experienced a resumed opportunity for social contact. This is neural evidence that brains may be wired for social contact in this area; when we are deprived of social contact, this area becomes potentiated or primed in wait of resumption of social interaction. As well, it is inferred from the animal study (across species there is preserved existence of the DA DRN cells, thus the relevance of this research to humans), that activation of DA DRN cells produces a psychological experience of an emotion akin to loneliness, which is highly aversive. The aversive feeling then prompts the behavior of seeking social engagement and interaction. The researchers were able to control for change of environment (isolated to non-isolated) by testing the animals for specific interest in a new object added to an environment, versus motivation to be social with other animals in a changed environment. The motivation to socially engage showed a rebound effect for animals who had recently experienced a condition of social isolation.

To further control for error, researchers used optical inhibition of DA DRN cells, to then observe the sociability behaviors of the animals who experienced social isolation. As expected, under condition of inhibition of the dopaminergic cells of the DRN, the animals did not show the sociability typically observed when these cells are activated following isolation periods. For people who are socially isolated and subjectively experience loneliness, it is such a highly aversive experience that these human beings likely desire relief from it, in order to function at their best. Furthermore, research revealed that status is also important to the magnitude of the effect of manipulation of the DA DRN cells (Matthews et al., 2016). A history of dominant status and subjective feelings of loneliness produces a stronger adaptive response to loneliness, relative to what is seen in subordinate status subjects. This may explain why men of an intersecting dominant status (i.e., White male) may be particularly sensitive in some cultures such as the United States, to social isolation and feelings of loneliness.

Mass Shooter Data

The number of mass shootings in the United States between 1982 and November 7, 2018, recorded by race and ethnicity of the shooter(s) shows that 60 out of 106 mass shootings were enacted by White shooters (https://www.statista.com/statistics/476456/mass-shootings-in-the-us-by-shooter-s-race/). The same statista site reports between 1982 and November 7, 2018, only three mass shootings were enacted by a lone female shooter (https://www.statista.com/statistics/476445/mass-shootings-in-the-us-by-shooter-s-gender/). During the same time period, 102 mass shootings were carried out by male shooters. Thus, the White male shooter is commonly the perpetrator of public mass murder shootings receiving extensive media coverage in U.S. culture.

Another author has preferred to emphasize the maleness of this phenomenon over White racial identity; he also highlighted that majority world peoples (non-White identified persons who are classified as minorities in the United States) more disproportionately enact multiple murders in the U.S. within private settings (Engber, 2017). However, Engber neglects making reference to intersectionality as significant to understanding the human experience. Because it appears to be a cultural intersection of whiteness and maleness in these instances, that is salient to mass public murders in the United States.

One specific case of White male mass murder suicide captured media attention and the minds of society because of the uniqueness of his choice of victims, elementary school children. Following the massacre, the following words of the perpetrator were made public:

I have been desperate to feel anything positive for someone for my entire life
(Ortiz, 2018)

The incident was the mass murder suicide by a mentally and emotionally
disturbed young White male who was devoid of human contact; he murdered
20 children, and 6 teachers at an elementary school, following having also
murdered his sleeping mother. He is also on record as having said he had
nothing but scorn for humanity. He was reportedly obsessed with mass murder (Ortiz, 2018).

Cingulo Opercular Network

Research has revealed that the subjective aversive chronic feeling of loneliness enacts a self-preservation mode of being (Layden et al., 2017). Researchers measured resting state functional connectivity (FC) by use of functional magnetic resonance imaging equipment. An area of the brain was
activated during tonic alertness (Coste & Kleinschmidt, 2016), and the Cingulo Opercular Network (CO) was more activated in healthy individuals who
scored highly on Perceived Social Isolation (PSI) (Layden, et al., 2017). The
PSI was assessed via the UCLA Loneliness Scale (RUCLA) (Russell, 1996).
Functional connectivity (FC) cells only within the CO were activated during
the participants' perception of threat. Cells from outside of the network but
projecting to it, showed reduced FC firing. A reduction in FC-based firing of
frontal lobe circuits that project into the CO has been explained in the literature as concurrent with lowered executive function and lower impulse control
(Layden et al., 2017).

During instances of self-preservation, the individual is vigilant for any
signs of social threat from others, thereby making it more difficult to focus
outside of self, such as to show empathy for others (Cacioppo, Chen, &
Cacioppo, 2017). This is informative regarding the personalities and behaviors of some dominant status individuals who are perceived as disagreeable
individuals. For example, one psychologist has attempted to analyze the
mind of U.S. president, Donald Trump (McAdams, 2016). McAdams referenced Trump's strong motivation to pursue positive emotional experiences
such as social approval (as seen when he appears before crowds of his supporters), fame, and wealth; these behaviors are consistent with the extro-
verted person who seeks pleasure-rich experiences, which cause the release
of dopamine in the brain. McAdams extensively detailed Trump's disagree-
ableness and anger, linking these to Trump's social dominance. While
McAdams is thorough in explaining the personality of Trump in relationship
to social science–based evidence of personality studies, missing from his
analysis is in-depth reference to the cultural neuroscience of Trump's toxic
masculine ideology, misogyny, xenophobia, and implicit and explicit racially

charged jokes (e.g., "Pocahontas"), and violent speech (Greene, 2019; Saramo, 2016). When combined with anger and social rejection, such characteristics could have negative outcomes for persons who are targets of such biases in the mind of an authoritarian type leader.

Donald Trump was referenced as stating, when telling his life narrative, that early on in life he felt a sense of danger and a need for toughness, rooted in a belief that the world cannot be trusted (McAdams, 2017). This is consistent with the research regarding the impact of social isolation on more dominant status beings (Matthews et al., 2016). Trump's beliefs are consistent with the research findings of hypervigilance among people who rate high in Perceived Social Isolation.

Cognitive control is required for the maintenance of tonic alertness; it is specifically governed by the cortical area called the cingulo opercular network (Sadaghiani & D'Esposito, 2015). Cognitive control is necessary on a day-to-day basis for humans as they must interact with their environment and accomplish complicated behaviors. The cingulo opercular network is one of two networks that allows for the maintenance of cognitive control. The two networks have been discovered by researchers to function separately in the type of cognitive control that they mediate; the cingulo opercular network (CO) maintains longer term stable general vigilance, whereas the fronto-parietal (FP) network is activated during shorter term fluctuating cognitive control (Dosenbach et al., 2008; Sadaghiani & D'Esposito, 2015) such as in the moment-to-moment situations in which humans may need to adjust their cognitive control. The personalities that have developed in dominant status individuals, such as a Donald Trump, who are frequently on alert in anticipation of threats of social rejection (stemming from general feelings of isolation) may partly be explained by the functioning of their CO. The CO is comprised of the anterior insula/frontal operculum, anterior prefrontal cortex, dorsal anterior cingulate, and thalamus (Sadaghiani & D'Esposito, 2015). Together, these comprise a cognitive control network.

African-Centered Psycho-Social Cultural Perspectives

Thus far, this chapter has presented the results of research from mainstream journals and other sources, produced by researchers and journalists who operate from Eurocentric ideological cultural perspectives. A critical reading of the previous studies referenced here, reveals what scholar Marimba Ani detailed as a representation of the Eurocentric cultural seed (Ani, 1994). Ani named the seed the *asili* of the culture, which gives rise to specific cultural thought and specific cultural life-force or energy. Western-Eurocentric cultural perspectives have primarily been used to define and describe the mind and behavior; perspectives of African-centered social scientific scholars who detail the significance of spirit/soul to the human condition have been more marginalized, though they provide a wealth of cultural knowledge to inform the cultural neuroscience literature (Deterville, 2016; Myers et al., 2018).

Western-centered brain researchers provide for the reader, the neuroanatomy that is linked to the resulting emotions and behaviors such as feelings of isolation and tonic alertness. Scientists also describe a fragile masculine sense of self that can produce neurotic responses in men and boys. However, the findings of these studies can also be related to Ani's description of the *asili* of Eurocentric culture that is *utamawazo*. *Utamawazo* is the type of thinking within Eurocentric culture and history that produces a prioritization of objectivity, materialism, quantification, and rationality, minus an acknowledgment and appreciation of human spirit and collectivism.

Using an African-centered cultural neuroscience perspective, one may discuss the research findings of this chapter differently. For example, given that humans evolved areas of the brain that promote a motivation to seek social engagement, i.e., the dorsal raphe nucleus, how have Eurocentric cultures or worldviews contributed to the display of behaviors and emotions that counter the frequency of pursuit of a healthy need for positive social engagement and genuine connection to others?

Cultural neuroscience emphasizes the role of culture in the activity and processing of neural activity. Mass murders within U.S. culture, perpetuated frequently by White masculine-identified shooters must be examined for their connection to culture and brain. The same can be said for the incidents of impulsive and compulsive sexual assaults perpetrated by powerful Eurocentric patriarchal men. Furthermore, usage of terms such as *toxic masculinity,* created under a Eurocentric paradigm (Haider, 2016), often do not deeply interrogate from whence and why the toxic masculinity has culturally derived. An in-depth analysis of worldviews emanating from distinct *asili,* can inform about the origin of toxic beliefs linked to violence, patriarchy, and problematic expressions of masculinity (Ani, 1994).

Rhetorical Ethics

> I hope people call me insane [two smiley face emojiis] would that just be a big ball of irony? Yeah . . . I'm insane, but the only thing you people do after these shootings is "hopes and prayers" . . . or "keep you in my thoughts." He added, Every time . . . and wonder why these keep happening. (Levenson, Pagliary, & Kamp, 2018)

The above quote was posted on *Instagram* by a male shooter at the time he was inside the Thousand Oaks club, firing shots. The shooter's words are eerie, as he references what African-centered scholar Marimba Ani explained as rhetorical ethics. Ani defined the term rhetorical ethics as culturally structured European hypocrisy (Ani, 1994).

In United States societal culture, it has become commonplace following a mass shooting for members of local and national communities to hold vigils and recite prayers for the victims and their families. This behavior fits the category of ritualistic behaviors that are symbolic of rhetorical ethics; the tears and words of sympathy uttered at the vigils and in the media rather quickly subside with no resulting substantive actions to prevent the next shooting. Then when the next shooting occurs, the same rhetoric and symbolic gestures occur again with no transformative actions taken to prevent subsequent tragedies.

Research findings regarding the empathic brain are complex (De Vignemont & Singer, 2006); areas of the brain such as the anterior cingulate cortex (ACC) and the anterior insula (AI) have been shown to activate in response to seeing a person in pain, if that person is positively regarded by the evaluator (Singer et al., 2006). Yet in the same research, men who negatively cognitively evaluated a person, showed activation in the reward/pleasure area of the brain when seeing the negatively evaluated person in pain. Male research participants revealed via questionnaire that a pleasurable feeling was connected to thoughts of revenge (Singer et al., 2006). These findings are related to the actions of the Columbine murderers in the United States, who shot several classmates at close range, after asking some of them questions at gunpoint, and sometimes laughing at and taunting their victims.

For Isaiah Shoels, a Columbine murder victim, and sole African American killed, it was reported by classmates who were in the library at the time, that the murderers stated the following regarding Isaiah:

> There's that little nigger son of a bitch right there; let's get him. (Goldstein, Sanchez, & Fletcher, 1999)

In the same report, Michael Shoels, Isaiah Shoel's father, is quoted as feeling remorse that Isaiah had informed him of being the brunt of some racial situations at school; however, he had advised Isaiah to just stay focused and look beyond them. The murderers' words regarding Isaiah Shoels, and other students who they held in contempt as athletes or Christians, suggest the Columbine murderers may have experienced reward/pleasure activation in the brain when shooting their victims.

Afrocentric scholars have written extensively about cognitions regarding a cultural other (Ani, 1994; Kilomba, 2010) as mentally conceived during Eurocentric thought by some White persons. Afrocentric scholars state that the self-image of Eurocentric White men, in this case, needs the cultural other to affirm their own identity. Thus, the majority of the world's people, such as Isaiah Shoels, could not be conceived of as equal, nor as a human. Instead, the cultural other is conceived of as an object. Objects are viewed as disposable. Thus, cultural neuroscientific researchers who describe and explain brain areas associated with empathic responses, are remiss when they do not delve into questions that interrogate the concept of the cultural other. White men in the United States have mass murdered victims who would be classified under the western grand narrative and Eurocentric thought as cultural others by their murderers (Blinder & Sack, 2017). It is possible to conduct research on perceptions of these murders among White western acculturated males. This would be a significant step to transcend engagement in rhetorical ethics following such murders. Studies might explore the interaction of aversive feelings of loneliness and existing thoughts regarding some humans as cultural others, such as in the murder of Isaiah Shoal. Such research could shed light on the patterns of thinking that connect to normalization of violence against certain oppressed groups.

The following shootings have occurred in the United States against groups commonly viewed in U.S. historical culture to be cultural others: African Americans mass murdered in a Black church in South Carolina by a White male; predominantly LGBT persons murdered in Florida at a nightclub by a White male; Jewish older adults murdered in a synagogue by a White male. Each shooting was followed by normalized rhetorical ethics, followed by no substantive change in culture, policy, or substantive relevant brain research among survivors or White males in the country regarding their perceptions and emotions about these events.

Psycho-Spiritual Wellness and Mass Killing

Comparatively, males who do not identify as White in U.S. culture, have been less prevalent as perpetrators of deadly mass public shootings that garner widespread media attention. This is not meant to suggest that gun violence is not a significant social problem within some communities of color in which males are victims and perpetrators of gun violence. In fact, Black on Black violence in marginalized impoverished communities has been extensively discussed, with the macrosystemic reasons for its existence (Muhammad, 2010). As well, there have been a few notable U.S. mass shooting tragedies in which the perpetrators were men of color. One of such cases can be examined using related fields of study known as African-centered Black/psychology (ACBP) and transpersonal psychology.

This final section of this chapter focuses on the ideology of scholars of African-centered psychology who have pushed for bridging the gap between African-centered psychology and transpersonal psychology to advance approaches to healing and wellness (Deterville, 2016). Transpersonal psychology is defined as a western psychology rooted in the philosophy of transcendentalism, theism, and beliefs in oneness of consciousness, i.e., all things in the universe are connected. The perspectives of transpersonal psychology have much in common with the epistemology of African-centered psychology; yet as noted by Deterville (2016), African-centered psychology is conspicuously absent from western-focused scholarship in transpersonal psychology.

African-centered psychology is a system of thought and action used to examine the processes that allow for the illumination and liberation of the spirit. Although Africa is a diverse continent of cultures and nations, there are unifying principles, values, and traditions that manifest within broader Pan-African communities. It is these unifying principles, values, and traditions that are centered in the psychological analyses of African-centered psychology (Nobles, 2006). African-centered psychology also includes a focus on oneness or communalism, emphasizing that the collective is the most significant component of existence. Both transpersonal western focused psychology and African-centered psychology emphasize communal self-knowledge, or a communal sense of personhood as vital to mental well-being (Deterville, 2016).

In cultural neuroscience literature, similarly to the transpersonal psychology literature, researchers have failed to include the variety of African epistemological, cosmological, cultural, and philosophical variables that may be investigated for their cultural impact on the brain's processing and ensuing thoughts, emotions, and behavior. In the case of Black male serial shooters John Muhammad and Lee Malvo, respectively an adult and teen, they may be studied using African-centered psychological nosology. African-centered psychology offers insight to how their experiences of early childhood abandonment, search for belonging, exposure to militarization, dominance and power images, video-gaming, and mass media culture could have contributed to their killing spree during three weeks in October 2002 in the Washington D.C., metropolitan area (Myers et al., 2018; Webster, 2004; Davis, 2017). These Black males' life experiences leading up to their violent episode are salient under the western grand narrative socialization of masculinity and racism.

It is reported regarding John Muhammed, that both of his marriages ended in divorce. The second divorce was bitter, resulting in his separation from his children, who were most important to him as reported by those who knew him. People who knew him stated his children were his life. One of Muhammed's army associates described him as a changed man after his kids were taken from him. Specifically, he likened Muhammed's behavior to having a nervous breakdown, spending some days crying all day, and obsessed with getting his children back (Davis, 2017). Though notable that Muhammed's mother died when he was five, his life, in totality, suggests he may have been seeking belonging by joining the Islamic faith and by enlisting in the Army National Guard, where he had frequent conflict with his fellow U.S. soldiers (Davis, 2017). Though he could be charming, he was able to manipulate (forging passports) and dominate for his own purposes, as he did with Lee Malvo, who he trained to be a killer and to be completely submissive to Muhammed as a father figure.

The 24-years-younger Lee Malvo had a history of being repeatedly abandoned by his mother; he had an absent biological father. He was described as having a desire to please adults. Malvo's adult-pleasing personality, as one psychologist described, is a malleable type of personality for being turned into a killing machine by someone skilled in tactical deception as was John Muhammed. Malvo was described as having a desperate need to belong to something greater; he had a fear of abandonment (Webster, 2004). The following words were published from a suicide-like note Malvo provided to one of his acquaintances:

> Was my purpose here on the God forsaken planet to be banned, shamed and disapproved, why am I hear [sic] . . . I've had a hard life believe it or not, no father and a mother who hate [sic], no that's understatement, she has disbarred me from her. . . . As I have a father [Muhammad] who I know is going to have to kill me for a righteous society to prevail. (Webster, 2004)

Malvo's older cousin, who lived with him for a portion of his life, also revealed Malvo would sometimes sadly withdraw into himself and ask, "Why me?" regarding his lack of a real family (Webster, 2004). An examination of the life and words of Malvo and Muhammad across the stages of their lives leading up to the killing spree of 2002, reflect that neither was in a positive state of psycho-spiritual wellness (Deterville, 2016).

Psycho-spiritual wellness is a process of co-active relationship-based spirituality (Deterville, 2016). Thus, according to both the African-centered psychology and transpersonal psychological epistemologies, Muhammad and Malvo, like all the men detailed in this chapter, lacked development of a communal personhood through development of a healthy, stable, self-other interpersonal relationship.

Adding the cultural neuroscience literature to the fields of transpersonal and African-centered psychology provides a more complete analysis of the harmful impact of loneliness and isolation, particularly as manifest in western acculturated males. Though not elsewhere thoroughly explicated in the long list of mass shootings by Western-acculturated men, the impact of isolation, abandonment, rejection, and loneliness is significant for targeted future research. More widespread knowledge of how human loneliness impacts the brainstem area of the dopamine raphe nucleus is needed.

Furthermore, in the case of the emotionally isolated men of African descent presented in this section, Malvo and Muhammad, Frantz Fanon's discussion of the use of violence by the oppressed is relevant. Fanon's theory of the psychology of oppression is applicable, as we closely examine Muhammad's stated objective for the killing spree. Muhammad premeditated his actions because he reasoned the magnitude of fear that would be spread by the random shootings, would enable him to extort $10 million from the U.S. government. He believed the $10 million could then be used to recruit and train other Black men to create an army to take over the country (Davis, 2017).

Though this revelation about the motive was given relatively scant analysis in mainstream press, it is significant as it pertains to the work of Fanon, who wrote extensively about the psychology of colonialized oppression (Bulhan, 1985). Fanon explained violence used as resistance to oppression because the oppressed have been the victims of violence, oppression, and dehumanization at the hands of their oppressors.

This prompts the question: Why did John Muhammad's brain produce thoughts of a need for a militarized, well-trained army of Black men to takeover the United States? On the surface, his thinking could be categorized as the delusions of a deranged serial killer. However, in Fanon's *Wretched of the Earth*, Fanon (2005) wrote of violence being used by the oppressed as a means of finally trying to achieve freedom from a sort of inferiority complex, negative emotionality, and disempowered action. Fanon wrote of fearless acts of violence to resist oppression and to restore self-respect taken away by oppressors who have persistently enacted violence upon the oppressed.

Muhammad's second marriage was over, and his children had been taken away from him. By the accounts of an army buddy of Muhammad's, the disruption of the self-other relationship with the children, devastated Muhammad. Yet, the loss of his children was legally sanctioned by the U.S. courts. Fanon's account and what we know from the cultural neuroscientific, transpersonal, and African-centered psychological explanations of the aversive effects of loneliness and separation from others (Matthews e. al., 2018; Deterville, 2016; Myers et al., 2018) are informative. John Muhammed's vision of a Black male army takeover is consistent with a motivation for cathartic release, in the form of revolutionary violence against oppression. Fanon described this type of violence as not only cathartic, but as actions that allow the oppressed to recreate or restore themselves, their political identity, and their freedom and self-determination (Bulhan, 1985). The murdered D.C. humans were tragically sacrificed because of the lack of psycho-spiritual wellness of the shooter and his mentor. Malvo confessed he was conditioned by Muhammad, to master the practice of detachment from his emotions when pulling the trigger, feeling nothing whenever he murdered random innocent persons (Webster, 2004). John Muhammed was executed by the state for the murders, while Malvo is still imprisoned for his actions. However, restoration of spirit is relevant, as described within the optimal psychology approach (Myers, 2013). Myers has addressed the need for a cultural realignment through cogno-affective restructuring, soul illumination, and refinement of character to restore spirit.

African-centered scholarship explicates the meaning of "tornadoes of the mind" (Nobles, Baloyi & Sodi, 2016), which though not presented in mainstream volumes such as the *Diagnostic and Statistical Manual of Psychiatric Disorders (DSM)*, does provide insight towards understanding the pathology inherent to a cultural worldview and socialization that interferes with psycho-spiritual wellness. Nobles, Baloyi, & Sodi described "tornadoes of the mind" as "spirit defilement," or damage for African people. The disconnection created by the spirit defilement is accompanied by a sense of not being wholly human by internalizing unchallenged beliefs that one is inferior and lacking in self-sacredness.

Conclusion

"Tornadoes of the mind" relates to the overall information presented in this chapter regarding some socially rejected men's violent and predatory behaviors. The disconnection to others can lead to a deprivation of stimulation and shrinkage (Stahn, 2019) in areas of the brain which govern humans' need for social inclusion, connection, and authentic community. The results of brain research published in peer-reviewed journals is not read by the masses. Unfortunately, often academics are writing for other academics. While this is welcome and beneficial for expanding the literature, it does not help to inform the people on the frontlines regarding some men's isolation-based behaviors, Eurocentric *utamawazo*, and emotional pain. The cultural approach of such African-centered community health models to restore spirit, should also be further investigated for impact at the neuronal level and network level of areas such as the cingulo opercular network (CO).

Chapter Ten

Environmental Injustices

Renowned scholar of the sociopolitical nature of water, Terje Tvedt, has proclaimed that no one can escape the power of water (Tvedt, et al., 2007). However, chances are, people living in more economically privileged spaces, think very rarely or not at all about the quality of the water they use daily for drinking, cooking, or cleaning. Likewise, their preoccupation with air quality and lead paint levels inside their domiciles may be nonexistent. Scholars concerned about such neurotoxins among the less privileged, have developed strategies to determine the prevalence of these risk factors, so they may further estimate the population impact on the neurodevelopment of children. The impact of environmental chemicals such as methylmercury, organophosphate pesticides, and lead can result in loss of full-scale IQ points in children; the impact is exacerbated for children living in poverty relative to those living in advantaged environments (Bellinger, 2012).

The work of researchers who study climate change is instrumental to understanding the connection of humans and their worldwide cultural practices to hydroclimatic fluctuations. Scientists have used advanced computer models and long-term observations of the ancient rings of trees to observe historical patterns of drought. Using such methods, scientists have revealed the longtime impact of human-influenced global warming on hydroclimate. Droughts of the past and seemingly into the future are addressed by the scientific findings. From this research, three distinct time periods have been detailed as significant to global warming and resulting impact on water levels (Marvel et al., 2019).

The three time periods have been revealed to be first, years 1900–1949, marked by an increase in global warming. Some regions of the world experienced drought while others became wetter during this period. The second period was from 1950–1975, a time during which aerosol sprays were reported to be at high levels of release into the air, possibly impacting conditions, though there was no identifiable patterns of drought, as in period one. Period three from the mid-1970s through the end of the 20th century was deemed of inconclusive causation, although greenhouse gas emissions and global temperatures continued to rise. Marvel et al. (2019), however, remain open to possibilities of alternative explanations to appear over the next 10 years; yet the scientific models project pervasive drying to come. The impact of the severe fluctuations of water existence is further damaging for those challenged by poverty who have stress, lack of exposure to enrichment opportunities, and overall lack of physical resources causing hardship (Bellinger, 2012).

FANON: THE PSYCHOLOGY OF OPPRESSION

The world's population is not equally susceptible to exposure to neurotoxins, nor equitably able to access resources such as healthy and abundant water. This is relevant to cultural neuroscience, as the impact of lack of access to clean and abundant water supplies among people of disenfranchised communities, has consequences for their brain health. Consistent and easy access to clean fresh water should be regarded as a human right; failure to have access to clean, fresh, healthy water is inhumane. Thus, a discussion of water is significant to the writings of Fanon on the psychology of liberation from oppression for people throughout the world.

Frantz Fanon is associated, long after his death, with being a voice for the voiceless, an advocate for taking revolutionary action to alter oppressed existence (Utsey, Bolden, & Brown, 2001). Fanon and other scholars expressed the need for collectivism and unity of thought and action to address widespread oppression and suffering. Therefore, increased collective knowledge and unification of effort is an initial step towards addressing the freshwater global scarcity crisis. Lack of combined effort among the people of the world has serious implications for available freshwater, to the detriment of biodiversity and global human welfare.

Water for Life

The human body is composed on average of about 65 percent water. Yet, daily, this is unlikely at the forefront of humans' thoughts. Nor at the forefront of our thoughts, is what would happen if there was cessation of the consumption of water in all forms to include even drinks that contain water. Death by dehydration is a process affecting all cells of the body, including brain cells. Over time, chronic dehydration would result in a shrinkage of brain tissue. This would eventually impact an area of our brain called the hypothalamus, which regulates thirst motivation, and helps maintain homeostasis. Throughout our daily living, we lose water through urination, sweating, defecation, and use of water needed in the body for us to function. People in places relatively directly removed from conscious concern about freshwater availability, may be unaware there is a global water crisis, why it exists, and the related mortality and morbidity rates.

Researchers Mekonnen & Hoekstra (2016), reported that previous annual global water scarcity assessments underestimated the water scarcity experienced. This is due to lack of inclusion of data regarding seasonal fluctuations in water consumption and availability of freshwater. Based upon monthly assessments, Mekonnen & Hoekstra found that 4 billion people, half of whom live in India and China, experience severe water scarcity for at least one month of the year. However, they stated that still half a billion people of the world experience water scarcity all year round.

Water Stress, Water Scarcity, and Water Risk

Broadly, water stress refers to both drought and flooding stress. It has been reported that major crops yielded by planters can be reduced by more than 50 percent as a result of water stress (Rahman & Hasegawa, 2011). Primary water stress derives from water deficits, i.e., drought and its resulting impact on soil. The eventual effect of water stress's impact on plants and food supply in general is famine. The plants of arid regions are challenged to withstand the water stress; they go through a series of adaptive biochemical and physiological responses to survive.

Water stress can also refer to the ability, or lack thereof, to meet human and ecological demand for water (World Resources Institute, 2019). It is a broad term that has been used to encompass physical aspects of water resources, such as water scarcity. Scholars have also indicated it can include discussions of the quality of the water that humans access, the flow of water through the environment, and overall access to water (Schulte, 2014). Though commonly, the terms have been used interchangeably, researchers have created graphics and reports to distinguish water stress in relationship to more specific terms such as water scarcity and water risk. It is imperative that businesses, educators, activists, and researchers are using common language when engaging the terms. Water stress is a broader term that includes water scarcity. Water can be plentiful in an area yet still be polluted or contaminated water. Industries and companies can better understand water risk by understanding water stress and water governance (Schulte, Morrison, Orr, & Power, 2014).

The different sectors of society, organizations, and cultures in general face varying degrees of water risk and possible deleterious outcomes depending upon factors such as water scarcity, pollution, poor governance, inadequate infrastructure, or climate change (Schulte, 2014). It is optimal for all sectors to collectively strategize to overcome the stress and health challenges of water risk, stress, and scarcity. Scholars have argued for multiple approaches and collective strategies for optimally addressing water management challenges to benefit the masses (Diringer, Thebo, Cooley, Wilkinson . . . et al., 2019).

Traditional Healers

Of specific cultural significance, the ensuing reduction in crop yields from water stress, has consequences for traditional healers who provide significant healthcare in some cultures. For example, traditional healers of Mali have been reported to still widely use natural plant-based remedies to treat serious illnesses, rather than relying upon western medicines (Tattersall, 2007). Traditional healers clean and cure with plants based on remedies that have been handed down for many generations. Traditional medicines that incorporate dried roots, leaves, and grains are just a few examples of crops that could be affected by water stress in some impacted regions of the world. Another point of consideration is cost, as plant-based cures are less expensive to cultivate and sell, require no prescription, and have a wider level of acceptance in areas such as Mali. The government of Mali is one of few in Africa to formally recognize the benefits of traditional healers. Scientists test the traditional healers' methods and give them a seal of approval (Tattersall, 2007).

In the early 2000s, researchers undertook an ethnobotanical survey to collect information from traditional healers regarding their use of medicinal plants in Kancheepuram district, a northeast region of the state of Tamil Nadu in India (Muthu et al., 2006). Researchers were interested in gathering information from the healers about indigenous knowledge of native plants used to treat health conditions. Questionnaires and personal interviews were conducted from the field. Traditional healers of the region reported using 85 species of plants across 76 genera and 41 plant families as they treated a variety of diseases. The most common diseases addressed with medicinal plants were skin diseases, poison bites, and stomach and nervous disorders. The people of the region were reported as reliant on medicinal plants for their primary healthcare treatment (Muthu et al., 2006). As of 2019, Tamil Nadu faced its third successive year of water drought. Water demand has increased in Tamil Nadu's capital city of Chennai by 47 percent in the last decade, from 750 MLD in 2008 to 1,100 MLD in 2018 (Narasimhan & Babu, 2019). In 2018, rainfall in Chennai had been at the lowest level of 75.55 centimeters, relative to a level of 149.5 centimeters in 2017. The water reservoirs are nearly dry, and rainfall is mostly nonexistent in the region.

Collective activity among businesses to try and mitigate the water risks has been reported; such activities range from asking employees to work from home to controlling the water flow from the taps and reducing the number of toilets (Narasimhan & Babu, 2019). While asking employees to work from home appears as a good strategy for water management by businesses, it produces increased water stress for families. When working from home, employees risk consuming more water from their already scarce water supply at home. The government, restaurants, and real estate developers are also strategizing options for how to manage the water crisis in Tamil Nadu.

Approximately 800 miles north and slightly east of Tamil Nadu is the state of Odisha. The region is generally described as of a tropical climate, where winters are not severe. Krishna (2019) reported the narrative of an older adult female resident of Gobindapur village in Odisha's Bhadrak district. The woman carries a bucket of water from the hand pump to her house 40 times a day, the distance being about 400 meters. Physically, by the end of the day, her body is sore and fatigued. Piped water connections do not exist in her village (Krishna, 2019). Given these challenges within the cultures described, what are possible psychological, physical, and spiritual effects?

Water: Psychological, Physical, and Spiritual

Hydration state is determined by the balance between water output relative to water input. Dehydration exists when water input is deficient to replace water output. The less water in blood, the greater the concentration of particles that have not been dissolved, referred to as osmolality. Osmolality increases during dehydration and decreases when fluid has accumulated. Dehydration is assessed when urine osmolality is greater than 800 milliosmoles per kilogram of water; optimal hydration exists when the 24-h urine osmolality ≤ 500 milliosmoles per kilogram of water; middle hydration is defined when 24-h urine osmolality is between 500 and 800 milliosmoles per kilogram of water (Zhang et al., 2018). Emergency hospitalizations have been particularly prevalent amongst both children and the elderly, resulting from dehydration (Whitney, Santucci, Hsiao, & Chen, 2016; Sfera, Cummings, & Osorio, 2016). Given that brain mass consists of 75 percent water, it is logical that researchers study the impact of dehydration on cognitive performance.

Cognition

Vulnerability and resulting cognitive impairment from even mild dehydration exists, though with sometimes mixed results for type of cognitive versus mood impairment (Pross, 2017). As well, there is a relative paucity of research findings based on adolescents and older adults when trying to understand more about the effects of mild dehydration. However, what is known is that lack of water access and resulting water crises could likely have negative consequences for children and older adults as vulnerable populations, particularly since they are often dependent upon others to achieve their daily water intake.

Young adults have been studied for effects of dehydration on cognition. Via testing of college students in Baoding (a city in central Hebei province of China) researchers investigated the effects of dehydration and water supplementation on cognitive performances. Students were required to refrain from drinking water for 36 hours, so researchers could obtain both cognitive performance measures and any physical structural changes in the brain (Zhang et al., 2018). Six different cognitive tests were administered to the students, using primary cognitive ability software from the Institute of Psychology, Chinese Academy of Sciences (Beijing, China).

The study is typical of research in the psychological sciences, as the participants were college students. Yet future testing of ordinary citizens of the area might be further enlightening, given the widespread structural changes planned. President Xi Jinping's plan is to construct Xiong'an New District, to address population pressures on nearby Beijing. The proposed project was planned to fall under the jurisdiction of Baoding city and planned to be approximately three times the size of New York (Qin, 2017). President Xi Jinping has also issued a call for increased efforts to tackle pollution (Reuters, 2018). How might this plan for a new smarter, greener, and more beautiful environment impact better quality and abundance of water access, and address neurotoxin levels among developing Chinese citizens, relative to the past? This is a biosocial question of interest that is relevant to cultural neuroscience.

Prior to the start of ground breaking for the project, Baoding city has had existing air quality and water stress problems. Baoding city has consistently ranked lowest in China for two to three years for its air quality (more than once named China's most polluted city) and residents worry about how the Xiong'an New District project will impact the area's water availability. Water scarcity, water pollution, and the over-extraction of groundwater are foreboding given the aims of the Xiong'an New District project to produce a more environmentally smart and beautiful environment (Qin, 2017).

For areas of China such as Chao Lake in southeastern China's Anhui province, the water's smell due to algae is hardly bearable for residents; this is despite the fact that environmentalists in China have stated that air quality, by nature, is more easily observed, but water pollution can often be hidden from public view or is not as obvious to the eye. In the case of Cho Lake, the water pollution is obvious to the nose. However, the commonly hidden nature of water contamination has consequences for policymakers' ability to obtain the data needed about China's main watersheds' levels of pollution and consequences for their planning to successfully deliver clean, drinkable water to hundreds of millions in China (Qin, 2016).

Psychology has been referred to as a discipline that produces WEIRD science, which is an acronym for western, educated, industrial, rich, democratic (APA, 2010). The acronym highlights the reality that findings from psychological science research are not representative of the world's population of people. The economically disenfranchised of some of the poorer villages of China, are aware that education is their way out of poverty; yet achieving the dream of attending university is difficult for many. This is despite the country having successfully reduced poverty with its aid to low-income families under China's anti-poverty campaign (China Daily/Asia News Network, 2018).

Cultural neuroscience is an area of study that should engage researchers in the study of effects of dehydration, food insecurity, and pollution on cognitive performance for persons challenged by poverty across cultures. The Chinese government moved 68 million people out of poverty between 2013–2018 and plans to help another 30 million to rise from poverty before the end of year 2020 (China Daily/Asia News Network, 2018). These millions of people impacted by the campaign are prime participants for cultural neuroscientific studies of changes to their cognitive and emotional processing within the culture, following the anti-poverty campaign efforts. Despite the success of the anti-poverty campaigns, there are rural villagers of China that have been left behind; among them, are some villagers whose cognitive framing and learned helplessness include no hope that they will ever be lifted from poverty (Pinghui, 2019).

In rural villages of China, the *Water Poverty Index* (WPI) has been used as a method for evaluating the extent of water shortage in regions (Sullivan, 2001). The WPI uses five components: resources, access, capacity, use, and environment. Rural communities of Sheshu, Fanyao, Dongcao, Qiaodi, and Gouershang have been listed as communities experiencing a water poverty situation (Liu et al., 2018). Humans of these areas are not commonly studied in neuroscience but should be cognitively and emotionally assessed to advance research in cultural neuroscience.

Physical

Regarding the older adult woman of Gobindapur village in Odisha's Bhadrak district, who has been reported as carrying buckets of water over 40 times a day, research sheds light on the physical consequences of this behavior within her tropical climate. Water comprises 55 percent of body weight in older adults; in addition to the daily living hardship of water stress, the implications for her physical effect is also important. This includes her overall pattern of water intake, the complex mechanisms of maintaining water homeostasis in her body, and the impact of variation in her water intake on her health and energy, weight, human performance, and functioning (Popkin,

Anci, & Rosenberg, 2010). An older adult carrying buckets of water over 400 meters, 40 times a day in tropical weather is a health risk and is inhumane. There are three types of heat-related disorders: heat cramps, heat exhaustion, and heatstroke. Thermoregulatory mechanisms naturally exist to maintain homeostasis, yet prolonged exposure to excessive heat and elevated body temperature can tax the thermoregulatory mechanisms to the point of failure.

Laboratory-based physiological studies have indicated that older adults' ability to sense heat, consume fluids as needed, and their physiological (e.g., blood distribution, sweating) responses during exposure to heat may be compromised (Mack et al., 1994). These findings were based on otherwise healthy older adults, relative to younger adults to whom they were compared. Also, as early as the1950s, researchers discovered that during physical activity, older adults sweat less, even though they maintain the same numbers of sweat glands as they age (Hellon & Lind, 1956). Sweating less has severe consequences for the ability of bodies of older adults to cool as needed; therefore, exposure to high heat and physical exertion (among people already socioeconomically stressed and disenfranchised) can be exacerbated when they face hydroclimactic challenges within their environment.

Researchers have prioritized describing the effects of heat on older adults' human physiology and the factors that increase their risk of heat stress (Kenny et al., 2010). From their research, Kenny et al. (2010) found that the following variables put people at risk for heat-related disorders: being over 60 years old, obesity, hypertension, pulmonary or cardiovascular disease, and chronic diabetes. Furthermore, they found increased risk of death due to heat exposure was related to lower levels of education, lower income, being of non-White origin, and social isolation. These findings align with the writings of Fanon about the oppressed, as well as medical anthropologists who have referenced the social origins and expressions of illness (Singer, 2004). Such is also directly relevant to the field of cultural neuroscience, as it aims to probe deeper into environment, culture, biology, and neuroscience to understand humans' lived experiences. As such, water stress extends far beyond the immediate consequences of not having adequate usable water, but also has consequences for the exacerbation of other chronic conditions often found among the marginalized. Evidence of further marginalization was found in the Kenny et al. (2010) research; other contributing factors to likelihood of experiencing heat-related disorders was homebound lifestyle, lack of contact with other people, and decreased mobility.

On the other end of the developmental spectrum of older adults, are infants and young children. How might a health challenge such as dehydration, pose dangers for babies' developing brains? Findings from a study of newborns re-hospitalized for dehydration in the United States, suggests that the answer to this question may depend upon social class, as researchers found no significant adverse long-term neurological effects in the re-hospitalized newborns (Escobar et al., 2017). A close reading of the study revealed that the dehydrated newborns (long term follow-up to age 5) and their parents were families of privilege. The sample was an insured population with a somewhat high education level, and high rates of breastfeeding. The families also had ready access to several support services (follow-up clinics and phone advice banks staffed by registered nurses) and no barriers to prompt rehospitalization. This research too then, is consistent with WEIRD biased science (APA, 2010).

The following are facts from a UNICEF (2017) report: one in four children will live in areas of extreme water stress by 2040; 530 million children live in extremely high flood occurrence zones; 200 million hours are lost each day by women and girls carrying water. The report further details the life-
threatening risks for children due to water stress, rising temperatures that allow bacteria and pathogens in their water to flourish, and rising sea levels that salinate freshwater. When children are not killed by disease, dehydration, diarrhea, and contaminated water they may survive still with stunted bodies and brains, thereby impacting their ability to properly absorb needed nutrients and properly learn. Furthermore, although the crisis of water is global, and unification of strategic efforts to combat this is mandatory, currently it remains inequitable who are the people most severely impacted, based on region of the world.

Although water scarcity is a global phenomenon, the tragedy strikes harder in certain geographic regions such as parts of Nigeria, Somalia, South Sudan, and Yemen (UNICEF, 2017). Drought, famine, and malnutrition impact nearly 1.4 million children in places like Yemen. In parts of Ethiopia, already by 2017, it was expected that over 9 million people there would not have safe drinking water at their disposal (UNICEF, 2017).

Unfortunately, the existence of scientific brain studies of children and their families of such regions is still elusive. Thus, for example, it is likely to be several years before scientists who produce cultural neuroscientific studies based on Ethiopian samples will appear. In fact, it has only been since a joint Ethiopian/Norwegian training program in neurosurgery was initiated in June 2006 that progress has been made even in critical healthcare such as neurosurgery in Ethiopia, to understand and treat brain traumas (Lund-Johansen et al., 2017). The institutionally founded program has been the main external contributor to neurosurgical capacity building in Ethiopia. A total of 21 Ethiopian neurosurgeons were trained in support of a sustainable environment, whereby they can then teach others of the country. The training included a network of five centers in the city of Addis Ababa. Brain drain on Ethiopia and other nations of Africa has been the subject of discussion, as many natives of the countries receive study abroad grants to medically train in Europe or the United States, but following their training, do not return to practice in their home countries (United Nations Conference on Trade and Development, 2012).

Flint, Michigan

The United Nations Conference on Trade and Development (UNCTD) 2012 report focused on the least developed countries (LDCs). Non-western regions of the Nile River basin have also been the subject of documentaries on water stress and the global water crisis (Tvedt et al., 2007). Yet, because the water crisis and environmental injustices are global, areas of the United States must also be included for discussion. One of the more recent ongoing incidents involving lead exposure through the U.S. drinking water is from the city of Flint, Michigan.

To save money, the city of Flint decided to change its primary water source of Lake Huron, thereby putting its citizens at water risk. Their alternative water source became the Flint River. However, many of the later water samples from the river tested poorly for lead levels. Blood lead levels in children were significantly increased (Bondy & Campbell, 2017). The consequences of this are not trivial, as lead is an environmental contaminant.

Housing built prior to the late 1970s in the United States, especially if never renovated, have been found to still possess lead paint in some areas; as well, they can have drinking water service lines made from lead, lead solder, or lead inclusive plumbing materials. Though in 2017 the city reported to its residents that the water was again safe to drink, still as of April 2019, 2,500 lead service lines throughout the plumbing system were still in need of replacement after 8,000 had already been replaced (Ahmad, 2019). In a comprehensive review of the literature, it is evident from studies dating back to 1943, that there are cognitive effects of childhood lead exposure (CDC, 2012). The possible severity of impact of lead exposure is so significant that most reports concur there is no safe blood lead threshold for adverse effects of lead on infant or child neurodevelopment that can be identified.

In the United States, the adverse health consequences of lead contaminated water were recognized as early as 1845 (Karalekas, Ryang, & Taylor, 1983); yet the Flint water crisis began in 2014. This represents environmental injustice. Environmental injustice is defined as situations in which specific social groups such as communities of color and low socioeconomic persons are disproportionately affected by environmental hazards (Brulle & Pellow, 2006). Environmental activists and researchers highlight the resulting effects of the injustices on the people's health and environment. Also, environmental justice calls for the elimination of unequal environmental protection and environmental inequality of laws, regulations, governmental programs, enforcement, and policies (Maantay, 2002).

Filmmaker Michael Moore, a native of Flint, Michigan, publicly stated that if the water-based injustice of his hometown had occurred anywhere else, it would have been addressed long before (Carucci, 2017). His comments represent the ideology of scholars and activists of environmental justice in referencing the historical working-class nature of the people of Flint. He described the residents as hardworking people of meager resources, who contributed significantly to the growth and development of Flint. His reference to the lower socioeconomic status of his hometown in comparison to other more socioeconomically affluent areas such as Westchester, New York, and Northern Virginia suburbs of Washington, D.C., highlights the environmental injustice of the contaminated water, due to its occurrence in a more disenfranchised U.S. community. U.S. Census Bureau data from 2017, revealed Flint as the poorest city of its size in the United States, with nearly 39 percent of residents and 60 percent of the children living in poverty (Ahmad, 2018). As of 2019, the Flint water crisis and residual efforts to bring the water and plumbing system to healthy status have been ongoing for five known years. Exposure to contaminated water can result in vomiting, diarrhea, and intestinal inflammation as harmful consequences of human exposure to bacteria. Bacteria make use of potent and toxic molecules to gain access to the brain and bodies of host humans and animals. Once inside, they may be capable of attacking a wide variety of cell types, or they may be specific to harming neural cells, thereby referred to as neurotoxins (Popoff & Poulain, 2010).

Leeanne Waters, a Flint resident and mother of four, collected 800 water samples from homes. Waters found through her research and communications with the Environmental Protection Agency (EPA), university researchers, and medical professionals, that lead contamination levels in some areas of the city were twice as high as what the EPA considered hazardous waste (Persio, 2018). Lead and bacteria were at such high levels in the water samples because the city had not proactively applied necessary corrosive controls to the pipes, which could have prevented lead from getting into the water supply. Ms. Waters, prior to her research, had questioned why her eyelashes had fallen out at one time. All her children had shown signs of lead contamination, and one of her children was diagnosed with lead poisoning.

Lead in water can cause permanent brain damage in children and other health complications (Sanders, Liu, Buchner, & Tchounwou, 2009). What is promising, is that researchers have studied adult neural cells. They have discovered there is hope for the introduction of genetic and epigenetic manipulation of adult neural stem cells to produce new neurons and glia for damaged or diseased neural tissue (Jacquet, Patel, et al., 2009). However, given social injustices in access to healthcare and even participation in clinical trials, these genetic and epigenetic manipulations of adult neural stem cells may not be delivered to marginalized people in need of such interventions.

An African-Centered Cultural Neuroscience of Water and Well-Being

To date, the scholarship in the field of cultural neuroscience has not included a diversity of cultural experiences and practices that represent the vast cultures of Africa. In opposition to the WEIRD science nature of psychology and other STEM discipline scholarship (APA, 2010), water will be discussed in this section in relation to the biopsychosocial, cultural, and spiritual health needs of humans.

Mali

In some parts of the world, such as Dogon country in Mali, West Africa's largest nation, the people have become accustomed to the local hydrological cycle of drought most of the time, with exceptions of rare great rainfall (Tvedt et al., 2007). Lake Antogo exists among the Dogon people of Mali; the lake comes and goes every year. Except for the annual fishing ritual during the sixth month of the dry summer season, fishing is prohibited in the Bamba area. During the annual fishing ritual at Lake Antogo, men and boys from throughout Mali trek to the lake to participate in a fishing frenzy. It takes approximately 15 minutes for the participants to empty the lake of all fish; (Tvedt et al., 2007). The Dogon people regard the lake as sacred because of its rarity in Mali, which primarily consists of the Sahara Desert and the dry steppes of the transitional zone of the Sahel. During the pre-climate change era, the area had plush greenery, and the water was believed to be filled with good spirits. The annual fishing ritual is strongly based on ancestor worship.

After approximately 30 minutes, gunshots signal the end of the annual fishing ritual. Each captured fish is combined and given to the oldest man of Bamba (Bertolino, 2019). The revered elder's job is to properly distribute the haul of fish among all villages represented. The fishing ritual of *Antogo* symbolizes peace and unity of the Dogon villages. The *Antogo* of the Dogon also represent a good example of the philosophy that separation leads to suffering.

A neurologist and neuropsychologist collaborated to highlight ancient teaching from Buddha and mindfulness regarding the benefits of practicing togetherness and interconnectedness with the world (Hanson & Mendius, 2009). In the *Antogo* ritual, the frenzied run into the water to grab fish is a sacred act of togetherness within the culture, rather than a competition. The anticipation of the event leads to an adrenalin rush; this accompanies further pleasurable effects inside the brain and body because of the absence of threat and anxiety due to the togetherness and excitement.

Unfortunately, because of the remoteness of the Bamba village and the marginalized status of the residents (relative to well-funded western scientists), it is unlikely that cultural neuroscience will soon incorporate culturally sensitive quality studies of the *Antogo*, or water stress of the region, for how these experiences impact the minds and neural activation patterns of the Dogon people. Yet, these are the types of cultural, spiritual, and cognitive brain studies that would add tremendous value to what we know about how neural patterns and well-being are shaped by long-standing communal cultural practices.

The Nile River Basin

Along the Nile River basin, multiple nations are impacted by a water crisis and water risk, stemming from conflict over who will control the water of the river. The most directly impacted people of the Nile River basin are not well-represented in empirical studies of the culture of stress and environmental injustice in relation to neural processing and resulting emotions. Likewise, disenfranchised populations from areas such as Flint, Michigan, are not represented in biomedical imaging research as participants nor as cultural neuro-scientific case studies. Flint residents' experience with water contamination for continuous years is a cultural experience that should be examined for its potential biochemical and neural impact and potentially long-term psychological impact.

Water universally and powerfully impacts all humans. It is also vital for all plants and non-human animals. Via studying the words of non-western trained spiritualists, anti-WEIRD scientists can gain insight. An African spiritualist's perspective calls for an understanding of the spiritual power of water as a giver and sustainer of life. The call is for global education about the spiritual power of water now and into the future, similarly to how water has been historically revered among several indigenous cultures. Such worldviews of respect for nature and cultural practices can shape decision-making and well-being.

The pervasive capitalist cultural practices of commercialization and taxation of water impacts global life. The harm from the commercialization and disrespect of water as a sacred entity, has resulted in water stress, health hazards, and global environmental danger. Toxic materials that travel through water and the environment, when taken in by plants, animals, and humans cause a loss of sacredness, a reduction in natural consciousness, and reduction of optimal functioning.

The Andes

Increased awareness of ancient solutions to modern problems of water scarcity is imperative. For example, pre-Incan cultural practices of the tropical Andes have been revisited for the development of nature-based water harvesting technologies. In times of extreme drought, ancient and indigenous means (1,400-years-old) of infiltration enhancement have provided solutions (Ochoa-Tocachi, Bardales, Antiporta, et al., 2019). Using the system, water can be diverted from headwater streams onto the mountainous slopes of the region during the wet season. This process enhances the water yield and the length of downward flow of water for availability during the dry season; this ancient and indigenous infiltration system allows water to be retained an average of 45 days before it resurfaces in time for dry season flow. This ancient system acts as a complement to the work of conventional engineering efforts to combat water insecurity.

Haiti and Peru

In nations such as Haiti and Peru, there are examples of bio-cultural usage of water and plants in ritual bathing practices. Individuals engage in the bathing practices for healing and for protection (Daniels, 2016). All four natural elements are a part of ritual bathing practices: water, plants, smoke/fire, and mud. Gran Salin, for example, is a small fishing town in northern Haiti. It is a natural site where freshwater and saltwater meet. Such water spots exist in Haiti where seekers of healing come to submerge themselves in the water and be visited by spirits who will aid them. An example is the sacred waterfall of *Sodo* (Haitian Creole). Thousands of Haitians and foreign travelers visit the waterfall to bathe in it. This is done to address their physical illnesses, social problems, and psychological conditions (Daniels, 2016).

Finally, in Peru, *ayahuasca* is among the most well-known medicinal plant of the indigenous Americas. The indigenous people of the Amazon regions view it as sacred medicine. During *ayahuasca* treatments, visitation to waterfalls or rivers may be incorporated into the health plan provided by the *curandera* (healer or shaman). The force, temperature, and movement of the waterfall is energizing for revitalization. Persons suffering from lethargy, listlessness, and stress can benefit from the treatment (Daniels, 2016). *Ayahuasca* baths (herbal, mud/clay, flower) before or after a healing ceremony are done to rid of negative energies and unproductive thoughts.

Conclusion

For humans on the planet who have made sacred uses of water a regular part of their cultural practices, how has it shaped their development and possible epigenetic influences on their brain processes? The psychological and physiological effects of such cultural practices are worthy of empirical investigation because of the engagement in practices to release unhealthy elements of one's mind and body. Non-western mindfulness practices and the African-centered worldview both stress the interconnectedness of all cultures of the planet and connection with and reverence for nature. Though survival strategies have evolved in support of individualism, such a way of being in modern times can lead to greater psychological suffering (Hansen & Mendius, 2009). The unification of world communities is health beneficial; the unification of world communities with nature may lead to a reconnection to the value of water, to decreased mental and physical suffering, increased brain health, and benefits to humanity (Bwoya, 2019).

Chapter Eleven

Forever Fanon

Often when the iconic Fanonian text, *The Wretched of the Earth*, is referenced, his opening sectional commentary regarding necessity of violent retaliation by the oppressed towards their oppressors has been interpreted and highlighted; Butts (1979), well-articulated how such a preoccupation misses the grander message of the text. As well, because of the historical time period and national contexts of *The Wretched of the Earth*, some may not only wonder of its relevance to current global events, but further question its relevance to discussions of cultural neuroscience. However, Fanon asserted that everything can be explained to the people, if one really wants the people to understand.

THE BRAIN AS BIOSOCIAL ORGAN

Fanon's assertion further aims to summarize the objective of this current work, *Our Biosocial Brains*. The central nervous system is complex. Given the rapid changes in the healthcare fields, bio-engineering, biotechnologies, neuroscience, bio-imaging and the futuristic work anticipated in these fields, it is imperative that the disenfranchised people of the world (discussed in this book) increasingly become integrated into the research explorations of the brain as a biosocial organ. There are implications for their lives now and into the future for understanding even basic anatomy and functioning of the brain, and how the brain and body will be increasingly manipulated by scientists and experiences in the future sociocultural world (Bess, 2016). We will see growing impact of climate change, increased competition for fewer natural resources, greater economic disparity, and resulting expansion of inequities in healthcare and safe housing (Klare 2002; 2012). Nations of Africa and Asia have been predicted to be impacted even more severely than other areas.

The underlying meaning of the phrase, *the brain is a biosocial organ* is not novel. Ancient philosophers spoke that the flow of thoughts has the power to sculpt our brains. What we are exposed to in our sociocultural world impacts our thoughts. Humans' brains continue to respond to experiences of power, bias, and inhumane treatment. Already in the United States, the mass murders from gun violence have saturated media such that this is a logical subject for investigation in developmental brain research. Concerning the children of the Sandy Hook elementary tragedy who witnessed and survived the gun violence and hundreds more children daily exposed to violent deaths, who will follow-up with them longitudinally? Research evidence exists that such early life stress of exposure to violence relates to neurocognitive deficits of the frontal lobe and deficits of the stress response and other neuroendocrine responses (Perkins & Graham-Bermann, 2012). According to this research, childrens' executive functioning and self-regulatory challenges may interfere with their academic performance and mental health.

The current work has aimed to educate, prompt discussion, and raise critical consciousness about diversifying the nascent field of cultural neuroscience. There is a need for greater conscious awareness of our brains as arguably our most important body part, always under the influence of cultural input. Critical consciousness of this among researchers, has the power to develop important and culturally sensitive innovative research.

A transformation of thoughts produced in the brain can lead to new behaviors. The objective is to motivate development of more diverse research questions with more diverse groups, as the field of cultural neuroscience advances. Fanon (2005) and other African-centered scholars have written about the psychology of oppression. Therefore, there is also a goal to increase numbers of ethical researchers who center brain science in conjunction with advancing a sociocultural neuroscience of liberation. Increased togetherness or unification of the oppressed to act in the best interest of their joint liberation, aligns with the ideology of Fanon in *The Wretched of the Earth*. This unity also aligns with positive mental and emotional health (Hanson & Mendius, 2009). Thus, Fanon's work is still relevant beyond his era of colonialism and advocacy for affected colonized nations. It is relevant to global populations of oppressed and disenfranchised groups such as members of LGBTQ communities, poverty-challenged people, women, indigenous people, Black and other non-White people, immigrants, and the various intersections of all these groups.

Further research is needed to expand upon findings regarding existing potential coping mechanisms among lower social class individuals, that result in their being more compassionate and attuned to distress in others, relative to the lesser compassion shown by their upper-social-class counterparts (Stellar, Manzo, Kraus, & Keltner, 2012). This was evident from the findings presented in this book from my work with poverty-challenged Black women in North Carolina. Although the women are poverty-challenged, they primarily expressed aspiration to do work that can benefit others of their community. How might such social class-based difference appear in neuro-imaging research? Insight to this question has implications for expanding the awareness of any potential neural processes to attract funding and generate widespread positive community change that is impactful in communities.

In contemporary terms, the varying groups of disenfranchised people of the earth can be perceived as their own nation of people in need of psycho-logical liberation, in need of decolonization of the minds. Kgatla (2008) has referenced colonization of the mind as subtle political, economic, cultural, and religious manifestations by powerful elitist inhumane beings, who even-tually possess and control the minds of the oppressed. The colonized mind is one that has been made delusional like the minds of their oppressors, who Fanon described as possessing pro-White, anti-Black paranoia (Butts, 1979). Colonization of the mind has two purposes: 1) to change the oppressed peoples' perceptions of themselves and their own cultures, and 2) to cause the oppressed to idolize the cultures, behaviors, and identities of their oppres-sors. The liberation of the people necessitates organization, education, and decolonized action (Fanon, 2005).

Fanon eventually recognized that the psychoanalytic approach, which was his primary framework of training, was inadequate for addressing op-pression and resulting psychological disorder. The psychoanalysis of his time dismissed a notion of socio-cultural and institutional influences on eventual development of neurosis, commonly known today as anxiety. Fanon saw racist-based power and its related extensions of bias and inhumanity as the cause of psychological disorder in both the oppressed and the oppressor. The neuroses (anxiety) described by Fanon as produced by racism, is an early example of recognition of cultural neuroscience. Thus, it could be argued that Fanon was one of the pioneers in linking psychiatry, African-centered psychology, neuroscience, cultural studies, and race and ethnic studies. In *The Wretched of the Earth*, a section entitled "On National Culture" explains the connection between the combat for culture and the people's struggle for liberation (Fanon, 2005).

By training, Frantz Fanon was a physician who specialized in psychiatry. As such, it was mandatory that he understand the brain and how its function-ing may be enhanced or compromised by medical as well as illegal psycho-active substances. Psychiatrists are trained to use a variety of treatments beyond medications, such as psychotherapy, psychosocial interventions, and other brain-based treatments such as electroconvulsive shock therapy. Fanon has been described as espousing a socio-cultural psychiatric frame of refer-ence (Butts, 1979). Therefore, during his time working as a hospital adminis-trator at Blida Hospital during the years 1953–1956, he implemented several clinical reformations to the hospital's practices. The reforms Fanon made were aligned with humanistic rather than dehumanization of the patients. For example, he minimized the use of patient restraints, supported open wards for some patients who did not require a more restrictive setting, and disallowed references to *native* versus European classifications of patients (Butts, 1979). He eventually resigned from this position, however, as he became more of an activist physician with increased Black consciousness and sense of responsibility to act. He desired to make more substantive political, socioeconomic, and cultural changes in the face of the injustices he saw in Algeria.

A widespread adherence to the ideology and application of several of the ideas from *The Wretched of the Earth* has relevance for changing the minds of the disenfranchised to reject characterizations of themselves as savage, dangerous, inferior, other. To pair the ideas from *The Wretched of the Earth* to a cultural neuroscience framework is necessary. Every person, no matter whether they have power or status, have brains that have been shaped by how they have been socialized to perceive themselves in the world. Experiences of dehumanization across time, space, and intersecting categories of oppression have been highlighted throughout the chapters of this current project, to more deeply consider the impact this may have on brain and behavior. As well, the benefits to marginalized people lie in their collective information gathering and sharing, while prioritizing optimal psychological belief systems.

In *The Wretched of the Earth*, Fanon described three stages of development of Black consciousness in the colonized writer: 1) assimilationist literary products, 2) conflicted writing that waivers between humor, allegory, anguish, and self-loathing, and 3) combat writing used not only to proclaim one's culture and people, but also to galvanize the people for a new reality in action (Fanon, 2005). It is the third descriptive stage of Fanon's process that represents this current text, *Our Biosocial Brains.*

As stated in a previous chapter on collectivists' and individualists' brains, depending on the culture one has lived, one or the other of these classifications may be deemed primarily characteristic of a society. Yet for the most disenfranchised of the world, Fanon asserted that it matters not whether an oppressed group's national culture is celebrated above another oppressed culture, because the goal of the oppressed should extend beyond borders in taking actions to fight oppression and gain genuine liberation (Fanon, 2005). He argued that the oppressed need not expend great energy in comparing or ranking their individual nation states of cultures; instead, the focus should be on the commonality of oppression of the disenfranchised by those in power (Fanon, 2005). Yet he also made clear the challenge for the oppressed to move beyond seeing themselves as different "tribes" who continue to prioritize their individual group's best interests. Making said changes towards unification and increased human social interaction among themselves has the potential for reshaping the brain because researchers have presented the importance of interacting with other people regarding human cognition, development, and well-being (Hari, Henriksson, Malinen, & Parkkonen, 2015).

Research evidence has also revealed that those with social power show greater approach motivation than the socially powerless; this relates to their left prefrontal cortex activation that initiates approach motivation, whereas right-sided prefrontal cortex activation links to avoidance motivation (Boksem, Smolering, & DeCremer, 2012). If oppressed people are to act after becoming educated to understand and subsequently collectively organize, they will still need to believe they are socially powerful to take the action (Zimmerman, 1995). Fanon stated that describing and discussing independence among the people will not be enough to eliminate the harmful impact of colonization of the mind; discussion only is not enough to propel the people to action. He expressed that the oppressed must become material and psychological masters to radically transform their society (Fanon, 2005). According to cultural neuroscience, in so doing, the result would be a radical transformation of their neural functioning; left-sided prefrontal dominance is an expected neural transformation, once people are healed from oppression of social powerlessness.

Fanonian Ideology and Cultural Neuroscience

In 1961 when *The Wretched of the Earth* was initially published, Fanon stated in it, that the peoples of Africa had only recently come to know themselves (Fanon, 2005). This, he described, was the result of the psychology of oppression enacted by the privileged elite. The psychology of the oppression he described, involved the use of capitalist exploitation and other barriers to a more utopic or optimal existence. During and after decolonization of the mind, Fanon foretold the oppressed to be more unified and motivated to resist oppression.

However, the privileged who have the power to disenfranchise, have many institutionalized policies to meet their objectives. Fanon wrote of how the elite may block oppressed groups' ability to unify and coordinate their efforts, thereby sustaining power over millions of people, resulting in hunger, homelessness, ignorance, and inhumanity (Fanon, 2005). He wrote of the changes he witnessed in the formerly oppressed, once they began to understand, and decolonize their minds. He commented upon groups who were formerly enemies, who would become allies in the fight against their common oppressor. Scientists have made contributions to the neuro-imaging literature by experimentally investigating brain localization of cooperatively focused cognition and behavior (Abe et al., 2019).

Researchers in Japan used an experimental design to test for the existence of cooperation-based areas of the brain (Abe et al., 2009). The researchers' primary question was which parts of the brain are specifically involved in assisting humans during cooperative tasks? For the cooperative task in the experiment, participant-dyads were separately placed inside functional MRI (fMRI) machines to have their brains scanned while they tightly gripped a sensor device. The fMRI was used to monitor the alignment of the two participants' grips via the sensor device's connection to the fMRI. Cursor alignment for the two research participants was observed. The complexity of the design required the participant dyad to predict the grip force exerted by the other person, and to adjust their grip accordingly to align their cursors.

Researchers found that the cooperative task activated brain regions related to the mentalizing system. Activation of the anterior part of the right temporo-parietal junction (where the temporal and parietal lobes of the brain meet) showed a significant positive correlation with the degree of participants' cooperation during the joint task. Therefore, the right temporo-parietal junction is involved in controlling the flow of information about cooperative tasks. The researchers were interested in determining if there are different brain areas involved in individually mentalizing a task versus cooperatively mentalizing a task. Thus, a complex design was required.

For the individual testing component, participants were instructed to mentalize moving their cursor to a designated location, and then adjust their grip to move it. They were also instructed to only observe (no movement) a pre-recording of the research procedure, in which a cursor was being moved. The complexity of the research design allowed the researchers to gather data regarding the brain regions activated during individual versus cooperative tasks, as well as tasks involving engagement in a task versus only observation of a task. The (Abe et al., 2009) findings about the temporo-parietal locale, are neural evidence that the human brain evolved to have designated locations for thinking about and working with others. Fanon's call for oppressed people to organize and act is in accordance with the evolution of a brain area that is devoted to mentalizing and behaving in cooperation.

Mentalizing is defined as the ability to read the mental states of other agents and engages many neural processes (Frith & Frith, 2006). The unification of oppressed people is recommended, based on their shared perspective taking and awareness about their status in the world. The human brain can represent the self's mental state and the mental state of others. The brain can also represent the relationship between one's own mental state and that of others (Frith & Frith, 2006). This makes it possible for humans to communicate ideas.

As Fanon expressed, decolonization creates a new person because of the process of liberation from untruths of inferiority. African philosophers have emphasized a search for the truth via restoration of health and empowerment (Oelofsen, 2015); restoration of health is needed following the damage done to the psyche from colonization of the mind. African philosophy does not dwell on a romanticized past prior to the damage done, but instead focuses on healing from a trauma of oppression to move forward with a new truthful self-understanding and identity.

The medial prefrontal cortex and medial posterior parietal cortex have consistently shown neural activation during neuroimaging studies of personal identity. These brain areas activate for research participants when thinking, "Who am I?" (Pfeifer & Peake, 2012). Neuro-imaging studies have also investigated brain activation during socioemotional thoughts such as, "What do others think about me?" or, "Where do I fit in?" The following brain areas have been listed as related to these socioemotional thoughts: tempo-parietal junction and posterior superior temporal sulcus, temporal poles, anterior insula, ventral striatum, anterior cingulate cortex, middle cingulate cortex, and ventrolateral prefrontal cortex (Pfeifer & Peake, 2012). However, the mentalizing, emotional expression, and emotional regulation that are so central to self-development are based on neuro-imaging studies that are lacking in diverse representations of people who have experienced varying traumas of disenfranchisement. These persons have been the focus of the current text and of Fanon's works, *The Wretched of the Earth* and *Black Skin, White Masks*. More empirical work is needed that is inclusive of these populations.

Past, Present, and Future

Scholars of cultural studies and of neuroscience often operate in silos, rather than collaborating to strategize and innovate solutions to pressing issues of the global world. A visitation of the ideology of Fanon reveals his works' relevance to the present. There is also a kind of Afrofuturism in Fanon's treatment of systemic social problems taken from his writings of the 1950s and 1960s. Afrofuturism is no longer regarded as just a subgenre of science fiction. Afrofuturism has been referenced as a larger aesthetic body of work to which a diverse representation of artists have contributed (Yaszek, 2006). Artists of several genres and media have contributed to Afrofuturism in a type of practice of *Ubuntu* an African-centered worldview of "I am because we are." The diverse contributors to Afrofuturism share a common goal of projecting Black futures based on positive truths of the Afro-diasporic past of experiences. Such representation also existed in Fanon's *The Wretched of the Earth*.

Afrofuturism has a political mission, which was highly characteristic of Fanon's work. For example, in the first section of Fanon's *The Wretched of the Earth*, he incorporates Aime Cesaire's poetry and refers to the poetry as having prophetic significance in its description of oppression-derived violence. By using words of Cesaire, Fanon represents Afrofuturism. The poem reflected how enslaved Africans and their descendants experienced conditions of threat, violence, depression, rage, and overall lack of well-being.

Fanon portrayed to the reader via Cesaire's poetry, the historical authenticity of the experience of the oppressed. Throughout *The Wretched of the Earth*, Fanon wrote how experiences of colonization lead to the damaged psyches of the oppressed, with consequences far into the future of descendants.

Afrofuturism has been described as not just about reclaiming the history of the past, but about reclaiming the history of the future as well (Yaszek, 2006). The healing necessary to create new minds, new people, new healthy communities that can move forward, requires a return to the past to defy the lies of colonialism, Jim Crow, apartheid, The Trail of Tears, the Holocaust, slavery, conversion therapies, and other atrocities. Yet this creation of newly liberated men and women in Fanon's time, and currently, will not occur swiftly. A return to the past to deeply study the methods of change and ideology is informative for future liberation.

In *The Wretched of the Earth*, in his chapter entitled, "Grandeur and Weakness of Spontaneity," Fanon references the unemployed, the disenfranchised, the criminal, the vagrant, the second-class citizens. Fanon described these groups as being devoted to the liberation struggle, once they are approached and made aware. He saw these groups as redeeming themselves in their own eyes and before history, returning to action as they took their vital place as people on the move (Fanon, 2005).

O'Shea (2019) posed the question of how do the disenfranchised manage to create themselves in the current world in which their identities are predetermined by false narratives developed by the more powerful? One such powerful sphere that has shaped the perceptions of and minds of the disenfranchised is digital technologies such as the internet and access to social media. Gramlich (2019) reported that teens in general use the same forms of social media irrespective of demographics; yet teens of lower income families use Facebook more than higher-income teens. Seventy percent of the teens who live in households earning less than $30,000 a year use Facebook. However, just 36 percent of teens whose income is over $75,000 use Facebook. Thus, teenagers' internet use behavior is not uniform. Their usage varies by gender, class, race, and ethnicity. Regarding concerns of colonization of the mind or psychology of oppression, it is worth noting that half of teen girls, compared to only 39 percent of teen boys, report being persistent, chronic online users. Similarly, Latino teens significantly (54 percent) report constant internet usage compared to their White counterparts (41 percent) (Anderson & Jiang, 2018). What are the biosocial brain implications of this?

For disenfranchised groups who have historically experienced institutionalized discrimination and oppression, research has addressed their abusers' use of digital technologies as contemporary tools of racist culture (Back, 2002). This is relevant to the theme of this book and past writings of Fanon. White nationalist movements have been successful in incorporating digital technology into modern day racist cultural cyberspace. It is also important to note though, that this and other research on the harmful impact of digital technologies may have overshadowed the good that may also benefit disenfranchised populations.

O'Shea (2009) emphasizes in her work regarding digital technologies, how it can benefit even the disenfranchised, if society is willing to return to the past to advance the future. She makes a case for making sense of the past to claim the present and move forward. Her vision is a bringing of digital technologies under control, to build a more democratic future for members of the culture. One example O'Shea presents from Fanon, to exemplify the benefit of reaching back to the past, is Fanon's descriptions of Algerians reclaiming radio to use as a tool of expression. Fanon described how initially in Algeria, the oppressed despised the radio, because it was regarded as the master's tool of control and oppression. However, as the people began to understand its significance, they were able to appreciate their own new usage of it as a tool of organization and information for the people in the struggle.

Sankofa means to "go back and fetch it"; scholars have stated that Blacks engage in *Sankofa* processes more than their White counterparts (Jones & Leitner, 2015). Interestingly, using a past orientation such as *Sankofa* mediates psychological outcomes for Blacks. However, the impact of *Sankofa* is also complex; for example, *Sankofa* processes may be less useful during psychological threats. Depending on what stressors are endured for Black persons, their reliance on the processes may be sources of psychological threat or may be useful coping mechanisms.

O'Shea (2019) advocated for a reclamation of digital technologies to empower the people, rather than to manipulate or injure. O'Shea's work aligns with the research of other scholars who have used the term "radical digital citizenship" (Emejulu & McGregor, 2019). They define radical digital citizenship as a process through which individuals and groups critically analyze the social, political, and economic consequences of technologies in everyday life. Radical digital citizenship harkens back to the philosophy and collectivist ideology of Fanon, in which he advocated for deliberation and action. Radical digital citizenship strives to build alternative and liberating technologies and technological practices. In the radical digital citizenship literature, the emphasis is placed on politicizing digital technologies in support of social justice and equitable citizenship. This form of radical citizenship was used to engage, make visible, and liberate the narratives of men and women of the #metoo movement, and the #blacklivesmatter movement (Mundt, Ross, & Burnett, 2018; Campbell, 2018).

Given the high levels of screen time and digital technology available across much of the globe, scientists have questioned the possible effect of this cultural phenomenon on cognition. Overall, the impact of digital devices, gaming, and the internet on brain health has shown mostly mixed findings from relatively harmless to harmful (Pasquinelli, 2018). More longitudinal brain research is needed that focuses on the varieties of types of digital technologies, following their usage over time among diverse samples of marginalized people.

Ethnopsychiatry

Ethnopsychiatry has been defined as the study of mental illness using a cross-cultural framework; the cross-cultural framework considers cultural similarities and differences in definitions, classification, causality, and treatment (Gadit, 2003). In the mid-1950s, Fanon came to the realization that he had to resist traditional psychiatry. Its Eurocentric nature was not suited for the oppressive dehumanization experienced by the Algerians he was charged with interviewing and making psychiatric diagnosis. What he witnessed within the colonized cultural context, was that his patients were often labeled criminal, lazy, liars, who were deemed innately inferior to Europeans. There was nothing existent in the traditional psychiatry, which understood or accommodated a psychology of oppression, such as what Fanon faced while working in Blida-Joinville hospital.

Therefore, Fanon established and practiced a radical ethnopsychiatry rooted in the people he studied, rather than used to exploit indigenous disenfranchised people for his own career goals. He immersed himself in the culture of the people he studied and treated, so he could truly know them. As well, because of the peoples' experiences of colonization, Fanon was aware of the need to also heal and liberate by restoring human dignity to his patients (Bulhan, 1985). He is referenced as describing madness in the Algerian context of oppression and colonization as the pathology of liberty. Fanon's radical ethnopsychiatry was one that explained that his patients' confinement, rejection, and victimization led to mood and anxiety disorders; he also reported phantom hallucinations and delusions that came forth in some of his patients' minds, resulting from their maltreatment. Contemporary research on the brains of humans who have endured hallucinations and delusions during solitary confinement in prisons is a testament to the negative harmful psychological effects on the brain, stemming from such inhumanity (Smith, 2018b). As members of protected status from scientific researchers, incarcerated humans are relatively absent from behavioral neuroscientific research. Certified African-centered psychologists who are known to do ethical work, would make ideal scientists for doing cultural neuroscience research with formerly incarcerated humans, once they are *free* citizens again. This sort of research is likely many years away, because adequate training and certification to ethically conduct such research must be developed among a critical mass of researchers. Yet it is worth the pursuit.

Fanon was unwavering in his mission to correct any misconceptions regarding mental illness among the people of the African Diaspora. He and his colleague, Dr. Sanchez, engaged in cross-cultural psychology by comparing the attitudes of North Africans to that of Europeans regarding mental illness (Bulhan, 1985). They noted differences in how mental illness was viewed in the two cultures. They described Europeans as perceiving mentally ill persons as diseased and in need of isolation from others. North Africans, however, explained the mental illness as stemming from accidental random humans being under the control of certain spirits. The North Africans did not believe the mentally ill should be isolated, distrusted, or punished. They believed aggressive problematic spirits needed to be appeased or confronted. Such cultural aspects of people were not dismissed by Fanon in his advocacy of a more ethno-psychiatry. As with other psychiatrists, Fanon well understood the biological aspects of mental illnesses; however, he advocated for recognition of culture and context as significant for their impact on the patients' brains and the nature of the manifestations of mental illness (Jamison, 2010). Fanon highlighted the need to put mental illness into its socio-historical and cultural perspective, while never losing sight of the human who is taken over by madness.

Ethnopsychiatry also involves the restoration of respect and integrity to indigenous cultures' conception of mental illness, and to their holistic frameworks of engagement with a mentally ill person (Bulhan, 1985). Fanon and his colleague, Dr. Sanchez, advocated for an ethnopsychiatry as a humane psychiatry that reflects care and respect for the human. In contemporary times, the field of psychiatry has been critiqued and viewed with skepticism due to accusations and evidence of inhumane and socially unjust practices with the mentally and emotionally vulnerable (Whitaker & Cosgrove, 2015).

Still Wretched: Solidarity of the Disenfranchised

The explication of what it means to be human has been well-articulated in the literature of African philosophy and Afro communitarianism (Chimakonam & du Toit, 2018). This ideology can be used to explore more deeply what it means to humanize the field of cultural neuroscience as it continues to develop. Those in cultural studies and neuroscience should consider study of the *Ubuntu* worldview and African philosophy. However, to date, neuroscience has not fully recognized the importance of others' history, context, culture, and community for shaping the mind.

Inhumane treatment of others can be further examined by interrogating perceptions and beliefs. What behaviors flow from persons' beliefs about what it means to be human? The focus in neuroscience has remained at the level of the molecular, cellular, and neural circuitry rather than more broadly and deeply understanding humans in community and across their sociocultural histories. Yet, all marginalized peoples of the world, several of whom have been discussed in this book, can be said to represent one community.

When Fanon said everything can be explained to the people, on the condition that you really want them to understand, it was relevant in the past and today. Neuroscience can benefit from greater recognition and understanding of humans' inter-dependent relationships and the implications of this for the central nervous system.

Afro-Communitarianism and African-Centered Consciousness

In the philosophy of Afro-communitarian, personhood comprises the creation of a person through community. Personhood centers ethical behavior, moral duties, and responsibilities. What makes us human, according to Afro-communitarianism, is humans' capacity for self-realization through meaningful, interpersonal relationships (Oelofsen, 2015). Comparatively, when African-centered psychologist Wade Nobles asked the question, what does it mean to be human (Nobles, 2015), his explanation is of consciousness beyond the physical level of the electromagnetic energy of the cells. Nobles' explication of the concept of illumination of the human spirit describes an inner transformation to arrive at a state of illumination. Once humans reach an inner transformation into illuminated consciousness, the types of interpersonal relationships described under Afro-communitarianism is more likely.

What has not been thoroughly explored to date in mainstream neuroscience, are the underlying neural aspects of reaching the consciousness which Nobles (2015) describes. Practitioners and researchers have studied cultural practices such as kundalini yoga, Hatha yoga, and African dance in relationship to higher consciousness and stress reduction as measured by the significance of darkness to consciousness and measuring cortisol levels in saliva (Bynum, 2012; West et al., 2004). Nobles provides a thorough cultural overview of intergenerational African consciousness within the context of the African worldview, stating that consciousness at the human level is always a collective experience passed from one collective generation, or one being to the next, irrespective of geographical location (Nobles, 2015). He stated that the consciousness of each succeeding generation vibrates at a new or changed speed. Nobles' framework regarding consciousness has implications for development of psychosocial justice-based interventions that may disrupt negative environmental pressures such as intergenerational poverty and trauma.

At micro levels of interest, future studies would improve if they were to include more assessment of biomarkers in humans who have experienced chronic social inequality and related changes in consciousness that can be identified via brain imaging technologies (Pitts-Taylor, 2019). Cultural neuroscience involves examination of proteins, genes, brain cells, and tissue as they are impacted by environmental factors such as chronic social inequality. Research investigating families' low versus high socioeconomic status

(SES) has been conducted to examine how the status correlates with children's stress reactions as measured by biomarkers in the children. This research revealed that with body mass index as a moderating variable, children of lower SES families show low grade inflammation detected by elevated C-reactive protein (CRP), a biomarker of chronic stress exposure (Schmeer & Yoon, 2016).

The world is comprised of individualists and collectivists who are interconnected with reciprocal influences on one another. This is increasingly evident when we witness global water risk, pollution, wars, climate change issues, and epidemic human loneliness. The importance of interpersonal relations for the self is vital from the African-centered worldview; this worldview sees the individual as necessarily socially embedded as did Fanon in his ideological framework of radical ethnopsychiatry and liberation. Contrary to what some scholars have expressed, advocacy for Afro-communitarianism need not be regarded as advocacy for the disappearance of the individual as significant (Eze, 2009). The socially embedded human in healthy interpersonal relationships is good for humans' brains, bodies, minds, and spirits.

Marginalized groups who live in different spaces on the planet are not a monolithic group. They do not possess the same socio-histories. However, what they do have in common is that all have the same neuroanatomy and capability for neuroplasticity. Their psychobiology will be shaped by enactment of or exposure to inhumanity, bias, and power as well as exposure to a more optimal healthy psychology of experiences (Myers, 1993; 2003). Attention to the intersectionality of humans' multiple identities and experiences is critical for the field of cultural neuroscience. Writer Audre Lorde has been referenced as stating there is no hierarchy of oppression (Lorde, 1983). In the case of this book's theme, our brains do not rank categories of oppressions because all experiences have potential to impact cellular, molecular, and synaptic levels. Yet, more neuroscience is needed to explore the impact of powerlessness, bias, inhumanity, and cases of resilience across diverse cultural groups. The time is long overdue for neuroscientists and cultural studies scholars to increasingly collaborate to conduct non-Eurocentric focused research.

Chapter Twelve

Future Directions

This final chapter is based on a U.S. working group's BRAIN 2025 report to the advisory committee of the director of the National Institutes of Health (Bargmann & Newsome, 2014). On April 2, 2013, then U.S. president Barack Obama, launched the BRAIN Initiative, an acronym for Brain Research through Advancing Innovative Neurotechnologies. The charge to the working group was to detail a 10-year plan for the acceleration of the development and application of innovative technologies that will aid the construction of dynamic pictures of brain function, including its neuronal and circuit activity over time and space (Bargmann & Newsome, 2014). The charge also emphasized the need for continued interdisciplinary teamwork to reach impressive and innovative neuroscientific goals. The following are listed in the report, as requisite fields for meeting the charge: neuroscience, genetics, physics, engineering, informatics, nanoscience, chemistry, and mathematics. Conspicuously absent is reference to cultural psychology and cultural studies; in just a few places of the 146-page report, one will find cursory mentioning of behavioral scientists' significance to the team of scientists to be involved in the 10-year initiative. Culture is not integral to the objectives for the initiative. Upon close examination of the seven goals of the BRAIN Initiative, it seems that increased perspectives that transcend traditional neuroscientific priorities and traditional western worldviews are needed to deeply address the implications of the brain as a biosocial adaptable organ.

Integrating diverse worldviews and experiences with science, technology, engineering, and math (STEM) is necessary to attract more underrepresented minority students (URM) to interest in STEM research careers. STEM research topics that have attracted more diverse students to STEM pursuits are 1) individualism/collectivism and brain activity, 2) biological markers of same-sex attractionality and identity, 3) atypical patterns in gender identity, and 4) the impact of discrimination-based stress on cardiovascular activity, stress hormones, and immune markers in African-American students (Weekes, 2012). I highlighted each of these STEM research topics in this book. Greater diversity of perspectives has the potential to advance the methods and hypotheses pursued in alignment with the BRAIN initiative's goals. Comparable to Fanon's advocacy for, and practice of a radical ethnopsychiatry, a radical ethno-socio-cultural neuroscience is recommended as future direction for brain research.

BRAIN INITIATIVE 2025: A SCIENTIFIC VISION

The years of the BRAIN Initiative are 2016–2026. As indicated in the report, the first five years of the initiative are dedicated to emphasizing technology development. The second five years will emphasize discovery-driven science. My discussion here will address the areas of the report, including the goals, that may be expanded to advance a radical ethno-sociocultural neuroscience. The process which culminated in the June 2014 BRAIN initiative report began approximately a year earlier in the spring/summer of 2013. The work began with a review of the landscape of the field of neuroscience.

During spring/summer 2013 there were four workshops, 48 expert participants, and time allotted in the process for public commentary. In autumn/winter of 2013 there were conversations, presentations, and feedback obtained from leadership and general membership of the Society for Neuroscience, from other professional neuroscience societies, and from public and private partners. An interim report was produced with research priorities for the fiscal year 2014. The final spring 2014 report contained deliverables, milestones, implementation, and budgets to carry out the BRAIN initiative. A flaw in the process of creating the BRAIN initiative from the perspective of an ethno-cultural neuroscience is the lack of diversity of perspectives that contributed to the report. It is logical that expert participants, leaders of and members of neuroscience-focused societies should be integral to the BRAIN initiative; yet, how can only well-educated, socioeconomically privileged members of a culture set the agenda for brain research into the future, without a deeper engagement with the masses of the most disenfranchised members of the population?

In a section on education, contained in the report, it is briefly mentioned how important it is that non-neuroscientists be educated about neuroscience. Yet no specificity was given for how this might best occur across diverse spaces and groups of humans. As well, alternatively, the report lacks emphasis on the need for neuroscientists to be educated about cultural influences and the brain. Members of all diverse communities have experiences that shape brain processes including the specifics of cellular, molecular, and neural circuit dynamics. Awareness in neuroscience of the experiences of the disenfranchised who have experienced bias, powerlessness, and inhumanity or resiliency, will spark different questions, insights, and neurotechnological advancements to promote innovative research.

Goals

The working group established the following seven goals for the BRAIN 2025 initiative (Bargmann & Newsome, 2014):

Identify and provide experimental access to the different brain cell types to determine their roles in health and disease.

Generate circuit diagrams that vary in resolution from synapses to the whole brain.

Produce a dynamic picture of the functioning brain by developing and applying improved methods for large-scale monitoring of neural activity.

Link brain activity to behavior with precise interventional tools that change neural circuit dynamics.

Produce conceptual foundations for understanding the biological basis of mental processes through development of new theoretical and data analytical tools.

Develop innovative technologies to understand the human brain and treat its disorders; create and support integrated human brain research networks.

Integrate new technological and conceptual approaches produced in goals 1–6 to discover how dynamic patterns of neural activity are transformed into cognition, emotion, perception, and action in health and disease.

Several of the goals are applicable to research questions that may be developed using a radical ethno-cultural neuroscience framework. Yet, wherever behavioral science is referenced in the BRAIN initiative report, it is cursory, lacking consideration of inclusion of more diverse human populations.

Researchers have reported that advances in neuroimaging techniques (such as magnetoencephalography (MEG), electroencephalography (EEG), functional MRI (fMRI), diffusion tensor imaging (DTI), voxel based morphomentry (VBM), and optical imaging, are continuing to bring the field of neuroscience closer to solving the hard problems of consciousness (Brogaard & Gatzia, 2016). Advances in neuroimaging techniques coupled with new developments in theoretical and data analytical tools (Goal 5) may be beneficial for being able to investigate the mind-body spirit connection using more empirical approaches than in the past. Thus, under Goal 5, some of the thoughts and behaviors that contribute to human suffering may be studied with the objective to learn how to disrupt them or prevent them from initiating in the mind. Studying hard problems of consciousness should extend beyond an objective to interrupt the onset of psychiatric diseases such as schizophrenia, mood disorders, and Alzheimer's disease (AD), and improving upon circuit diagrams and deep brain stimulation for Parkinson's disease (PD). AD and PD are serious disorders of neurodegeneration and are the two most common of such diseases (Xie, Gaon, Xun, & Meng, 2014). Thus, it is not surprising that AD and PD are frequently referenced in the working group's BRAIN initiative report. However the question remains as to the likely intersectionality of research participants who will provide data for the future studies that will proliferate from the BRAIN initiative. Will the initiatives beyond 2026 have broad demographic representation of humans for generalizability beyond WEIRD populations (Henrich, Heine, & Norenzayan, 2010)? This remains to be seen.

The experts express in the report, a need for research using a diversity of species. They express the aim to advance research using both human and non-human samples in parallel. Diversity is also stated as a priority regarding the need for neuroscientific experimentation with different cell types (Goal 1). The topics I address in this text are not directly referenced in the BRAIN initiative report, although in several places the working group mentions the relevance of behavioral sciences, and brain and behavior to the scientific vision. Although the report calls for interdisciplinary teams to advance innovative neuro-technologies and discovery-driven science, the thinking has not yet expanded to include radical perspectives and questions non-traditionally regarded as capable of advancing brain research. Arguably, the field of neuroscience (particularly in western society) is still far from incorporating a radical cultural neuroscience that is poised to address the impact of chronic experiences of bias, powerlessness, and inhumane treatment and ongoing challenges in the brain and body, such as from water risk in developing and impoverished locales. However, using large scale monitoring of neural activity (Goal 3) of diverse groups who have experienced such social challenges is important. Some marginalized populations of humans are relatively grossly understudied in neuroscience and in basic and applied psychology.

Ethnic and class identity are socio-cultural, not biological. So, it is not surprising that the theme of *Our Biosocial Brains* may not be viewed as traditionally relevant to neuroscientists who aim to map neural circuits, and measure fluctuating patterns of electrical and chemical activity flowing within neural circuits. Yet it is argued here that cultural studies and neuroscience need one another to advance the work that both aim to do. It is noteworthy too, that animal research remains prevalent in neuroscientific research, such that this too may prove significant regarding the mainstreaming of ethno-radical neuroscientific studies of humans becoming competitive for widespread funding to create a significant paradigm shift.

Repeatedly, the BRAIN initiative report references a need for researchers and medical professionals to understand how fluctuating patterns of electrical and chemical activity flow within neural circuits to create unique cognition and action. A radical cultural neuroscience would be bold enough to include more studies of power, bias, and dehumanization beliefs in cognitive neuroscience. For consideration, what if the future of neuroscientific research might include deeper investigations into racist, sexist, transphobic, or homophobic beliefs? Once such is discovered, suppose it could be followed by use of interventional tools that change neural circuit dynamics related to those negative thoughts? Such questions are not specifically posed in the BRAIN initiative report. However, such research of cognitive biases followed by study of experimentally produced reduction of these biases, might be studied for their relevance to neural circuits. This aligns with Goal 4 of the BRAIN initiative report (Bargmann & Newsome, 2014).

Radical Ethno-Sociocultural Neuroscience

Western traditional neuroscience may be reluctant to delve deeply into a radical ethno-sociocultural neuroscience because of concerns of being labeled race-science (Saini, 2019) or accusations of politicizing supposedly objective science. It is also understandable that people who do not identify as White, middle-class, educated, cis-gender, and heterosexual might be cautious about participating in brain research, given the racist history of biomedical and scientific studies. Yet Wilson (1993) stated that Eurocentric science is commonly presented as apolitical and objective even when it is not. The striving for objectivity is honorable, yet the actuality of this in research has remained elusive when we critically examine the hypotheses and interpretations of findings in scientific research.

Cultural neuroscience (CN) opens the door for a different approach to evaluating the biosocial nature of the brain. As a specific term of use, the approach of CN originated from non-western worldviews. A perusal of westernized departments of neuroscience in the United States do not reveal cultural neuroscience as salient nor specifically named by mainstream neuroscientists. As well, some who have been critical of the western grand narrative in the field of neuroscience, are even still of the opinion that using a term such as "cultural neuroscience" is problematic because it marginalizes the variable of interest, rather than diversifying neuroscience to normalize and incorporate culture (Abiodun, 2019).

However, the journey still lies ahead for culturally salient research to become centered content in neuroscience. Thus, until that time, a push for funding and conferences expressly labeled cultural neuroscience is a need. This can be likened to the year 1968 when the Association of Black Psychologists was created because of the cultural bias and racism existent within the

American Psychological Association. Even today, both associations still exist as independent associations that occasionally collaborate on initiatives. Currently, a relevant area of research to cultural neuroscience in the United States is the work of behavioral scientists who study social neuroscience; social neuroscience has even been a topic of a recent full issue of a peer-reviewed journal (Amodio & Keysers, 2018).

The special issue on social neuroscience includes studies in which different researchers pose the following questions in separately published studies: What can rodents teach us about empathy (Meyza & Knapska, 2018)? Is there a role for interoception in self-other distinction (Palmer & Tsakiris, 2018)? What does neuromodulation and lesion studies tell us about the function of the mirror neuron system and embodied cognition (Keysers, Paracampo & Gazzola, 2018)? What is the role of the lateral prefrontal cortex in moral goal pursuit (Carlson & Crockett, 2018)?

Yet still, a close reading of the above-mentioned studies, reveals that the researchers do not utilize more radical liberatory frameworks in the research, such as what was advocated by Fanon in his radical ethnopsychiatry. The researchers tend to avoid the social implications of their discoveries for disenfranchised marginalized humans. For example, in empathy research using rodents, special emphasis was placed on behavioral paradigms and data regarding the neuronal correlates of emotional contagion (Meyza & Knapska, 2018). Future directions of such research should further explore the human implications of such research, beyond psychiatric disorders, even as these are important too, to address among marginalized humans.

In the Meyza & Knapska study, it was expected that the rodent models might enhance understanding of social deficits in neuropsychiatric disorders, specifically characterized by impairments of empathy. The researchers did not give attention to lack of empathy as it plays out in the social world of non-psychiatric negative human behaviors directed at those perceived as other. Researchers, however, did mention the evolutionary continuity of the empathy trait in humans, yet did not address non-clinical examples of human atrocities against one another, such as what has occurred throughout human history. The special issue did include a study of race-based and status-based human perceptual biases, with discussion of the implications for prejudice reduction interventions (Mattan, Wei, Cloutier, & Kubota, 2018).

There is existing human research of racially biased differences in neural empathic responses (Avenanti, Sirigu, & Aglioti, 2010). For example, using transcranial magnetic stimulation, researchers have explored sensorimotor empathic brain responses. The research participants were of Black and White racial identity. They exhibited implicit but not explicit in-group preference and race-specific autonomic reactivity to the pain of others. When observing the pain of in-group models, there was inhibition of the perceivers' corticospinal system, similarly as if they too were feeling the pain. This was not felt towards individuals culturally marked as an outgroup member based on skin color. There was a strong positive correlation between lack of empathic reactivity and implicit racial bias. Even though humans can show empathy to strangers, racial bias and stereotyping may override this reaction when the person in pain is a member of a specific perceived outgroup. These types of studies increasingly need funding and further exploration using neuro-technologies and discovery-driven science. The radical socio-cultural neuro-science of the future may be able to eliminate racial bias via neuromodula-tion of the structures and circuits that correspond to feelings of disgust, anger, or fear of perceived racial others. The Bargmann & Newsome (2014) groups' BRAIN initiative report suggests such possibilities that align with one of the goals in the report (Goal 6).

Traditional neuroscience, for ethical reasons has had to historically rely upon animal research for experimental advancement of the science. Culture has not been a topic of relevance in this basic neuroscience. In this book, *Our Biosocial Brains*, animal research was not emphasized because of the cen-trality of culture, bias, power, and injustice to the theme. Findings based on animal research, however, were presented in this work where most relevant. For example, animal studies of isolation presented in chapter 9, included inferences about humans' feelings of loneliness based on animals' behaviors following experimentally controlled periods of isolation from other animals. Therefore, it is to be expected that animal research will remain relevant to conclusions to be made within a radical ethno-sociocultural neuroscience

Neuroscientists may be accustomed to thinking about and conducting research at the levels of cellular, molecular, and neural circuitry. Historically, the consideration of culture and the social world's impact on the nervous systems have not been as equitably considered. Mainstream scientists may not expect the cell types under examination during procedures such as elec-tron microscopy to look differently based upon experiences developing in a collectivist versus an individualist culture. Instead, basic traditional neurosci-ence has primarily maintained a focus on the message that humans share the same anatomical circuits, brain regions, and synaptic interactions irrespective of cultural environments.

Contemporary science could do better to emphasize that the pattern of neural connections and interactions of circuits and synapses can vary from person to person. The brain is an adaptable biosocial organ, even to the level of the specifics inside a neuron, and between neurons. Individuals and groups of individuals with shared sociocultural experiences may reflect the impact of shared experiences through their nervous systems. The argument present-ed in this book is not to be equated to race science, nor essentialism, but instead the interaction between nature's and nurture's influences on the ner-vous system. *Our Biosocial Brains* has highlighted epigenetic changes of interest to neuroscientists, with specific attention paid to the psychology of bias, oppression, power, and inhumane treatment for their neural signifi-cance. Scientists are aware that experiential variations produce differences in perception, motivation and emotion, cognition, learning and memory, and behavior. It is time to expand the type of research being done and the ques-tions posed about these variations and resulting effects.

Frantz Fanon has been referred to as a radical revisionist regarding his work in mental health and psychological liberation. *Black Skin, White Masks* and *The Wretched of the Earth* are the more widely known of his books. Fanon was a physician of psychiatry and was not working in the field of neuroscience; yet, he and African-centered psychologists were referenced in *Our Biosocial Brains* because of their outspokenness on behalf of disenfran-chised people of the world, and their advocacy for prioritizing humanity and spirit in the sciences. Most relevant to the information presented in *Our Biosocial Brains*, Fanon used his clinical training to describe the psychology of racism and oppression, detailing how both the oppressed and their oppres-sors become mentally ill because of the racism, dehumanization, and oppres-sion being enacted or received. As scientists envision and implement the BRAIN Initiative 2025, the issues of concern to Fanon decades ago should be integral to brain science.

What is the place of a radical ethno-sociocultural neuroscientific revision-ist in the STEM sciences? Particularly, what is her place in cultural neurosci-ence as a developing field, to promote greater understanding and apprecia-tion of brain research that investigates the brain as a biosocial organ in populations other than western, educated, industrial, rich, democratic cul-tures of humans? What is her role in advancing the work of neuroscientists, by posing new types of questions? What is her role in contributing to the team of chemists, mathematicians, biologists, bioengineers, physicians, and neuroscientists? How can she more greatly enter these scientific fields as well? How can she pursue liberatory work, rather than assimilate into unorig-inal questions and methods of investigation? There is a place for revisionists within the field of neuroscience.

The radical ethno-sociocultural neuroscientist must pursue a different fu-ture for brain research that will seek answers to address power, bias, and inhumane treatment throughout the world. Bioengineers and other scholars have projected rapid and widespread changes in how humans will think, feel, behave, and manifest illness and need for care (Bess, 2016). This is due to advances in cerebral organoid development, more sophisticated imaging technologies, optogenetics, and neural engineering techniques. Humans will also increasingly want to experiment with bio-enhancements (Bess, 2016). Yet what becomes of the most marginalized in the bio-enhanced world of the near future? Will there still be *othering*, but of a different type than we can now imagine? Who will get left behind in the bio-engineered society of the future, based on social status or perhaps even having outdated, non-enhanced neural capabilities? How will those with less, or who are mentally or physically different, be treated in the bio-enhanced world? Bess raises such questions for consideration. Studying sociocultural problems in humans, with the goal of finding interventions that can disrupt harmful patterns of thinking and behaviors is ideal. Imaging such as fMRI or novel research into biomarkers provide promise for displaying significant changes in cortical and subcortical neural activation patterns resulting from epigenetic influences.

Bargmann & Newsome have provided colleagues and the public with a nearly 150-page report of their working group's scientific vision for the future of brain research. In it, they state our brains provide us with the ability to react against injustice and to imagine a different future. The language used in the report is specific in their stated vision, that if carried through as planned, will be monumental. The following is language from the report:

> Finally, we hope through the BRAIN Initiative to create a culture of neuroscience research that emphasizes worldwide collaboration, open sharing of results and tools, mutual education across disciplines, and added value that comes from having many minds address the same questions from different angles. (Bargmann & Newsome, 2014, 19)

The Brain Initiative 2025 also acknowledges the continuing importance of ethics for research participants (human and non-human) and accountability to taxpayers for the expense of the scientific vision. The initiative will require new and distinct funding of $300–$500 million per year. If done in a manner that is ethical, innovative, and inclusive, this is an invaluable investment.

Conclusion

Neuroscience remains a field with limited presence of educators, researchers, and students who do not identify as White and male. However, bringing more diverse people and regions of the world into the field of neuroscience is both exciting as a challenge and goal for the BRAIN Initiative 2025 and beyond. Because of advances in neuro-technologies, there are fewer limits on addressing social problems via science and medicine today, than it was in Fanon's time. There is hope for future expansion of neuroscience. We might look to a field such as economics as an example of openness and growth. Economics now acknowledges the significance of behavioral economics, though once it was marginalized in economics. In time, perhaps cultural neuroscience will become a common and welcome addition within neuroscience, where researchers center the question in their research programs: "What does it mean to be a human with a very biosocial brain?"

References

Aaroe, L., Petersen, M. B., & Arceneaux, K. (2017). The behavioral immune system shapes political intuitions: Why and how individual differences in disgust sensitivity underlie opposition to immigration. *American Political Science Review, 111 (2),* 277–294 doi: https://doi.org/10.1017/S0003055416000770.

Abe, M. O., Koike, T., Okazaki, S., Sugawara, S., Takahashi, K., Watanabe, K., & Sadato, N. (2019). Neural correlates of online cooperation during joint force production. *NeuroImage, 191,* 150–161. https://doi.org/10.1016/j.neuroimage.2019.02.003.

ABC News (November 22, 2016). Standing Rock Sioux Tribe cites history of government betrayal in pipeline fight. Retrieved from, https://www.whas11.com/article/news/nation/standing-rock-sioux-tribe-cites-history-of-government-betrayal-in-pipeline-fight/354893412.

Abiodun S. J. (2019). "Seeing Color," A discussion of the implications and applications of race in the field of neuroscience. *Frontiers in Human Neuroscience.* 13:280. doi: 10.3389/fnhum.2019.00280.

Abutaleb, Y. (2019). What's inside the hate-filled manifesto linked to the alleged El Paso shooter. *Washington Post.* Retrieved from, https://www.washingtonpost.com/politics/2019/08/04/whats-inside-hate-filled-manifesto-linked-el-paso-shooter/?utm_term=.3ff71ba55417 August 16, 2019.

Adams, G., Dobles, I., Gómez, L. H., Kurtiş, T., & Molina, L. E. (2015). Decolonizing psychological science: Introduction to the special thematic section. *Journal of Social and Political Psychology, 3(1),* 213–238. doi:10.5964/jspp.v3i1.564.

Adler, N. E., D. M. Cutler, J. E. Jonathan, S. Galea, M. Glymour, H. K. Koh, & D. Satcher. (2016). Addressing Social Determinants of Health and Health Disparities. Discussion Paper, Vital Directions for Health and Health Care Series. National Academy of Medicine, Washington, DC. https://nam.edu/ wp-content/uploads/2016/09/addressingsocial-determinants-of-health-and-health-disparities.pdf.

Adler, N. E. & Rehkopf, D. H. (2008). U.S. disparities in health: descriptions, causes, and mechanisms. *Annual Review of Public Health, 29,* 235–252. DOI: 10.1146/annurev.publhealth.29.020907.090852.

Agence France-Press. (2018, November 10). Khashoggi corpse dissolved in acid: Report. *Deccan Herald.* https://www.deccanherald.com/international/khashoggi-corpse-went-down-702367.html

Ahmad, Z. (2019). Roughly 2,500 lead service lines left to replace in Flint. *Michigan Live.* https://www.mlive.com/news/flint/2019/04/roughly-2500-lead-service-lines-left-to-replace-in-flint.html .

Ahmad, Z. (2018). Flint again most impoverished city in the nation, new census data shows. *Michigan Live*. https://www.mlive.com/news/flint/2018/09/more_than_half_of_flints_child.html.

Akuno, K. & Nangwaya, A. (2017). *Jackson rising: The struggle for economic democracy and Black self-determination in Jackson, Mississippi*. Montreal, QB: Daraja Press.

Alexander, M. (2012). *The new Jim Crow: Mass incarceration in the age of colorblindness*. New York, NY: The New Press.

American Psychological Association (2010). *Publication manual of the American Psychological Association*. Washington D.C.: American Psychological Association, pg. 74–75.

American Psychological Association (2010). Are your findings 'WEIRD'? *Monitor on Psychology, 41(5)*, 11. https://www.apa.org/monitor/2010/05/weird .

American Psychological Association (August 2005). Legislative efforts to eliminate native-themed mascots, nicknames, and logos: Slow but steady progress post-APA resolution. Retrieved from, https://www.apa.org/pi/oema/resources/communique/2010/08/native-themed-mascots.

Ames, D. L. & Fiske, S. T. (2010). Cultural neuroscience. *Asian Journal of Social Psychology, 13(2)*, 72–82. doi:10.1111/j.1467-839X.2010.01301.x.

Amodio, D. & Keysers, C. (2018). Social neuroscience. *Current Opinion in Psychology, 24*, 1–98. https://doi.org/10.1016/j.copsyc.2018.04.010 .

Anderson, M. & Jiang, J. (2019). Teens, social media & technology 2018. *Pew Research Center*. https://www.pewinternet.org/2018/05/31/teens-social-media-technology-2018/.

Anderson, R. E., McKenny, A. M., Koku, L., & Stevenson, H. C. (2018). EMBRacing racial stress and trauma: Preliminary feasibility and coping responses of a racial socialization intervention. *Journal of Black Psychology, 44(1)*, 25–46. https://doi.org/10.1177/0095798417732930.

Ani, M. (1994). *Yurugu: An African-centered critique of European cultural thought and behavior*. Trenton, NJ: Africa World Press Inc.

Asim, J. (2007). *The N word: Who can say it, who shouldn't, and why*. Boston, MA:Houghton Mifflin.

The Association of Black Psychologists (n.d.). The ABPsi board certification in African centered/Black psychology(CAC/BP). https://www.abpsi.org/programs.html

Avenanti, A., Sirigu, A., & Aglioti, S. M. (2010). Racial bias reduces empathic sensorimotor resonance with other-race pain. *Current Biology, 20 (11)*, 1018–1022. https://doi.org/10.1016/j.cub.2010.03.071.

Azar, B. (2010). Your brain on culture. *Monitor on Psychology. 41 (10)*. Retrieved from, http://www.apa.org/monitor/2010/11/neuroscience.aspx.

Babcock, E. D. (2016). Using brain science to transform human services and increase personal mobility from poverty. *The US Partnership on Mobility from Poverty*. https://www.mobilitypartnership.org/using-brain-science-transform-human-services-and-increase-personal-mobility-poverty.

Babcock, E. D. (2014). Using brain science to design pathways out of poverty. *EMPath Economic Mobility Pathways*. Retrieved from, https://s3.amazonaws.com/empath-website/pdf/Research-UsingBrainScienceDesignPathwaysPoverty-0114.pdf.

Back, L. (2002). Aryans reading Adorno: Cyber-culture and twenty-first-century racism. *Ethnic and Racial Studies, 25, (4)*, 628–651. doi:10.1080/01419870220136664.

Bailey, M. & Trudy (2018). On misogynoir: Citation, erasure, and plagiarism. *Journal of Feminist Media Studies, 18 (4)*, 762–768. https://doi.org/10.1080/14680777.2018.1447395.

Baldwin, J. (2017). *I am not your negro*. Vintage, Media Tie In edition.

Bargmann, C. & Newsome, W. (2014). BRAIN 2025: A scientific vision. Retrieved from, https://braininitiative.nih.gov/sites/default/files/pdfs/brain2025_508c.pdf July 11, 2019.

Barker G. (2005). *Dying to be men: Youth, masculinity and social exclusion*. New York, NY: Routledge.

Barker S. A. (2018). N, N-Dimethyltryptamine (DMT), an endogenous hallucinogen: Past, present, and future research to determine its role and function. *Frontiers in Neuroscience, 12*, 536. doi:10.3389/fnins.2018.00536.

Barnes, S. L. (2013). To welcome or affirm: Black clergy views about homosexuality, inclusivity, and church leadership. *Journal of Homosexuality, 60(10),* 1409–1433. doi: 10.1080/00918369.2013.819204.

Baum, F., MacDougall, C., & Smith, D. (2006). Participatory action research. *Journal of Epidemiology and Community Health. 60 (10),* 854–857. doi:10.1136/jech.2004.028662.

Baumeister, R. F. & Leary, M. R. (1995). The need to belong, desire for interpersonal attachments as a fundamental human motivation. *Psychological Bulletin, 117,* 497–529. http://dx.doi.org/10.1037/0033-2909.117.3.497.

BBC News (January 10, 2018). Harvey Weinstein scandal: Who has accused him of what? *BBC.* Retrieved from, https://www.bbc.com/news/entertainment-arts-41580010 August 17, 2019.

Bellinger, D. C. (2012). A strategy for comparing the contributions of environmental chemicals and other risk factors to neurodevelopment of children. *Environmental Health Perspectives, 120 (4),* 501–507. doi: 10.1289/ehp.1104170.

Bendixen, M. & Gabriel, U. (2013). Social judgment of aggressive language: Effects of target and sender sex on the evaluation of slurs. *Scandinavian Journal of Psychology, 54(3),* 236–242. doi: 10.1111/sjop.12039.

Berger, A. A. (2000). The meanings of culture. *M/C: A Journal of Media and Culture 3(2).* Retrieved from http://www.api-network.com/mc/0005/meaning.php.

Berman, M. (2017, June 17). Minnesota officer acquitted in shooting of Philando Castile during traffic stop, dismissed from police force. The Washington Post. https://www.washingtonpost.com/news/post-nation/wp/2017/06/16/minn-officer-acquitted-of-manslaughter-for-shooting-philando-castile-during-traffic-stop/

Bertolini, M. (2019). Antogo: The sacred Dogon fishing ritual. *Reportage.* https://www.reportage.co.uk/featured-stories/antogo-the-sacred-dogon-fishing-ritual/.

Bertrand, N. & Sterbenz, C. (2015, June 23). Official autopsy reveals Freddie Gray died from a single 'high-energy injury' like those seen in shallow-water diving incidents. Business Insider. https://www.businessinsider.com/freddie-gray-autopsy-is-released-2015-6

Bess, M. (2016)*. Our grandchildren redesigned: Life in the bioengineered society of the near future.* Boston, Massachusetts. Beacon Press.

Blanchett, W. J. (2006). Disproportionate representation of African American students in special education: Acknowledging the role of white privilege and racism. *Educational Researcher, 35(6),* 24–28. https://doi.org/10.3102/0013189X035006024 .

Blanchette, I. & Richards, A. (2010). The influence of affect on higher level cognition: A review of research on interpretation, judgement, decision making, and reasoning. *Cognition and Emotion, 24(4),* 561–595. https://doi.org/10.1080/02699930903132496.

Blazina, C., Eddins, R., Burridge, A., & Settle, A. G. (2007). The relationship between masculinity ideology, loneliness, and separation-individuation difficulties. *Journal of Men's Studies,15 (1),* 101–109. https://doi.org/10.3149/jms.1501.101.

Blinder, A. & Sack, K. (January 10, 2017). Dylann Roof is sentenced to death in Charleston church massacre. *The New York Times.* Retrieved from https://www.nytimes.com/2017/01/10/us/dylann-roof-trial-charleston.html.

Boksem, M. A. S., Smolders, R., & De Cremer, D. (2012). Social power and approach-related neural activity. *Social Cognitive & Affective Neuroscience,7,* 516–520. doi:10.1093/scan/nsp006.

Boksem M. A. S., Tops M., Wester A. E., Meijman T. F., & Lorist, M. M. (2006). Error-related ERP components and individual differences in punishment and reward sensitivity. *Brain Research, 1101,* 92–101.

Bondy, S. C. & Campbell, A. (2017). Water quality and brain function. *International Journal of Environmental Research and Public Health, 15(1),* 2. doi:10.3390/ijerph15010002 https://www.ncbi.nlm.nih.gov/pmc/articles/PMC5800103/.

Bonvillian, C. (2018, September 14). Bakersfield mass shooter believed wife cheated on him, court documents say. AJC. https://www.ajc.com/news/national/bakersfield-mass-shooter-believed-wife-cheated-him-court-documents-say/Ibt8va2Lsdta0d6PYyLAKM/

Boyd, R. (December 2006). The puzzle of human sociality. *Science, 314,* 1555–1556. http://xcelab.net/rm/wp-content/uploads/2008/10/boyd-evolution-human-cooperation-review.pdf.

Brannon, R. (1985). A scale measuring attitudes about masculinity. In A. G. Sargent (Ed.), *Beyond sex roles* (pp. 1–48). St. Paul, MN: West.

Bremner J. D. (2006). Traumatic stress: Effects on the brain. *Dialogues in Clinical Neuroscience, 8(4)*, 445–461.

Brogaard, B. & Gatzia, D. E. (2016). What can neuroscience tell us about the hard problem of consciousness? *Frontiers in neuroscience, 10*, 395. doi:10.3389/fnins.2016.00395.

Brown, S. & Fischer, K. (2017). A dying town. *The Chronicle of Higher Education,* Retrieved from https://www.chronicle.com/interactives/public-health.

Brulle, R. J. & Pellow, D. N. (2006). Environmental justice: Human health and environmental inequalities. *Annual Review of Public Health, 27,* 103–124. doi: 10.1146/annurev.publhealth.27.021405.102124.

Buck, D. M., & Nedvin, M. A. (2017). The impact of mating motives on anti- transgender prejudice. North American Journal of Psychology, 19(3), 641–658.

Budkin, D. M. & Nedvin, M. A. (2017). The impact of mating motives on anti-transgender prejudice. *North American Journal of Psychology, 19(3),* 641–658.

Bulhan, H. A. (1985). *Frantz Fanon and the psychology of oppression.* Springer Science+Business Media: New York, NY.

Burgest, D. R. (1973). The racist use of the English language. *The Black Scholar, 5(1),* 37–45.

Business Wire. (December 4, 2016). Energy Transfer Partners and Sunoco Logistics Partners respond to the statement from the Department of the Army. *Business Wire.* Retrieved from, https://www.businesswire.com/news/home/20161204005090/en/Energy-Transfer-Partners-Sunoco-Logistics-Partners-Respond February 9, 2019.

Butts H. F. (1979). Frantz Fanon's contribution to psychiatry: The psychology of racism and colonialism. *Journal of the National Medical Association, 71(10),* 1015–1018.

Bwoya, T. (n.d.). Listening to the spirit of water. *Center for Humans and Nature.* Retrieved from, https://www.humansandnature.org/listening-to-the-spirit-of-water June 30th 2019.

Byne, W. (2014). Forty years after the removal of homosexuality from the DSM: Well on the way but not there yet. *LGBT Health,1(2),* 1–3. https://doi.org/10.1089/lgbt.2014.1504.

Bynum, E. B. (2013). *Why darkness matters: The power of melanin in the brain, 2nd ed.* Scotts Valley, CA: CreateSpace Independent Publishing Platform.

Byrne, R. W. & Whiten, A. (Eds.). (1988). *Machiavellian intelligence: Social expertise and the evolution of intellect in monkeys, apes, and humans.* New York, NY, US: Clarendon Press/ Oxford University Press.

Cacioppo, J. T., Chen, H. Y., & Cacioppo, S. (2017). Reciprocal influences between loneliness and self-centeredness: A cross-lagged panel analysis in a population-based sample of African American, Hispanic, and Caucasian adults. *Personality and Social Psychology Bulletin, 43(8),* 1125–1135. https://doi.org/10.1177/0146167217705120.

Cacioppo S., Capitanio J. P., & Cacioppo, J. T. (2014). Toward a neurology of loneliness. *Psychological Bulletin. 140(6),* 1464–1504. doi: 10.1037/a0037618.

Cahill, L., Prins, B., Weber, M., & McGaugh, J. L. (1994). Beta-adrenergic activation and emotional memory for events. *Nature 371*:702–204 doi: 10.1038/371702a0.

Calmore, J. O. (2005). Whiteness as audition and Blackness as performance: Status protest from the margin. *Washington University Journal of Law and Policy,* 18. https://openscholarship.wustl.edu/cgi/viewcontent.cgi?referer=&httpsredir=1&article=1257&context=law_journal_law_policy

Campbell, C. (September 3, 2018). This land is my land takes a different view of the wild west than red dead redemption. Retrieved from, https://www.polygon.com/2018/9/3/17800798/this-land-is-my-land-preview-native-american-western-stealth-game .

Campbell, P. (2018). Occupy, Black lives matter and suspended mediation: Young people's battles for recognition in/between digital and non-digital spaces. *Young, 26(2),* 145–160.

Carbon, C. C. (2014). Understanding human perception by human-made illusions. Frontiers in Human Neuroscience, https://www.frontiersin.org/articles/10.3389/fnhum.2014.00566/full

Carlson, R. W. & Crockett, M. J. (2018). The lateral prefrontal cortex and moral goal pursuit. *Current Opinion in Psychology, 24,* 77–82. doi: 10.1016/j.copsyc.2018.09.007.

Carucci, J. (2017). Michael Moore says Flint crisis would be solved if it were elsewhere. *Detroit Free Press.* https://www.freep.com/story/news/local/michigan/flint-water-crisis/2017/10/24/michael-moore-flint-water-crisis/797208001/.

Carver, C. S. & White, T. L. (1994). Behavioral-inhibition, behavioral activation, and affective responses to impending reward and punishment the BIS BAS scales. *Journal of Personality and Social Psychology, 67,* 319–333. https://doi.org/10.1037/0022-3514.67.2.319.

Center for the Study of Hate and Extremism (2019). Report to the nation: 2019 factbook on hate and extremism in the U.S. & internationally. Retrieved from, https://csbs.csusb.edu/sites/csusb_csbs/files/CSHE%202019%20Report%20to%20the%20Nation%20FINAL%207.29.19%2011%20PM.pdf.

Centers for Disease Control and Prevention. (2012). Lead in drinking water and human blood lead levels in the United States. *MMWR, 61(Suppl):*1–10. https://www.cdc.gov/mmwr/pdf/other/su6104.pdf.

Chaitlin, D. (2018, October 21). Trump campaign holding 'Big Texas Tailgater,' claims '100,000+' flocking to Houston rally. Washington Examiner. https://www.washingtonexaminer.com/news/trump-campaign-holding-big-texas-tailgater-claims-100-000-flocking-to-houston-rally

Chee, M., Zheng, H, Goh, J. O., Park, D., & Sutton, B. P. (2011). Brain structure in young and old East Asians and Westerners: Comparisons of structural volume and cortical thickness. *Journal of Cognitive Neuroscience, 23(5),* 1065–1079. https://doi.org/10.1162/jocn.2010.21513.

China Daily/Asia News Network (2018). China's anti-poverty campaign on track, aims to help more people. *The Straits Times.* https://www.straitstimes.com/asia/east-asia/chinas-anti-poverty-campaign-on-track-aims-to-help-more-people.

Chiao, J. Y. (2009). Cultural neuroscience: a once and future discipline. *Progress in Brain Research.* Elsevier Press, Oxford, UK. Retrieved from, http://www.lphslibrary.org/uploads/7/2/9/6/7296009/ib_psych_1.pdf.

Chiao, J. Y., Hariri, A. R., Harada, T., Mano, Y., Sadato, N., Parrish, T. B., & Iidaka, T. (2010). Theory and methods in cultural neuroscience. *Social Cognitive and Affective Neuroscience, 5 (2–3),* 356–361. https://doi.org/10.1093/scan/nsq063.

Chimakonam, J. O. & du Toit, L. (2018). *African philosophy and the epistemic marginalization of women.* United Kingdom: Routledge Taylor & Francis.

Clay, R. A. (2015). Eliminating class bias. *Monitor on Psychology, 46 (7),* 82 Retrieved from https://www.apa.org/monitor/2015/07-08/eliminating-bias.

Corbetta, M. & Shulman, G. L. (2002). Control of goal-directed and stimulus-driven attention in the brain. *Nature Reviews Neuroscience, 3(3),* 201–215. doi: 10.1038/nrn755.

Coste, C. P. & Kleinschmidt, A. (2016). Cingulo-opercular network activity maintains alertness. *Neuroimage,128,* 264–272. https://doi.org/10.1016/j.neuroimage.2016.01.026.

Cox, J. W., Bui, L., & Brown, D. L. (2015, December 16). Who was Freddie Gray and how did his death lead to a mistrial in baltimore? The Washington Post. https://www.washingtonpost.com/local/who-was-freddie-gray-and-how-did-his-death-lead-to-a-mistrial-in-baltimore/2015/12/16/b08df7ce-a433-11e5-9c4e-be37f66848bb_story.html

Cox, J. W., Clement, S., & Vargas, T. (2016). New poll finds 9 in 10 Native Americans aren't offended by Redskins name. *The Washington Post.* Retrieved from, https://www.washingtonpost.com/local/new-poll-finds-9-in-10-native-americans-arent-offended-by-redskins-name/2016/05/18/3ea11cfa-161a-11e6-924d-838753295f9a_story.html August 16 2019.

Craig, A. D. (2009). How do you feel—now? The anterior insula and human awareness. *Nature reviews. Neuroscience, 10 (1),* 59–70 PMID: 19096369.

Croom, A. M. (2015). Slurs, stereotypes, and in-equality: A critical review of "How Epithets and Stereotypes are Racially Unequal." *Language Sciences, 52,* 139–154. doi: 10.1016/j.langsci.2014.03.001.

Croom, A. M. (2014). The semantics of slurs: A refutation of pure expressivism. *Language Sciences, 41(PT B),* 227–242. http://dx.doi.org/10.1016/j.langsci.2013.07.003.

Croom, A. M. (2013). How to do things with slurs: Studies in the way of derogatory words. *Language & Communication, 33,* 177–204. http://dx.doi.org/10.1016/j.langcom.2013.03

.008.

Croom, A. M. (2011). Slurs. *Language Sciences, 33(3)*, 343–358. doi:10.1016/j.langsci.2010.11.005.

Cross, E. J., Overall, N. C., Low, R. S., & McNulty, J. K. (2019). An Interdependence Account of Sexism and Power: Men's hostile sexism, biased perceptions of low power, and relationship aggression. Journal of Personality and Social Psychology: Interpersonal Relations and Group Processes, 117, (2) https://doi.org/10.1037/pspi0000167

Cross, W. E., Jr. (1971). The Negro-to-Black conversion experience. *Black World, 20, 9*, 13–27.

Currie, J. & Schwandt, H. (2016). Mortality inequality: The good news from a county-level approach. *The Journal of Economic Perspectives, 30(2)*, 29–52. doi: 10.1257/jep.30.2.29.

Daniels, D. (May 4, 2014). *You're not a black gay man, stop jacking our slang*. http://www.musedmagonline.com/2014/05/youre-black-gay-man-stop-jacking-slang/.

Daniels, K. M. (2016). The coolness of cleansing: Sacred waters, medicinal plants and ritual baths of Haiti and Peru. *ReVista: Harvard Review of Latin America, 16(1)*, special edition on the Biology of Culture, 21–24. https://revista.drclas.harvard.edu/book/coolness-cleansing-sacred-waters-medicinal-plants-and-ritual-baths-haiti-and-peru-0.

Dasen, P. R. (2012). Emics and etics in cross-cultural psychology: Towards a convergence in the study of cognitive styles. In T. M. S. Tchombe, A. B. Nsamenang, H. Keller & M. Fülöp (Eds.), *Cross-cultural psychology: An Africentric perspective*. (pp. 55–73). (Proceedings of the 4th Africa Region Conference of the IACCP, University of Buea, Cameroun, August 1–8, 2009). Limbe, Cameroun: Design House. http://www.unige.ch/fapse/SSE/teachers/dasen/home/pages/emicsandetics.pdf.

DataUsa.io (n.d.). Forsyth county, NC. https://datausa.io/profile/geo/forsyth-county-nc#about.

Davis, M. (June 18, 2017). Deadly shooters prowled the streets targeting policemen and pregnant women. *Lifedeathprizes*. https://www.lifedeathprizes.com/real-life-crime/washington-sniper-john-lee-muhammad-23666.

Dekok, D. (September 25, 2018). Bill Cosby, in cuffs, imprisoned for up to 10 years for sexual assault. *Reuters*. https://www.reuters.com/article/us-people-cosby/bill-cosby-in-cuffs-imprisoned-for-up-to-10-years-for-sexual-assault-idUSKCN1M5190.

Deterville, A. (2016). African-centered transpersonal self in diaspora and psycho-spiritual wellness: A Sankofa Perspective. *International Journal of Transpersonal Studies, 35(1)*, 118–128.

De Vignemont, F. & Singer, T. (2006). The empathic brain: how, when and why? *Trends in Cognitive Sciences, 10(10)*, 435–441. doi: 10.1016/j.tics.2006.08.008.

Dikker, S., Wan, L., Davidesco, I., Kaggen, L., Oostrik, M., . . . et al. (2017). Brain-to-brain synchrony tracks real-world dynamic group interactions in the classroom. *Current Biology, 27(9)*, 1375–1380. doi: 10.1016/j.cub.2017.04.002. Epub 2017.

Diringer, S., Thebo, A., Cooley, H., Wilkinson, R. . . . et al. (2019). *Moving toward a multi-benefit approach for water management*. Oakland, CA: Pacific Institute. https://pacinst.org/wp-content/uploads/2019/04/moving-toward-multi-benefit-approach.pdf.

Dosenbach, N. et al. (2008). A dual-networks architecture of top-down control. *Trends in Cognitive Science, 12(3)*, 99–105. doi:10.1016/j.tics.2008.01.001.

dos Santos, R. G., Osório, F. L., Crippa, J. A. S., and Hallak, J. E. C. (2016). Classical hallucinogens and neuroimaging: A systematic review of human studies. Hallucinogens and neuroimaging. *Neuroscience & Biobehavioral Reviews, 71*, 715–728. doi: 10.1016/j.neubiorev.2016.10.026.

Dowd, K. (November 30, 2016). Standing Rock activists asking white people to stop treating pipeline protest like Burning Man. *San Francisco Chronicle*. Retrieved from, https://www.sfgate.com/news/article/Standing-Rock-protest-white-people-Burning-Man-10640250.php August 13 2019.

Dreshcher, J. (2010). Queer diagnoses: Parallels and contrasts in the history of homosexuality, gender variance, and the Diagnostic and Statistical Manual. *Archives of Sexual Behavior, 39*, 427–460. doi: 10.1007/s10508-009-9531-5.

Dunbar, R. I. M. & Schultz, S. (2007). Evolution in the social brain. *Science, 317(5843)*, 1344–1347. doi: 10.1126/science.1145463.

Eberhardt, J. (2019). Biased: *Uncovering the hidden prejudice that shapes what we see, think, and do.* New York, New York: Viking.

Elliott, R., Dolan, R. J., & Frith, C. D. (2000). Dissociable functions in the medial and lateral orbitofrontal cortex: Evidence from human neuroimaging studies. *Cerebral Cortex, 10(3),* 308–317. doi: 10.1093/cercor/10.3.308.

Emejulu, A. & McGregor, C. (2019). Towards a radical digital citizenship in digital education. *Critical Studies in Education, 60 (1),* 131–147, DOI: 10.1080/17508487.2016.1234494.

Engber, D. (October 6, 2017). Mass shooters aren't disproportionately White. *Slate.* https://slate.com/news-and-politics/2017/10/what-the-white-mass-shooter-myth-gets-right-and-wrong-about-killers-demographics.html.

Esch, T. & Stefano, G. B. (2011). The neurobiological link between compassion and love. *Medical Science Monitor, 17(3),* RA65–75 doi: 10.12659/MSM.881441.

Escobar, G. J., Liljestrand, P., Hudes, E. S., Ferriero, D. M., Wu, Y. W., Jeremy, R. J., & Newman, T. B. (2007). Five-year neurodevelopmental outcome of neonatal dehydration. *The Journal of Pediatrics, 151(2),* 127–133.e1. doi:10.1016/j.jpeds.2007.03.009.

Eversley, M. (October 29, 2016). Dakota Access pipeline protests draw contrasts to Bundy. *USA Today.* Retrieved from, https://www.usatoday.com/story/news/2016/10/28/dakota-access-pipeline-protests-continue-questions-fairness-emerge/92913148/ October 31 2018.

Eze, M. O. (2009). What is African communitarianism? Against consensus as a regulative ideal. *South African Journal of Philosophy, 27(4),* 386–399. DOI: 10.4314/sajpem.v27i4.31526.

Fagot, B. I., Rodgers, C. S., & Leinbach, M. D. (2000). Theories of gender socialization. In T. Eckes & H. M. Trautner (Eds.), *The Developmental Social Psychology of Gender* (pp. 65–89), Psychology Press, Danvers, MA.

Fairman, C. (February 14, 2010). Saying it is hurtful. Banning it is worse. *Washington Post,* B01.

Fanon, F. (2008). *Black skin, white masks.* London: Pluto Press. (Originally published 1952).

Fanon, F. (2005). *Wretched of the earth.* Grove Press. New York, NY. (Originally published 1961).

Farfán-Santos, E. (2011). Quilombolismo: Fighting and dying for rights. *Trans-scripts (1),* 131–151. Retrieved from http://sites.uci.edu/transscripts/files/2014/10/2011_01_10.pdf.

FCC (Federal Communications Commission) (January 14, 2013). *Consumer guide: Obscene, indecent, and profane broadcasts.* http://transition.fcc.gov/cgb/consumerfacts/obscene.pdf.

Fessler, D. M. T., Holbrook, C., & Gervais, M. M. (2014). Men's physical strength moderates conceptualizations of prospective foes in two disparate societies. Human Nature, 25(3), 393–409. https://doi.org/10.1007/s12110-014-9205-4

Fischman, G. E. (2000). *Imagining teachers: Rethinking gender dynamics in teacher education.* Lanham, MD: Rowan & Littlefield.

Forliti, A. (2017, June 26). Philando Castile's family reaches $3M settlement in death. Associated Press. https://apnews.com/d89912f174fa4f7ebec977629216adc1

France-Press. A. (November 3, 2018). Jamal Khashoggi's body was 'dissolved' after murder as 'biological evidence' in Saudi consulate's garden is cited. *South China Morning Post,* Retrieved from https://www.scmp.com/news/world/middle-east/article/2171503/kashoggis-body-was-dissolved-after-murder-turkish-official.

Freeman, J. B., Rule, N. O., & Ambady, N. (2009). The cultural neuroscience of person perception. *Progress in Brain Research, 178,* 191–201. doi: 10.1016/S0079-6123(09)17813-5.

French, J. H. (2013). Rethinking police violence in Brazil: Unmasking the public secret of race. *Latin American Politics and Society, 55(4),* 161–181. doi: https://doi.org/10.1111/j.1548-2456.2013.00212.x.

Frith, C. D. & Frith, U. (2006). The neural basis of mentalizing. *Neuron, 50 (4),* 531–534. doi:https://doi.org/10.1016/j.neuron.2006.05.001.

Fulton, B. R. (2011). Black churches and HIV/AIDS: Factors influencing congregations' responsiveness to social issues. *Journal for the Scientific Study of Religion, 50(3),* 617–630. Retrieved from, https://onlinelibrary.wiley.com/doi/pdf/10.1111/j.1468-5906.2011.01579.x.

Gadit, A. A. (2003). Ethnopsychiatry: A review. *Journal of the Pakistan Medical Association, 53 (10)*, https://jpma.org.pk/article-details/285.

Galinsky, A. D., Magee, J. C., Inesi, M. E. & Gruenfeld, D. H. (2006). Power and perspectives not taken. Psychological Science , 17 (12), 1068–1074. https://doi.org/10.1111/j.1467-9280.2006.01824.x.

Galinsky, A. D., Gruenfeld D. H., & Magee, J. C. (2003). From power to action. *Journal of Personality and Social Psychology, 85*, 453–466.

García-Sesnich, J. N., Flores, M. G., Ríos, M. H., & Aravena, J. G. (2017). Longitudinal and immediate effect of Kundalini Yoga on salivary levels of cortisol and activity of alpha-amylase and its effect on perceived stress. *International Journal of Yoga, 10(2)*, 73–80. doi:10.4103/ijoy.IJOY_45_16.

Garrett, P. & Baquedano-Lopez, P. (2002). Language socialization: Reproduction and continuity, transformation and change. *Annual Review of Anthropology, 31*, 339–361. doi: 10.1146/annurev.anthro.31.040402.085352.

Gavrilets, S.& Vose, A. (2006). The dynamics of Machiavellian intelligence. *Proceedings of the National Academy of Sciences, 103(45)*, 16823–16828 https://doi.org/10.1073/pnas.0601428103.

Gay and Lesbian Alliance Against Defamation (2010). *Media reference guide, 8th edition.* Retrieved from, http://www.glaad.org/files/MediaReferenceGuide2010.pdf?id=99.

Gibson, J. J. (1979). *The ecological approach to visual perception.* Boston, MA: Houghton Mifflin.

Gilman, S. L. & Thomas, J. M. (2016). *Are racists crazy? How prejudice, racism, and anti-semitism became markers of insanity.* New York, NY: New York University Press.

Glick, P. & Fiske, S. T. (1997). Hostile and benevolent sexism: Measuring ambivalent sexist attitudes toward women. *Psychology of Women Quarterly, 21(1)*, 119–135. doi: 10.1111/j.1471-6402.1997.tb00104.x.

Goff, P. A., Eberhardt, J., Williams, M. J., & Jackson, M. C. (2008). Not Yet Human: Implicit knowledge, historical dehumanization, and contemporary consequences. Journal of Personality and Social Psychology, 94 (2), 292-306. https://web.stanford.edu/~eberhard/downloads/2008-NotYetHuman.pdf

Goldstein, A., Sanchez, R., & Fletcher, M. A. (April 23, 1999). In choosing victims, gunmen showed their prejudice. *Washington Post.* Retrieved from https://www.washingtonpost.com/archive/politics/1999/04/23/in-choosing-victims-gunmen-showed-their-prejudice/15522b06-bb4f-4aa6-a513-6cf9b0de91d0/.

Gonzalez, S., France, R., & Melas, C. (October 4, 2018). The year since the Weinstein scandal first rocked Hollywood. *CNN.* Retrieved from, https://www.cnn.com/2018/04/05/entertainment/weinstein-timeline/index.html.

Gramlich, J. (2019). 10 facts about Americans and Facebook. *Pew Research Center.* https://www.pewresearch.org/fact-tank/2019/05/16/facts-about-americans-and-facebook/.

Grant, J. M. et al. (2011). *Injustice at every turn: A report of the national transgender discrimination survey.* Washington: National Center for Transgender Equalityand National Gay and Lesbian Task Force. https://www.transequality.org/sites/default/files/docs/resources/NTDS_Report.pdf.

Greene, V. (2019). "Deplorable" satire: Alt-right memes, white genocide tweets, and redpilling normies. *Studies in American Humor, 5(1)*, 231–69. doi:10.5325/studamerhumor.5.1.0031.

Greicius, M. D., Krasnow, B., Reiss, A. L., & Menon, V. (2003). Functional connectivity in the resting brain: A network analysis of the default mode hypothesis. *Proceedings of the National Academy of Sciences of the United States of America, 100*, 253–258. doi: 10.1073/pnas.0135058100.

Greicius, M. D., Srivastava, G., Reiss, A. L., & Menon, V.(2004). Default-mode network activity distinguishes Alzheimer's disease from healthy aging: Evidence from functional MRI. *Proceedings of the National Academy of Sciences of the United States of America, 101*, 4637–4642. doi: 10.1073/pnas.0308627101.

Grills, C. (2013). The context, perspective, and mission of ABPsi past and present. *The Journal of Black Psychology.* 39(3), 276–283. https://doi.org/10.1177/0095798413480685.

Guinote A. (2007). Power and goal pursuit. *Personality and Social Psychology Bulletin, 33*, 1076–1087.

Gusnard, D. A., Akbudak, E., Shulman, G. L., & Raichle, M. E. (2001). Medial prefrontal cortex and self-referential mental activity: Relation to a default mode of brain function. *Proceedings of the National Academy of Sciences of the United States of America, 98*, 4259–4264. doi: 10.1073/pnas.071043098.

Guthrie, J. T., Coddington, C. S., & Wigfield, A. (2009). Profiles of motivation for reading among African American and Caucasian students. *Journal of Literacy Research, 41(3)*, 317–353. doi:10.1080/10862960903129196.

Guthrie, R. V. (2004). Even the rat was white: A historical view of psychology (2nd ed.). Pearson Education. (Originally published 1976)

Haas, L. (2017, October 18). The origin of others by Toni Morrison review – the language of race and racism. The Guardian.https://www.theguardian.com/books/2017/oct/18/origin-of-others-toni-morrison-review

Haggins, K. & Jackson, T. (2016). Community defined practice: Emotional emancipation circles CIBHS evidence-based practices symposium. California Institute for Behavioral Health Solutions (CIBHS). Retrieved from, https://www.cibhs.org/sites/main/files/file-attachments/thurs_400_terrace_jackson_eec_pres_for_ebp_symposium_haggins_and_jackson.pdf.

Haider, S. (2016). The shooting in Orlando, terrorism or toxic masculinity (or both?). *Men and Masculinities, 19(5)*, 555–565. https://doi.org/10.1177/1097184X16664952.

Halberstadt, J., Sherman, S., & Sherman, J. (2010 epub). Why Barack Obama Is Black: A cognitive account of hypodescent. Psychological Science, 22(1), 29-33. https://doi.org/ 10.1177/0956797610390383

Hall, W. J., Chapman, M. V., Lee, K. M., Merino, Y. M., Thomas, T. W., Payne, B. K., . . . Coyne-Beasley, T. (2015). Implicit racial/ethnic bias among health care professionals and its influence on health care outcomes: A systematic review. *American Journal of Public Health, 105(12)*, e60–e76. doi:10.2105/AJPH.2015.302903.

Hamid, N., Pretus, C., Atran, S., Crockett, M. J., . . . et al. (2019). Neuroimaging "will to fight" for sacred values: An empirical case study with supporters of an Al Qaeda associate. *Royal Society Open Science, 6,* Retrieved from, https://royalsocietypublishing.org/doi/10.1098/rsos.181585.

Han, S., Northoff, G., Vogeley, K., Wexler, B. E., Kitayama, S. & Varnum, M. E. W. (2013). A Cultural neuroscience approach to the biosocial nature of the human brain. *Annual Review of Psychology. 64,* 335–359. doi: 10.1146/annurev-psych-071112-054629.

Haney, D. (March 9, 2017). Contractor nearly finished $1 million clean-up of pipeline protest camps. *KFGO.* Retrieved from, https://kfgo.com/news/articles/2017/mar/09/contractor-nearly-finished-1-million-clean-up-of-pipeline-protest-camps/ March 27, 2018.

Hansen, R. & Mendius, R. (2009). *Buddha's brain: The practical neuroscience of happiness, love, & wisdom.* Oakland, CA: New Harbinger Publications, Inc.

Hari, R., Henriksson, L. Malinen, S., & Parkkonen, L. (2015). Centrality of social interaction in human brain function. *Neuron, 88(1)*, 181–193. https://doi.org/10.1016/j.neuron.2015.09. 022 .

Harmer, C., Perrett, D. I., Cowen, P., & Goodwin, G. (2001). GM Administration of the beta-adrenoceptor blocker propranolol impairs the processing of facial expressions of sadness. Psychopharmacology, 154, 383-389. DOI: 10.1007/s002130000654

Harrell, J. (1999). *Manichean psychology.* Washington D.C.: Howard University Press.

Harris, L. T., & Fiske, S. T. (2006). Dehumanizing the Lowest of the Low: Neuroimaging responses to extreme out-groups. Psychological Science, 17(10), 847–853. https://doi.org/ 10.1111/j.1467-9280.2006.01793.x

Harrison-Quintana, J. & Lettman-Hicks, S. (2011). *Injustice at every turn: A look at Black respondents in the national transgender discrimination survey.* Washington: National Center for Transgender Equality and National Gay and Lesbian Task Force. https:// www.transequality.org/sites/default/files/docs/resources/ntds_black_respondents_2.pdf.

Hart, W. D. (2018). Constellations: Capitalism, antiblackness, Afro-pessimism, and black optimism. *American Journal of Theology & Philosophy, 39(1)*, 5–33. doi:10.5406/amerjtheophil.39.1.0005.

Harte, J. (October 5, 2016). Federal appeals court hears arguments over Dakota Access pipeline. *Reuters*. Retrieved from https://www.reuters.com/article/us-usa-pipeline-nativeamericans-hearing-idUSKCN12529S. October 14, 2018.

Hawkins, D. (July 31, 2017). "I don't care, she dying": Comedian Lil Duval says he would kill a sexual partner if he learned she was a transgender woman. *Washington Post*, Retrieved from https://www.washingtonpost.com/news/morning-mix/wp/2017/07/31/i-dont-care-she-dying-comedian-lil-duval-says-he-would-kill-a-sexual-partner-if-he-learned-she-was-transgender/.

Hellon, R. F. & Lind, A. R. (1956). Observations on the activity of sweat glands with special reference to the influence of ageing. *The Journal of Physiology, 133 (1)*, 132–44. DOI: 10.1113/jphysiol.1956.sp005571.

Henrich, J., Heine, S. J., & Norenzayan, A. (2010). The weirdest people in the world? *The Behavioral and Brain Sciences, 33,* 61–83. doi:10.1017/S0140525X0999152X.

Hilton, B. T. (2011). Frantz Fanon and colonialism: A psychology of oppression. *Journal of Scientific Psychology, 45–59*. Retrieved from, http://www.psyencelab.com/uploads/5/4/6/5/5465091/frantz_fanon_and_colonialism.pdf.

Hinton, P. (2017). Implicit stereotypes and the predictive brain: Cognition and culture in "biased" person perception. *Palgrave Communication 3,* 17086 doi:10.1057/palcomms.2017.86.

Hirschfelder, A. & Molin, P. F. (February 22, 2018). I is for ignoble: Stereotyping Native Americans. Retrieved from https://www.ferris.edu/HTMLS/news/jimcrow/native/homepage.htm.

Hoffman, K. M., Trawalter, S., Axt, J. R., & Oliver, M. N. (2016). Racial bias in pain assessment and treatment recommendations, and false beliefs about biological differences between blacks and whites. Proceedings of the National Academy of Sciences of the United States of America, 113(16), 4296–4301. https://doi.org/10.1073/pnas.1516047113

Hofstede, G. (1980). *Culture's Consequences: International differences in work-related values.* Beverly Hills, CA: Sage.

Hogeveen, J., Inzlicht, M., Obhi, S. S. (2014). Power changes how the brain responds to others. Journal of Experimental Psychology: General, 143 (2): 755–762. http://dx.doi.org/10.1037/a0033477.

Hong L. (2000). Toward a transformed approach to prevention: breaking the link between masculinity and violence. *Journal of American College Health, 48(6),* 269–279. https://doi.org/10.1080/07448480009596268.

Hooker, E. (1969). Parental relations and male homosexuality in patient and non-patient samples. *Journal of Consulting and Clinical Psychology, 33,* 140–142. http://dx.doi.org/10.1037/h0027188.

Hurlemann, R. et al. (2010). Human amygdala reactivity is diminished by the β-noradrenergic antagonist propranolol. *Psychological Medicine, 40,* 1839–1848 doi: 10.1017/S0033291709992376.

Hussey, K. A., Katz, A. N., & Leith, S. A. (2014). Gendered language in interactive discourse. *Journal of Psycholinguistic Research, 44(4),* 417–433. doi: 10.1007/s10936-014-9295-5.

Hutchinson, B. (2019, May 16). Viral video shows white Texas deputy mistakenly trying to arrest black man on warrant. ABC News. https://abcnews.go.com/US/viral-video-shows-white-texas-deputy-mistakenly-arrest/story?id=63078912

Hutson-Miller, K. M. (August 30, 2016). Show of support: Local tribes among those backing Standing Rock Sioux effort. *The Shawnee News Star*. Retrieved from, https://www.news-star.com/news/20160830/show-of-support-local-tribes-among-those-backing-standing-rock-sioux-effort September 26 2018.

Irobi, E. (2007). What they came with: Carnival and the persistence of African performance aesthetics in the African diaspora. *Journal of Black Studies. 37(6),* 896–913. https://www.jstor.org/stable/i40001844.

Isenberg, N. (1999). Linguistic threat activates the human amygdala. *Proceedings of the National Academy of Sciences of the United States of America, 96(18),* 10456–10459. https://doi.org/10.1073/pnas.96.18.10456.

Jacquet, B. V., Patel, M. et al. (2009). Analysis of neuronal proliferation, migration and differentiation in the postnatal brain using equine infectious anemia virus-based lentiviral vectors. *Gene Therapy, 16,* 1021–1033. doi:10.1038/gt.2009.58.

Jamison, D. F. (2010). Fanon revisited: Exploring the relationship between African-centered psychology and Fanonian psychology. *The Journal of Pan African Studies, 3(8),* 179–193.

Janusek, L. W., Tell, D., Gaylor-Harden, N., & Mathews, H. L. (2017). Relationship of childhood adversity and neighborhood violence to a pro-inflammatory phenotype in emerging adult African American men: An epigenetic link. *Brain, Behavior, and Immunity, 60,* 126–135. https://doi.org/10.1016/j.bbi.2016.10.006.

Jay, T. (2009). The utility and ubiquity of taboo words. *Perspectives on Psychological Science, 4(2),* 153–161. https://doi.org/10.1111/j.1745-6924.2009.01115.x .

Jenkins, E. J. (2002). Black women and community violence: Trauma, grief, and coping. *Women & Therapy, 25(3–4),* 29–44. http://dx.doi.org/10.1300/J015v25n03_03.

Jiang, J. et al. (2015). Leader emergence through interpersonal neural synchronization. *Proceedings of the National Academy of Sciences of the United States of America, 112*(14), 4274–4279. http://doi.org/10.1073/pnas.1422930112.

Johnsen, O. R. (2008). "He's a big old girl!" Negotiation by gender inversion in gay men's speech. *Journal of Homosexuality, 54(1/2),* 150–168. doi:10.1080/00918360801952044.

Johnson, S. & Galloway, S. (2018). Young Harvey Weinstein: The making of a monster. *The Hollywood Reporter.* Retrieved from, https://www.hollywoodreporter.com/features/young-harvey-weinstein-making-a-monster-1089069.

Jones, J. M. & Leitner, J. B. (2015). The Sankofa Effect: Divergent effects of thinking about the past for Blacks and Whites. In M. Stolarski, N. Fieulaine, & W. van Beek (eds.). *Time Perspective Theory: Review, Research and Application.* Basel, Switzerland: Springer International Publishing. DOI: https://doi.org/10.1007/978-3-319-07368-2_13.

Joyner, C. (1984). *Down by the riverside.* Chicago, Illinois: University of Chicago Press, pgs. 70–89.

Kaindl, S (2013) Bantu Stephen Biko and black consciousness: The struggle for equality in a racist South Africa.[Doctoral dissertation, University of Vienna]. http://othes.univie.ac.at/28390/1/2013-05-29_0509602.pdf

Karalekas, P. C., Ryan C. R., & Taylor, F. B. (1983). Control of lead, copper and iron pipe corrosion in Boston. *Journal of American Water Works Association, 75(2),* 92–95. https://doi.org/10.1002/j.1551-8833.1983.tb05073.x.

Karim, N., Greene, M. & Picard, M. (2016). The cultural context of child marriage in Nepal and Bangladesh: Findings from CARE's tipping point project community participatory analysis research report. *CARE.* Retrieved from, https://www.care.org/sites/default/files/documents/CARE_Tipping_Point_External%20Report_Web.pdf.

Kaufman, L. (May 20, 2013). For the word on the street, courts call up an online witness. *New York Times.* Retrieved from, http://www.nytimes.com/2013/05/21/business/media/urban-dictionary-finds-a-place-in-the-courtroom.html?pagewanted=all&_r=0.

Kelly, D. J., Quinn, P. C., Slater, A. M., Lee, K., Ge, L., & Pascalis, O. (2007). The other-race effect develops during infancy: evidence of perceptual narrowing. Psychological science, 18(12), 1084–1089. https://doi.org/10.1111/j.1467-9280.2007.02029.x

Keltner, D., Gruenfeld, D. H., & Anderson, C. (2003). Power, approach, and inhibition. *Psychological Review, 110,* 265–84. http://dx.doi.org/10.1037/0033-295X.110.2.265.

Kennedy, R. (2003). *Nigger: The strange career of a troublesome word.* New York, New York: Vintage Books.

Kenny, G. P., Yardley, J., Brown, C., Sigal, R. J., & Jay, O. (2010). Heat stress in older individuals and patients with common chronic diseases. *CMAJ: Canadian Medical Association journal = journal de l'Association medicale canadienne, 182(10),* 1053–1060. doi:10.1503/cmaj.081050.

Keysers, C., Paracampo, R., & Gazzola, V. (2018). What neuromodulation and lesion studies tell us about the function of the mirror neuron system and embodied cognition. *Current Opinion in Psychology, 24,* 35–40. https://doi.org/10.1016/j.copsyc.2018.04.001.

Kgatla, T. (2018). The decolonization of the mind and black consciousness community projects by the Limpopo council of churches. *Missionalia: Southern African Journal of Missiology, 46(1),* 146–162. doi:https://doi.org/10.7832/46-1-270.

Kilomba, G. (2010). *Plantation memories: Episodes of everyday racism.* Münster, North Rhine-Westphalia. Unrast.

Kim, S. & Cardemil, E. (2012). Effective psychotherapy with low-income clients: The importance of attending to social class. *Journal of Contemporary Psychotherapy, 42(1),* 27–35. doi: 10.1007/s10879-011-9194-0.

Kimmel, M.S & Mahler, M. (2003). Adolescent masculinity, homophobia, and violence random school shootings, 1982–2001. *American Behavioral Scientist, 46(10),* 1439–1458. https://doi.org/10.1177/0002764203046010010.

Kirkpatrick, D. D. & Hubbard, B. (November 1, 2018). Despite stigma of Khashoggi killing, crown prince is seen as retaining power. *The New York Times,* Retrieved from https://www.nytimes.com/2018/11/01/world/middleeast/with-saudi-prince-holding-on-to-power-us-seen-standing-by-him.html.

Kitayama, S., Duffy, S., Kawamura, T., & Larsen, J. T. (2003). Perceiving an object and its context in different cultures: A cultural look at new look. *Psychological Science, 14,* 201–206. doi: 10.1111/1467-9280.02432.

Klare, M. (2012). *The race for what's left: The global scramble for the world's last resources.* London, England. Picador.

Klare, M. (2002). *Resource wars: The new landscape of global conflict.* New York, New York. Holt Paperpacks.

Klebold, S. (2017). *A Mother's Reckoning: Living in the aftermath of tragedy.* Broadway Books.

Knyazev, G. G., Savostyanov, A. N., Bocharov, A. V., & Merkulova E. A. (2018). Resting state connectivity mediates the relationship between collectivism and social cognition. *International Journal of Psychophysiology, 123:*17–24. doi: 10.1016/j.ijpsycho.2017.12.002.

Kohli, R., Pizarro, M., & Nevárez, A. (2017). The "New Racism" of K–12 schools: Centering critical research on racism. *Review of Research in Education. 41(1),* 182–202. https://doi.org/10.3102/0091732X16686949.

Kouchaki, M., Dobson K. S., & Waytz, A. (2018). The link between self-dehumanization and immoral behavior. *Psychological Science, 29(8),* 1234–1246. https://doi.org/10.1177/0956797618760784.

Krishna, G. (2019). Water: A pipe dream. *Business Standard.* https://www.business-standard.com/article/opinion/water-a-pipe-dream-119032201095_1.html .

Kubota, J. T., Banaji, M. R., & Phelps, E. A. (2012). The neuroscience of race. *Nature neuroscience, 15*(7), 940–948. doi:10.1038/nn.3136.

Kulick, D. (2000). Gay and lesbian language. *Annual Review of Anthropology, 29,* 243–285. http://www.jstor.org/stable/223422.

Ladson-Billings, G. (2006). From the achievement gap to the education debt: Understanding achievement in U.S. schools. *Educational researcher, 35(7),* 3–12. https://doi.org/10.3102/0013189X035007003 .

Lai, C. K., Skinner, A. L., Cooley, E., Murrar, S., Brauer, M., Devos, T., & Simon, S. (2016). Reducing implicit racial preferences: II. Intervention effectiveness across time, Journal of Experimental Psychology: General, 145(8): 1001–1016. doi: 10.1037/xge0000179

Landau, E. (2009). Men see bikini-clad women as objects, psychologists say. CNN. https://www.cnn.com/2009/HEALTH/02/19/women.bikinis.objects/index.html

Laszlo, E. (2014). *The self-actualizing cosmos: The Akasha revolution in science and human consciousness.* Rochester, Vermont: Inner Traditions.

Lawson, E. S. (2018). Bereaved black mothers and maternal activism in the racial state. *Feminist Studies, 44 (3),* 713–735. DOI 10.15767/feministstudies.44.3.0713.

Layden, E. A., Cacioppo, J. T., & Cacioppo, S. (2018). "Loneliness predicts a preference for larger interpersonal distance within intimate space." *PLOS ONE,* https://doi.org/10.1371/journal.pone.0203491

Lei, X. (2006). Sexism in language. *Journal of Language and Linguistics, 5 (1),* 87–94. Retrieved from, https://pdfs.semanticscholar.org/d03a/fdaa103c8526b75523cdadbacfd

4a4d27041.pdf.

Lieberman, M. D., Hariri, A., Jarcho, J. M., Eisenberger, N. I., & Bookheimer, S. Y. (2005). An fMRI investigation of race-related amygdala activity in African American and Caucasian-American individuals. *Nature Neuroscience, 8.* doi: 10.1038/nn1465.

Levenson, E., Pagliery, J., & Kamp, M. (November 8, 2018). Thousand Oaks gunman was a Marine veteran who often visited the site of the shooting. *CNN.* Retrieved from, https://www.cnn.com/2018/11/08/us/thousand-oaks-gunman/index.html .

Lewis, M. K. & Marshall, I. (2012). *LGBT psychology: Research perspectives and people of African descent.* New York, New York: Springer Science.

Liu, W. M. (2017). White male power and privilege: The relationship between White supremacy and social class. *Journal of Counseling Psychology, 64*(4), 349–358. http://dx.doi.org/10.1037/cou0000227.

Liu et al. (2018). Water poverty in rural communities of arid areas in China. *Water, 10,* 505. doi:10.3390/w10040505.

Lobato, M. (2017). Brain maturation, cognition and voice pattern in a gender dysphoria case under pubertal suppression. *Frontiers in Human Neuroscience, 11,* 528. doi:10.3389/fnhum.2017.00528.

Lorde, A. (1983). There is no hierarchy of oppressions. *Bulletin: Homophobia and Education, 14(3/4),* 9.

Lu, K. & Ning, H. (2019). When do we fall in neural synchrony with others? *Social Cognitive and Affective Neuroscience, 14, (3),* 253–261. https://doi.org/10.1093/scan/nsz012.

Lund-Johansen, M., Laeke, T., Tirsit, A., Munie, T., Abebe, M., Sahlu, A., Biluts, H., & Wester K. (2017). An Ethiopian training program in neurosurgery with Norwegian support. *World Neurosurgery, 99,*403–408. doi: 10.1016/j.wneu.2016.12.051.

Maantay, J. (2002). Mapping environmental injustices: Pitfalls and potential of geographic information systems in assessing environmental health and equity. *Environmental Health Perspectives, 110 [Supplement 2],* 161–171.

McAdams, D. P. (June 2016). The mind of Donald Trump. *The Atlantic.* Retrieved from, https://www.theatlantic.com/magazine/archive/2016/06/the-mind-of-donald-trump/480771/ .

McCarthy, M. J., Gatehouse, S., Steel, M., Goss, B., & Williams, R. (2011). The influence of the energy of trauma, the timing of decompression, and the impact of grade of SCI on outcome. *Evidence-based spine-care journal, 2*(2), 11–17. https://doi.org/10.1055/s-0030-1267100

Mack G. W., Weseman, C. A., Langhans, G. W., . . . et al. (1994). Body fluid balance in dehydrated healthy older men: Thirst and renal osmoregulation. *Journal of Applied Physiology, 76,* 1615–1623. https://doi.org/10.1152/jappl.1994.76.4.1615.

Mahalik, J. R. et al. (1998). Men's gender role conflict and use of psychological defenses. *Journal of Counseling Psychology, 45 (3),* 247–255. http://dx.doi.org/10.1037/0022-0167.45.3.247.

Mani, A., Mullainathan, S., Shafir, S., & Zhao, J. (2013). Poverty impedes cognition. *Science, 341,* 976–980. doi: 10.1126/science.1238041.

Markus, H. R. & Kitayama, S., (1991). Culture and the self: Implications for cognition, emotion, and motivation. *Psychological Review, 20,* 568–579. doi :10.1037/0033-295X.98.2.224.

Marsh, N., Scheele, D., Feinstein, J. S., Gerhardt, H. et al. (2017). Oxytocin-enforced norm compliance reduces xenophobic outgroup rejection. *Proceedings of the National Academy of Science, 114 (35),* 9314–9319. https://doi.org/10.1073/pnas.1705853114.

Marvel, K., Cook, B. I., Bonfils, C. J. W., Durack, P. J., Smerdon, J. E., & Williams, A. P. (2019). Twentieth-century hydroclimate changes consistent with human influence. *Nature 569,* 59–65. https://doi.org/10.1038/s41586-019-1149-8.

Mattan, B. D., Wei, K. Y., Cloutier, J., & Kubota, J. T. (2018). The social neuroscience of race-based and status-based prejudice. *Current Opinion in Psychology, 24,* 27–34. https://doi.org/10.1016/j.copsyc.2018.04.010.

Matthews, G. A., Nieh, E. H., Vander Weele, C. M., et al. (2016). Dorsal raphe dopamine neurons represent the experience of social isolation. *Cell, 164(4),* 617–31. doi: 10.1016/j.cell.2015.12.040.

Matthiessen, C. (2009). Meaning in the making: Meaning potential emerging from acts of meaning. *Language Learning, 59 (S1)*, 206–229. doi:10.1111/j.1467-9922.2009.00541.x.

Mekonnen, M. M. & Hoekstra, A. Y. (2016). Four billion people facing severe water scarcity. *Science Advances, 2 (2)*, e1500323 doi: 10.1126/sciadv.1500323.

Meyza, K. & Knapska, E. (2018). What can rodents teach us about empathy? *Current Opinion in Psychology, 24*, 15–20. https://doi.org/10.1016/j.copsyc.2018.03.002.

Miller, R. L. (2007). Legacy denied: African American gay men, AIDS, and the black church. *Social Work, 52 (1)*, 51–61. doi: 10.1093/sw/52.1.51.

Miller, P. R. et al. (2017). Transgender politics as body politics: effects of disgust sensitivity and authoritarianism on transgender rights attitudes. *Journal of Politics, Groups, and Identities, 5(1)*, 4–24. https://doi.org/10.1080/21565503.2016.1260482.

Mitchell, J. P., Baraji, M. R., & Macrae, C. N. (2005). The link between social cognition and self-referential thought in the medial prefrontal cortex. *Journal of Cognitive Neuroscience, 17*, 1306–1315. doi: 10.1162/0898929055002418.

Mohammadi, M. R., & Khaleghi, A. (2018). Transsexualism: A different viewpoint to brain changes. *Clinical Psychopharmacology and Neuroscience: The Official Scientific Journal of the Korean College of Neuropsychopharmacology, 16(2)*, 136–143. doi:10.9758/cpn.2018.16.2.136.

Molina, N., HoSang, D. M., & Gutiérrez, R. A. (2019). *Relational formations of race: Theory, method, and practice.* Berkeley, CA: University of California Press.

Moore, T. O. (2010). *The science of melanin.* Redan, GA: Zamani Press.

Muhammad, K.(2010). *The condemnation of Blackness: Race, crime, and the making of modern urban America.* Cambridge, MA: Harvard University Press.

Mullainathan, S. & Shafir, E. (2014). *Scarcity: The new science of having less and how it defines our lives.* New York, New York: Henry Holt and Company, LLC.

Mullainathan, S., & Thaler, R. (2001). Behavioral economics. In *International Encyclopedia of Social Sciences* (pp. 1094–1100). Pergamon Press.

Mundt, M., Ross, K., & Burnett, C. M. (2018). Scaling social movements through social media: The case of Black Lives Matter. *Social Media + Society, 4(4)*, https://doi.org/10.1177/2056305118807911.

Murrow, G. B. & Murrow, R. (2015). A hypothetical neurological association between dehumanization and human rights abuses. *Journal of Law and the Biosciences, 2(2)*, 336–364. https://doi.org/10.1093/jlb/lsv015.

Muthu, C. et al. (2006). Medicinal plants used by traditional healers in Kancheepuram District of Tamil Nadu, India. *Journal of Ethnobiology and Ethnomedicine, 2(1)*, https://doi.org/10.1186/1746-4269-2-43.

Myers, L. J. et al. (2018). Optimal theory's contributions to understanding and surmounting global challenges to humanity. *Journal of Black Psychology, 44(8)*, 747–771. https://doi.org/10.1177/0095798418813240.

Myers, L. J. (2013). Restoration of spirit: An African-centered community health model. *Journal of Black Psychology, 39(3)*, 257–260. doi: 10.1177/0095798413478080.

Myers, L. J. (2009). Theoretical and conceptual approaches to African American psychology. In H. Neville, S. Utsey, and B. Tynes (Eds.). *Handbook of African American psychology* (pp. 35–46). Newbury Park, CA: Sage Publications.

Myers, L. J. (2006). Mental health strategies to eliminate health disparities: Towards the creation of a climate and culture of optimal health from an African (Indigenous) American perspective, *DePaul Journal of Health Care Law, 10 (1)*, 73–88.

Myers, L. J. (2003). *Our health matters: Guide to an African (Indigenous) American psychology and cultural model for creating a climate and culture of optimal health.* Columbus, OH: Ohio Commission on Minority Health.

Myers, L. J. (1993). *Understanding an Afrocentric World View: Introduction to an optimal psychology.* Dubuque, IA: Kendall Hunt Publishing.

Myers, L. J., Obasi, E. M., Jefferson, M., Anderson, M., Purnell, J., & Godfrey, T. (2000). Building multicultural competence around indigenous healing practices. In M. Constantine and D. Sue (Eds.), *Strategies for building multicultural competence in mental health and educational settings* (pp. 109–125). New York: John Wiley.

Nadal, K. L. (2013). *That's so gay! Microaggressions and the lesbian, gay, bisexual, and transgender community.* Washington DC: American Psychological Association.

Nadal, K. L. (2008). Preventing racial, ethnic, gender, sexual minority, disability, and religious microaggressions: Recommendations for promoting positive mental health. *Prevention in Counseling Psychology: Theory, Research, Practice and Training, 2(1)*, 22–27.

Nadal, K. L. Issa, M., Leon, J., Meterko, V., Wideman, M., & Wong, Y. (2011). Sexual orientation microaggressions: "Death by a thousand cuts" for lesbian, gay, and bisexual youth. *Journal of LGBT Youth, 8(3)*, 1–26. https://doi.org/10.1080/19361653.2011.584204.

Nadal, K. L., Rivera, D. P., & Corpus, M. J. H. (2010). Sexual orientation and transgender microaggressions in everyday life: Experiences of lesbians, gays, bisexuals, and transgender individuals. In D. W. Sue (Ed.*), Microaggressions and marginality: Manifestation, dynamics, and impact* (pp. 217–240). New York: Wiley.

Namkung, H. et al. (2017). The insula: An underestimated brain area in clinical neuroscience, psychiatry, and neurology. *Trends in Neuroscience, 40(4)*, 200–207. *doi: 10.1016/j.tins.2017.02.002.*

Narasimhan, T. E. & Babu, G. (2019). Tamil Nadu water woes: Chennai goes thirsty, industry feels the heat. *Business Standard.* https://www.business-standard.com/article/current-affairs/tamil-nadu-water-woes-chennai-goes-thirsty-industries-feel-the-heat-119061700389_1.html.

Narayan, D. (2000). Poverty is powerlessness and voicelessness. *Finance & Development, 37(4)*, Retrieved from http://www.imf.org/external/pubs/ft/fandd/2000/12/narayan.htm.

National Institute of Mental Health (2001). *Reliving trauma: Post-traumatic stress disorder.* Bethesda (MD): National Institute of Mental Health, National Institutes of Health, US Department of Health and Human Services; Extent. (NIH Publication No. 01-4597).

Naylor, B. (October 6, 2018). Brett Kavanaugh sworn in as newest Supreme Court justice. *National Public Radio Inc.,* Retrieved from https://www.npr.org/2018/10/06/654409999/final-senate-vote-on-kavanaugh-nomination-expected-saturday.

Neuberg, S. L., Kenrick, D. T., & Schaller, M. (2011). Human threat management systems: Self-protection and disease avoidance. Neuroscience and Biobehavioral Reviews, 35, https://www.researchgate.net/publication/46219699_Human_Threat_Management_Systems_Self-Protection_and_Disease_Avoidance

Nguyen, K. H. (2013). Hearing what we see: Censoring "nigga," vernaculars, and African American agentic subjects. *Howard Journal of Communications, 24(3)*, 293–308. doi:10.1080/10646175.2013.805988.

Nguyen, S. (2016, March 3). Nobel laureate Toni Morrison delivers the 2016 Norton lectures. *Harvard Magazine.* https://www.harvardmagazine.com/2016/03/toni-morrison-speaks-2016-norton-lecture

Nichols, D. E. (2018). N, N-dimethyltryptamine and the pineal gland: Separating fact from myth. *Journal of Psychopharmacology, 32(1)*, 30–36. doi: 10.1177/0269881117736919.

NIMH (2001). Post-traumatic stress disorder. https://www.nimh.nih.gov/health/publications/post-traumatic-stress-disorder-ptsd/ptsd-508-05172017_38054.pdf

Nobles, W. (2015). *The SAGE encyclopedia of African cultural heritage in North America* Thousand Oaks, CA: SAGE Publications, pg. 45–49. Inc. DOI: http://dx.doi.org/10.4135/9781483346373.n20.

Nobles, W. (2010). The function of traditional healing. *Imhotep Journal, 7*, 13–16.

Nobles, W. (2006). *Seeking the Sakhu: Foundational writings for an African psychology.* Chicago, Illinois: Third World Press.

Nobles, W. W. (2015). From Black psychology to Sakhu Djaer: Implications for the further development of a Pan African Black psychology. *Journal of Black Psychology, 41(5)*, 399–414. https://doi.org/10.1177/0095798415598038.

Nobles, W. W., Baloyi, L. & Sodi, T. (2016). Pan African humanness and Sakhu Djaer as praxis for indigenous knowledge systems. *Alternation Special Edition 18*, 36–59. http://alternation.ukzn.ac.za/Files/docs/23%20SpEd18/02%20Nobles%20F.pdf.

Novelly, T. (October 29, 2018). Police chief calls it a hate crime: Latest on the Louisville Kroger shooting. *Courier-Journal.* https://www.courier-journal.com/story/news/crime/2018/10/29/louisville-police-calls-kroger-shooting-hate-crime-more-updates/1804562002/.

Ochoa-Tocachi, B. F., Bardales, J. D., Antiporta, J. et al. (2019). Potential contributions of pre-Inca infiltration infrastructure to Andean water security. *Nature Sustainability, 2*, 584–593. doi:10.1038/s41893-019-0307-1.

Ochs, E. & Schieffelin, B. (1984). Language acquisition and socialization: Three developmental stories and their implications. In R. Shweder & R. LeVine (Eds.), *Culture theory: Essays in mind, self and emotion* (pp. 276–320), Cambridge University Press, New York.

Oelofsen, R. (2015). Decolonisation of the African mind and intellectual landscape. *Phronimon, 16 (2)*, 130–146.

Oh, H., DeVylder, J., & Hunt, G. (2017). Effect of police training and accountability on the mental health of African American adults. *American Journal of Public Health, 107(10)*, 1588–1590. doi:10.2105/AJPH.2017.304012.

Oliver, M. L., & Shapiro, T. M. (2006). *Black wealth, white wealth: A new perspective on racial inequality.* New York, NY: Taylor & Francis.

Ortiz, J. L. (December 9, 2018). Sandy Hook school shooter had "scorn for humanity," according to newly released documents. *USA Today.* Retrieved from, https://www.usatoday.com/story/news/2018/12/09/sandy-hook-shooter-adam-lanza-had-scorn-humanity/2259413002/.

O'Shea, L. (2019). *Future histories: What Ada Lovelace, Tom Paine, and the Paris commune can teach us about digital technology.* Brooklyn, New York: Verso.

Otten, M., Mann, L., van Berkum, J. J. & Jonas, K. J. (2017). No laughing matter: How the presence of laughing witnesses changes the perception of insults. *Social Neuroscience, (12)2*, 182–193, DOI: 10.1080/17470919.2016.1162194.

Ovalle, D. (2019, June 18). Miami jury convicts cop of misdemeanor for shooting at autistic man but acquits on felonies. Miami Herald. https://www.miamiherald.com/news/local/crime/article231656948.html

Palmer, C. E. & Tsakiris, M. (2018). Going at the heart of social cognition: Is there a role for interoception in self-other distinction? *Current Opinion in Psychology, 24*, 21–26. https://doi.org/10.1016/j.copsyc.2018.04.008 .

Pappas, S. (2012). Our brains see men as whole and women as parts. *Scientific American,* https://www.scientificamerican.com/article/our-brains-see-men-as-whole-women-as-parts/.

Pasquinelli, E. (2018). Are digital devices altering our brains? *Scientific American,* https://www.scientificamerican.com/article/are-digital-devices-altering-our-brains/ .

Paulsen, D. (2003). Murder in black and white. *Homicide Studies, 7 (3)*, 289–317. https://doi.org/10.1177/1088767903253707.

Peck, R. (Director). (2017). I am not your negro. [Film]. Magnolia Pictures.

Perkins, S. & Graham-Bermann, S. (2012). Violence exposure and the development of school-related functioning: Mental health, neurocognition, and learning. *Aggression and Violent Behavior 17(1)*, 89–98. https://doi.org/10.1016/j.avb.2011.10.001.

Persio, S. L. (2018). Who is Leeanne Walters? Activist who helped expose Flint water crisis wins top prize. *Newsweek.* Retrieved from, https://www.newsweek.com/who-leeanne-walters-activist-who-helped-expose-flint-water-crisis-wins-top-897326.

Peterson, N. A., Hamme, C. L., & Speer, P. W. (2002). Cognitive empowerment of African Americans and Caucasians: Differences in understanding of power, political functioning, and shaping ideology. *Journal of Black Studies, 32*, 336–351. http://dx.doi.org/10.1177/002193470203200304.

Pettit, B., & Western, B. (2004). Mass imprisonment and the life course: Race and class inequality in US incarceration. *American Sociological Review, 69(2)*, 151–169. http://dx.doi.org/10.1177/000312240406900201.

Pfeifer, J. H. & Peake, S. J. (2012). Self-development: Integrating cognitive, socioemotional, and neuroimaging perspectives. *Developmental Cognitive Neuroscience, 2(1)*, 55–69. https://doi.org/10.1016/j.dcn.2011.07.012.

Phelps, E. A., & LeDoux, J. E. (2005). Contributions of the amygdala to emotion processing: From animal models to human behavior. *Neuron, 48(2)*, 175–187. doi: 10.1016/j.neuron.2005.09.025.

Picard, M. & McEwen, B. S. (2018). Psychological stress and mitochondria: A systematic review. *Psychosomatic Medicine, 80(2)*, 141–153. doi: 10.1097/PSY.0000000000000545.

Pierce, C. (1970). Offensive mechanisms. In F. B. Barbour (Ed.), *The Black seventies* (pp. 265–282). Boston: Porter Sargent Publishers.

Pinghui, Z. (2019). Meet the Chinese villagers who fear they can never escape the poverty trap. *South China Morning Post.* https://www.scmp.com/news/china/society/article/2189274/meet-chinese-villagers-who-fear-they-can-never-escape-poverty.

Pitts-Taylor, V. (2019). Neurobiologically poor? Brain phenotypes, inequality, and biosocial determinism. *Science, Technology, & Human Values, 44(4),* 660–685 https://doi.org/10.1177/0162243919841695.

Popkin, B. M., D'Anci, K. E., & Rosenberg, I. (2010). "Water, hydration, and health." *Nutrition Reviews,* 68(8), 439-58. doi: 10.1111/j.1753-4887.2010.00304.x.

Potts, C. (2007). The expressive dimension. *Theoretical Linguistics, 33 (2),* 165–197. doi: https://doi.org/10.1515/TL.2007.011 .

Poussaint, A. F. (2002). Is extreme racism a mental illness? Yes. It can be a delusional symptom of psychotic disorders. *Western Journal of Medicine, 176(1),* 4. doi:10.1136/ewjm.176.1.4.

Premack, R. (October 27, 2018). Teens say they cringe when brands use these 11 outdated slang words here's what Gen Z is saying instead. *Business Insider,* Retrieved from https://www.businessinsider.com/goat-savage-lit-dope-bae-teens-gen-z-slang-words-2018-6.

Pross, N. (2017). Effects of dehydration on brain functioning: A Life-span perspective. *Annals of Nutrition and Metabolism, 70(1),* 30–36. https://doi.org/10.1159/000463060.

Qin, L. (2017). "Xiong'an New District: An old idea is finally accepted." *China Dialogue.* https://www.chinadialogue.net/culture/9937-Xiong-an-New-District-An-old-idea-is-finally-accepted/en

Qin, L. (2016). "Clear as mud: how poor data is thwarting China's water clean-up." *China Dialogue.* https://www.chinadialogue.net/article/show/single/en/8922-Clear-as-mud-how-poor-data-is-thwarting-China-s-water-clean-up

Rae, J. R., Gülgöz, S., Durwood, L., DeMeules, M., Lowe, R., Lindquist, G., & Olson, K. R. (2019). Predicting early-childhood gender transitions. *Psychological Science, 30*(5), https://doi.org/10.1177/0956797619830649

Rahman, I. & Hasegawa, H. (2011). *Water stress.* Rijeka, Croatia: InTech.

Ramasubramanian, S. & Oliver, M. B. (2007). Activating and suppressing hostile and benevolent racism: Evidence for comparative media stereotyping. *Media Psychology, 9,* 623–646. https://doi.org/10.1080/15213260701283244.

Reclaiming Native Truth (June 2018). Research findings: Compilation of all research. Retrieved from, https://www.reclaimingnativetruth.com/wp-content/uploads/2018/06/FullFindingsReport-screen.pdf August 16, 2018.

Reed, C. (2017). Colorism and its correlation with implicit racial stereotyping: An experimental action research study. *The Young Researcher, 1*(1), 16-26. Retrieved from http://www.theyoungresearcher.com/papers/reed.pdf

Reed, L. & Duncan, I. (September 21, 2018). What we know about Snochia Mosely, alleged shooter at Maryland Rite Aid warehouse. *Baltimore Sun.* Retrieved from, https://www.baltimoresun.com/news/maryland/harford/aegis/news/bs-md-moseley-20180920-story.html.

Reed, L. & Johnson, L. T. (2010). Serving LGBT students: Examining the spiritual, religious, and social justice implications for an African American school administrator. *The Journal of Negro Education, 79 (3),* 390–404. Retrieved from http://www.jstor.org/stable/20798357.

Reeve, J. (2018). Understanding motivation and emotion. Wiley. 2-7

Reindl V., Gerloff, C., Scharke, W., & Konrad, K. (2018). Brain-to-brain synchrony in parent-child dyads and the relationship with emotion regulation revealed by fNIRS-based hyperscanning. *Neuroimage, 178,* 493–502. doi: 10.1016/j.neuroimage.2018.05.060.

Reindl, V., Konrad, K., Gerloff, C., Kruppa, J. A., Bell, L., & Scharke, W. (2019). Conducting hyperscanning experiments with functional near-infrared spectroscopy. *Journal of Visualized Experiments,143,* 10.3791/58807. https://doi.org/10.3791/58807

Reuters. (May 20, 2018). China's President Xi Jinping calls for increased efforts to tackle pollution. *South China Morning Post.* Retrieved from, https://www.scmp.com/news/china/

policies-politics/article/2146945/chinas-president-xi-jinping-calls-increased-efforts August 20, 2019.

Richardson, V. (March 13, 2017). Dakota Access protest camps cleared after $1.1 million federal cleanup; four more dogs rescued. *Washington Times*. Retrieved from, https://www. washingtontimes.com/news/2017/mar/13/dakota-access-case-army-finishes-11-million-cleanu/ April 18, 2019.

Rieger, G., Linsenmeier, J. A. W., Gygax, L., & Bailey, J. M. (2008). Sexual orientation and childhood gender nonconformity: Evidence from home videos. *Developmental Psychology, 44(1)*, 46–58. doi: 10.1037/0012-1649.44.1.46.

Roberts, R. A., Bell, L. A., & Murphy, B. (2008). Flipping the script: Analyzing youth talk about race and racism. *Anthropology and Education Quarterly, 39(3)*, 334–354. https://doi.org/10.1111/j.1548-1492.2008.00025.x .

Robles, F. & Bosman, J. (2014, August 17). Autopsy shows Michael Brown was struck at least 6 times. https://www.nytimes.com/2014/08/18/us/michael-brown-autopsy-shows-he-was-shot-at-least-6-times.html

Rosch, E. & Mervis, C. (1975). Family resemblances: Studies in the internal structure of categories. *Cognitive Psychology, 7 (4)*, 573–605 http://matt.colorado.edu/teaching/categories/rm75.pdf.

Ross, C. T. (2015). A multi-level Bayesian analysis of racial bias in police shootings at the county-level in the United States, 2011–2014. *PLOS-ONE*, https://doi.org/10.1371/journal.pone.0141854.

Rozin, P., & Haidt, J. (2013). The domains of disgust and their origins: Contrasting biological and cultural evolutionary accounts. *Trends in Cognitive Science, 17*, 367-68. https://cpb-us-w2.wpmucdn.com/web.sas.upenn.edu/dist/7/206/files/2016/09/DisgustDomainsOrigin_TrendsCogSci2013-1aaumw9.pdf

Russell, D. W. (1996). UCLA loneliness scale (Version 3): Reliability, validity, and factor structure. *Journal of Personality Assessment, 66 (1)*, 20–40. http://dx.doi.org/10.1207/s15327752jpa6601_2 .

Ryff, C. D. & Keyes, C. L. M. (1995). The structure of psychological well-being revisited. *Journal of Personality and Social Psychology 69(4)*, 719–727. http://dx.doi.org/10.1037/0022-3514.69.4.719.

Sadaghiani, S. & D'Esposito, M. (2015). Functional characterization of the cingulo-opercular network in the maintenance of tonic alertness. *Cerebral Cortex, 25(9)*, 2763–2773. https://doi.org/10.1093/cercor/bhu072.

Saini, A. (2019). *Superior: The return of race science*. Boston, Massachusetts. Beacon Press.

Sanburn, J. (2014, November 25). All the ways Darren Wilson described being afraid of Michael Brown. Time. https://time.com/3605346/darren-wilson-michael-brown-demon/

Sanders, T., Liu, Y., Buchner, V., & Tchounwou, P. B. (2009). Neurotoxic effects and bio-markers of lead exposure: A review. *Reviews on Environmental Health, 24(1)*, 15–45. doi:10.1515/reveh.2009.24.1.15.

Sanguinetti, A. (2015). Diversifying cohousing: The retrofit model. *Journal of Architectural and Planning Research, 32(1)*, 68–90.

Sapolsky, R. (2017). *Behave*. London, UK: Penguin Books.

Saramo, S. (2017). The meta-violence of Trumpism. *European Journal of American Studies, 12(2)*, 1–17. http://dx.doi.org/10.4000/ejas.12129 .

Sasaki, J. Y. & Kim, H. S. (2016). Nature, nurture, and their interplay: A review of cultural neuroscience. *Journal of Cross-Cultural Psychology. 48(1)*, 4–22. doi: 10.1177/0022022116680481.

Schmeer, K. K., & Yoon, A. (2016). Socioeconomic status inequalities in low-grade inflammation during childhood. *Archives of Disease in Childhood, 101(11)*, 1043–1047. doi:10.1136/archdischild-2016-310837.

Schneider, M. A., Spritzer, P. M., Soll, B., Fontanari, A., Carneiro, M., Tovar-Moll, F., . . .(2014). *Driving harmonization of water stress, scarcity, and risk terminology*. (Discussion Paper) https://ceowatermandate.org/files/Driving_Harmonization_of_Water_Terminology_draft.pdf.

Schulte, P. (2014). Defining water scarcity, water stress, and water risk: It's not just semantics, https://pacinst.org/water-definitions/.

Schulte, P., Morrison, J., Orr, S., & Power, G. (2014). *Shared water challenges and interests: The case for private sector engagement in water policy and management* (Discussion Paper). Retrieved from https://ceowatermandate.org/files/private-sector-water-policy-engagement.pdf.

Schultz, C. (2015, February 23). A city of two tales. *Politico* magazine. https://www.politico.com/magazine/story/2015/02/tamir-rice-cleveland-police-115401

Sfera A., Cummings M., & Osorio, C. (2016). Dehydration and cognition in geriatrics: A hydromolecular hypothesis. *Frontiers of Molecular Biosciences, 3,*18. https://doi.org/10.3389/fmolb.2016.00018.

Shawtyjay. (January 14, 2014). *Female aint shit.* [Video file]. Retrieved from https://www.youtube.com/watch?v=C9p6oDZWCNA.

Silk, M. (2005). Religion and region in American public life. *Journal for the Scientific Study of Religion, 44 (3),* 265–270. https://doi.org/10.1111/j.1468-5906.2005.00285.x.

Simon, H. A. (1955). A behavioral model of rational choice. *Quarterly Journal of Economics, 69,* 99–118. https://doi.org/10.2307/1884852.

Singer, M. (2004). The social origins and expressions of illness, *British Medical Bulletin, 69 (1),* 9–16. https://doi.org/10.1093/bmb/ldh016.

Singer, T. et al. (2006). Empathic neural responses are modulated by the perceived fairness of others. *Nature 439,* 466–469. doi: 10.1038/nature04271.

Skiba, R. J., Michael, R. S., Nardo, A. C., & Peterson, R. L. (2002). The color of discipline: Sources of racial and gender disproportionality in school punishment. *The Urban Review, 34(4),* 317–342. http://dx.doi.org/10.1023/A:1021320817372.

Small, M. L., Harding, D. J., & Lamont, M. (2010). Reconsidering culture and poverty. *The Annals of The American Academy, 629,* 6–27. doi: 10.1177/0002716210362077.

Smith, C. (2018a). Lingering trauma in Brazil: Police violence against Black women, *NACLA Report on the Americas, 50(4),* 369–376, doi: 10.1080/10714839.2018.1550979.

Smith, D. G. (2018b). Neuroscientists make a case against solitary confinement. *Scientific American* Retrieved from, https://www.scientificamerican.com/article/neuroscientists-make-a-case-against-solitary-confinement/.

Smith P. K., Jostmann N. B., Galinsky A. D., & van Dijk W. W. (2008). Lacking power impairs executive functions. *Psychological Science, 19,* 441–447. doi: 10.1111/j.1467-9280.2008.02107.x.

Somé, S. (2002). *The spirit of intimacy: Ancient teachings in the ways of relationships.* New York, NY: Quill.

Speer, P. W. & Peterson, N. A. (2000). Psychometric properties of an empowerment scale: Testing cognitive, emotional, and behavioral domains. *Social Work Research, 24(2),* 109–118. https://doi.org/10.1093/swr/24.2.109 .

Spiers, H. J., Love, B. C., Le Pelley, M. E., Gibb, C. E., & Murphy, R. A. (2017). Anterior temporal lobe tracks the formation of prejudice. *Journal of Cognitive Neuroscience, 29 (3),* 530–544. https://doi.org/10.1162/jocn_a_01056.

Spencer-Oatey, H. (2012) "What is culture? A compilation of quotations. GlobalPAD Core Concepts." http://www2.warwick.ac.uk/fac/soc/al/globalpad/interculturalskills/

Stahn, A. C. (2019). Brain changes and response to long Antarctic expeditions. *The New England Journal of Medicine, 381:*2273-2275. doi: 10.1056/NEJMc1904905.

Stanley, J. (2018). *How fascism works.* New York, NY: Random House.

Stellar, J. E., Manzo, V. M., Kraus, M. W., & Keltner, D. (2012). Class and compassion: Socioeconomic factors predict responses to suffering. *Emotion. 12(3),* 449–459. doi: 10.1037/a0026508.

Stewart, W. F. & Schwartz, B. S. (2007). Effects of lead on the adult brain: A 15-year exploration. *American Journal of Industrial Medicine,* 50(10), https://doi.org/10.1002/ajim.20434

Sue, D. W, Nadal, K. L., Capodilupo, C. M., Lin, A. I., Torino, G. C., & Rivera, D. P. (2008). Racial microaggressions against Black Americans: Implications for counseling. *Journal of Counseling and Development, 86,* 330–338. https://doi.org/10.1002/j.1556-6678.2008.tb00517.x.

Sullivan, C. A. (2001). The potential for calculating a meaningful water poverty index. *Water International, 26*, 471–480. https://doi.org/10.1080/02508060108686948.

Swarns, R. L. (2015, September 20). *The science behind they all look alike to me. New York Times.* https://www.nytimes.com/2015/09/20/nyregion/the-science-behind-they-all-look-alike-to-me.html

Tarakeshwar, N., Stanton, J., & Pargament, K. (2003). Religion: An overlooked dimension in cross-cultural psychology. *Cross Cultural Psychology, 34(4)*, 377–394. doi: 10.1177/0022022103253184.

Tattersall, N. (2007). Mali's traditional healers unlock herbal cures. *Reuters.* https://www.reuters.com/article/us-mali-healers/malis-traditional-healers-unlock-herbal-cures-idUSL1689966920061129.

Terbeck, S., Kahane, G., McTavish, S., & Savulescu, J. (2012). Propanolol reduces implicit negative racial bias. *Psychopharmacology, 222(3)*, 419–424 doi: 10.1007/s00213-012-2657-5.

Thomas, J. D. (2016). Jeff Foxworthy's redneck humor and the boundaries of middle-class American whiteness. *SAGE-Open*, 1–15. doi: 10.1177/2158244016647772.

Thompson, E. H. & Pleck, J. H. (1986). The structure of male role norms. *American-Behavioral Scientist, 29*, 531–543. https://doi.org/10.1177/000276486029005003.

Tomassoni, T. (July 29, 2019). We are in great danger: In Amazon, indigenous Waiapi chief is killed by illegal miners. *NBC News.* Retrieved from, https://www.nbcnews.com/news/latino/we-are-great-danger-amazon-indigenous-waiapi-chief-killed-illegal-n1035806 August 16 2019.

Torgensen, S. (1986). Neurotic depression and DSM-III. *Acta Psychiatrica Scandinavica , 73* (s328), 317–34. https://doi.org/10.1111/j.1600-0447.1986.tb10521.x

Towncharts.com (2018). Winston-Salem, NC Demographics Data. Retrieved from, https://www.towncharts.com/North-Carolina/Demographics/Winston-Salem-city-NC-Demographics-data.html.

Triandis, H., Bontempo, R., Betancourt, H., & Verma, J. (1986). The measurement of etic aspects of individualism and collectivism across cultures. *Australian Journal of Psychology, 38(3)*, 257–267. http://dx.doi.org/10.1080/00049538608259013.

Tucker, D. M. & Williamson, P. A. (1984). Asymmetric neural control systems in human self-regulation. *Psychological Review, 91*, 185–215. http://dx.doi.org/10.1037/0033-295X.91.2.185.

Tvedt, T., Hannemann, E., Larsen, A. T., et al. (Producers), & Tvedt, T. (Director). (2007). *The future of water. Episode 2.* [Documentary]. Norway: Panopticon AS and University of Bergen.

Twenge, J. M., Martin, G. N., & Spitzberg, B. H. (2018). Trends in U.S. adolescents' media use, 1976–2016: The rise of digital media, the decline of TV, and the (near) demise of print. *Psychology of Popular Media Culture.* Advance online publication. http://dx.doi.org/10.1037/ppm0000203.

Tyber, J. M., Lieberman, D., Kurzban, R., & Descioli, P. (2009). Disgust: evolved function and structure. *Psychological Review, 120(1)*, 65–84. doi: 10.1037/a0030778.

UNICEF (2017). *Thirsting for a future: Water and children in a changing climate.* New York: New York. United Nations Children's Fund. https://www.unicef.org/publications/files/UNICEF_Thirsting_for_a_Future_REPORT.pdf.

United Nations Conference on Trade and Development-UNCTD (2012). *The least developed countries report 2012: Harnessing remittances and diaspora knowledge to build productive capacities,* pgs. 85–120. Retrieved from, https://unctad.org/en/PublicationChapters/ldcr2012_ch4_en.pdf.

Upchurch, D. M. & Wexler-Rainisch, B. K. (2012). Racial and ethnic profiles of complementary and alternative medicine use among young adults in the United States: Findings from the National Longitudinal Study of Adolescent Health. *Journal of Evidence-Based Complementary & Alternative Medicine, 17(3)*, 172–179. doi:10.1177/2156587212450713.

Utsey, S. O., Bolden, M. A., & Brown, A. L. (2001). Visions of revolution from the spirit of Frantz Fanon: A psychology of liberation for counseling African Americans confronting societal racism and oppression. In J. G. Ponterotto, J. M. Casas, L. A. Suzuki, & C. M.

Alexander (Eds.), *Handbook of multicultural counseling* (pp. 311–336). Thousand Oaks, CA, US: Sage Publications, Inc.

Vago, D. R. & Zeidan, F. (2016). The brain on silent: Mind wandering, mindful awareness, and states of mental tranquility. *Annals of the New York Academy of Sciences, 1373(1)*, 96–113. doi: 10.1111/nyas.13171.

van Stegeren, A. H., Goekoop, R., Everaerd, W., Scheltens, P., Barkhof, F., Kuijer, J. P., & Rombouts, S. A. (2005). Noradrenaline mediates amygdala activation in men and women during encoding of emotional material. *NeuroImage, 24* (3), 898–909. https://doi.org/10.1016/j.neuroimage.2004.09.011

Watson, F. (December 31, 2018). The uncontacted tribes of Brazil face genocide under Jair Bolsonaro. *The Guardian*. Retrieved from, https://www.theguardian.com/commentisfree/2018/dec/31/tribes-brazil-genocide-jair-bolsonaro August 16 2019.

Watson, K. (October 25, 2018). Deep division in Brazil's north-east, where 'life is real'. *BBC News*, Retrieved from https://www.bbc.com/news/world-latin-america-45965925.

Waytz, A., Hoffman, K., & Trawalker, S. (2014). A superhumanization bias in whites' perceptions of blacks. *Social Psychological and Personality Science, 6*(3), 352–359. https://doi.org/10.1177/1948550614553642

Weber, L. (2001). *Understanding race, class, gender and sexuality: A conceptual framework.* New York: McGraw-Hill.

Webster, D. (September 1, 2004). The making of a sniper. *Vanity Fair*. Retrieved from, https://www.vanityfair.com/news/2004/10/beltway-snipers-200410 (June 9, 2019).

Weekes, N. Y. (2012). Diversity in neuroscience. We know the problem. Are we really still debating the solutions? *Journal of Undergraduate Neuroscience Education, 11(1)*, A52–A54.

Wei, L., Zhang, S., Turel, O., Bechara, A., & He, Q. (2017). A tripartite neurocognitive model of internet gaming disorder. *Frontiers in Psychiatry, 8*, 285. doi:10.3389/fpsyt.2017.00285.

Weisbuch, M., & Ambady, N. (2008). Affective divergence: Automatic responses to others' emotions dependent on group membership. *Journal of Personality and Social Psychology, 95*, 1063–1079.

Weng, C. B., Qian, R. B., Fu, X. M., Lin, B., Han, X. P., Niu, C. S., & Wang, Y. H. (2013). Gray matter and white matter abnormalities in online game addiction. *European Journal of Radiology, 82(8)*, 1308–1312. doi: 10.1016/j.ejrad.2013.01.031.

West, J., Otte, C., Geher, K., Johnson, J. & Mohr, D. C. (2004). Effects of hatha yoga and African dance on perceived stress, affect, and salivary cortisol. *Annals of Behavioral Medicine, 28 (2)*, 114–118. https://doi.org/10.1207/s15324796abm2802_6.

Whitaker, R. & Cosgrove, L. (2015). *Psychiatry under the influence: Institutional corruption, social injury, and prescriptions for reform.* New York, New York: Springer.

Whiten, A., & Byrne, R. W. (1988). The Machiavellian intelligence hypotheses: Editorial. In R. W. Byrne & A. Whiten (Eds.), *Machiavellian intelligence: Social expertise and the evolution of intellect in monkeys, apes, and humans* (p. 1–9). Clarendon Press/Oxford University Press.

Whitney R. E., Santucci K., Hsiao, A., & Chen, L. (2016). Cost-effectiveness of point-of-care testing for dehydration in the pediatric ED. *American Journal of Emergency Medicine, 34*, 1573–1575. doi: 10.1016/j.ajem.2016.05.075.

Wicker, B. et al. (2003). Both of us disgusted in my insula: The common neural basis of seeing and feeling disgust. *Neuron, 40(3)*, 655–664. doi:https://doi.org/10.1016/S0896-6273(03)00679-2.

Wiley, J. W. (2013). *The nigger in you: Challenging dysfunctional language, engaging leadership moments.* Stylus Publishing: Sterling, Va.

Williams, C. (July 9, 2007). NAACP symbolically buries n-word. *Washington Post*. Retrieved from,http://www.washingtonpost.com/wpdyn/content/article/2007/07/09/AR2007070900609.html?noredirect=on.

Wilson, A. (1993). *The falsification of Afrikan consciousness: Eurocentric history, psychiatry, and the politics of white supremacy.* Brooklyn, NY: Afrikan World Infosystems.

Wilson, J. P., Hugenberg, K., & Rule, N. O. (2017). Racial bias in judgments of physical size and formidability: From size to threat. *Journal of Personality and Social Psychology, 113*(1), 59–80. https://doi.org/10.1037/pspi0000092

Winston, A. S. (2004). Defining difference: Race and racism in the history of psychology. Washington DC: American Psychological Association.

Woodyard, C. & della Cava, M. (November 8, 2018). What we know about Thousand Oaks gunman, Ian David Long, a marine veteran. *USA Today*. Retrieved from https://www.usatoday.com/story/news/nation/2018/11/08/ian-long-gunman-thousand-oaks-california-borderline-bar-grill/1928231002/ December 8, 2018.

World Resources Institute (August 6, 2019). *Updated global water risk atlas reveals top water-stressed countries and states* [Press Release]. Retrieved from https://www.wri.org/news/2019/08/release-updated-global-water-risk-atlas-reveals-top-water-stressed-countries-and-states.

Xie, A., Gao, J., Xu, L., & Meng, D. (2014). Shared mechanisms of neurodegeneration in Alzheimer's disease and Parkinson's disease. *Biomedical Research International*, 648–740. doi:10.1155/2014/648740.

Yancy, G. (2008). *Black Bodies, White Gazes: The continuing significance of race*. Lanham: Rowman & Littlefield.

Yancy, G. (2012). *Look! A White: Philosophical essays on whiteness*. Temple University Press, pg. 4.

Yaszek, L. (2006). Afrofuturism, science fiction, and the history of the future. *Socialism and Democracy, 20 (3)*, 41–60. https://doi.org/10.1080/08854300600950236.

Yuan K., Qin W., Wang G., Zeng F., Zhao L., Yang X., et al. (2011). Microstructure abnormalities in adolescents with internet addiction disorder. *PLoS ONE, 6(6)*, e20708. https://doi.org/10.1371/journal.pone.0020708 .

Zaki, J. & Ochsner, K. (2012). The neuroscience of empathy: Progress, pitfalls and promise. *Nature Neuroscience, 15(5)*, 675–680. doi:10.1038/nn.3085.

Zhang, J. et al. (2018). The effects of hydration status on cognitive performances among young adults in Hebei, China: A randomized controlled trial (RCT). *International Journal of Environmental Research and Public Health, 15(7)*, 1477. doi:10.3390/ijerph15071477.

Zhou, Y., Lin, F. C., Du, Y. S., Qin, L. D., Zhao, Z. M., Xu, J. R., & Lei, H. (2011). Gray matter abnormalities in internet addiction: A voxel-based morphometry study. *European Journal of Radiology, 79(1)*, 92–95. doi: https://doi.org/10.1016/j.ejrad.2009.10.025.

Zimmerman, M., A. (1995). Psychological empowerment: Issues and illustrations. *American Journal of Community Psychology, 23(5)*, 581–599. doi: 10.1007/BF02506983.

Index

abnormality, 73–74
ACBP. *See* African-Centered/Black psychology
ACC. *See* anterior cingulate cortex
actions, 47–48
Africa. *See specific countries*
African-Centered/Black psychology (ACBP): Afrocentricism for, 8; Afro-communitarianism and, 158–159; APA and, 165–166; Black on Black crime for, 3; CN of, xi, xiii; culture for, 5–6, 12–13, 149; environmental injustices for, 142–144; Fanon and, 9; identity for, 80–81; LGBTQ and, 5; native people and, 112; Negro-ape metaphor for, 26; othering for, 12–13, 17–21; psycho-social cultural perspectives in, 123–124; for *quilombolas*, 94–95; scholarship on, 6–7, 17, 29, 125–126; slavery for, 88–89; superhumanization for, 30; Tornadoes of the Mind for, 130; Transpersonal Psychology and, 126–130; *Ubuntu* for, 40, 112, 153, 157; for women, 51–52, 62
African cultural imperative, 48–49
African cultural wisdom, 45–46
African Diaspora, 3, 9, 37
African spiritual origins, 42–43
Afrifuturism, 153–154
Afro-communitarianism, 158–159
Afrofuturism, 153–154

age, 137–140
Alves, Damares, 103
Alzheimer's disease, 164
Amazon rainforest, ix, 102–104
American Psychological Association (APA), 75, 104, 106–107, 130, 165–166
amygdala, 18–19, 100–101
analysis, 41, 60–61, 69
ancestry, 6
Andes mountains, 143–144
anterior cingulate cortex (ACC), 17, 19–20
anxiety, 22
APA. *See* American Psychological Association
Archambault, Dave, II, 99
asili, 123–124
assimilation, 14
asymmetry, 92
authoritarianism, 79
avoidance motivation, 93
ayahuasca, 144

BE. *See* Behavioral Economics
behavior, 73–74, 81, 83, 87, 166; behavioral empowerment, 35–36; CN and, 51; with power, xii; rationalization of, 19; science of, 9–10
Behavioral Economics (BE), 31, 32, 32–33
BIA. *See* Bureau of Indian Affairs

About the Author

Michele K. Lewis is Department Chairperson and Associate Professor of Psychological Sciences at Winston-Salem State University in North Carolina. This is her third book. Her previous works are *Multicultural Health Psychology: Special Topics Acknowledging Diversity* and the co-authored book, *LGBT Psychology: Research Perspectives and People of African Descent.* She is a member of the Association of Black Psychologists, the Association of Black Brain and Behavior Scientists, and a research fellow with the Center for the Study of Economic Mobility, where she integrates her emphasis on the study of brain and behavior with African-centered/Black psychology (ACBP) and behavioral economics. She has led curriculum development and teaching for a Cultural Neuroscience Summer Institute for students funded by the National Science Foundation. She uses her understanding of cultural neuroscience to research, teach, and present on various contemporary and long-standing social problems. She has served as a faculty leader of study abroad programs to Chile and Morocco. She now annually leads students to study culture, race, and identity in Brazil.

Made in the USA
Las Vegas, NV
03 January 2022

40198695R00127